OUR MAN IN HIBERNIA

Ireland, The Irish and Me

CHARLIE CONNELLY

Little, Brown

LITTLE, BROWN

First published in Great Britain as a paperback original in 2010 by Little, Brown

A CIP catalogue record for this book
is available from the British Library.

ISBN 978-1-4087-0208-6

Typeset in Bembo by M Rules
Printed and bound in Great Britain by
Clays Ltd, St Ives plc

Papers used by Little, Brown are natural, renewable and
recyclable products sourced from well-managed forests and certified
in accordance with the rules of the Forest Stewardship Council.

Mixed Sources
Product group from well-managed
forests and other controlled sources
www.fsc.org Cert no. SGS-COC-004081
© 1996 Forest Stewardship Council
FSC

Little, Brown
An imprint of
Little, Brown Book Group
100 Victoria Embankment
London EC4Y 0DY

An Hachette UK Company
www.hachette.co.uk

www.littlebrown.co.uk

For Jude

CHAPTER ONE

There was an advert screened regularly on British television in the early nineties that you might remember. It was for Caffrey's Irish Ale and I can remember every second of it. The scene is a crowded bar and from the snatches of conversation heard above the squealing hip-hop of House of Pain's 'Jump Around' it's clear we're in New York. The place is packed, noisy, swaying and sweaty. We focus on a young man holding a pool cue, his dark, shoulder-length hair flopping over chocolate-brown eyes above a chin that's strafed meticulously with stubble and clearly destined for a future in razor blade adverts. 'We're trying to play pool here, boys,' he says in an Irish accent as he pokes and prods the crowd of drinkers in order to line up his shot.

Whether he succeeds in pulling off a thumping plant to wrap up the game or rips a tear in the baize and shanks the cue ball into the groin of a nearby drinker we don't find out, as the next thing we see is the same man at the bar trying to get the attention of the bar staff. 'Can I get a Caffrey's, please?' he shouts above the din.

And then the strangest thing happens. The 'please' hangs echoing in the air and suddenly the bar is gone. It and the heaving mass of braying New Yorkers have melted away and are replaced by what appears to be a windswept, lonely Irish mountain; House of Pain dissolving into a soaring lament on the oboe. Our man is no longer in the bar; he's out in the bogs somewhere in the west of Ireland, the wind teasing enviously at his immaculate hair. A full string section sweeps across the soundtrack as he gazes enigmatically into the middle distance before we cut to a shot of an old wooden fishing boat in a field, then an elderly man in a flat cap sitting by a pub window through which weak sunlight filters, then we're in slow motion as a green-shirted hurling team trudges up a village street, all flushed cheeks, muddy knees and spent effort. Next we see a flame-haired colleen in a brown overcoat striding away across a field, throwing a glance over her shoulder that hints at a mysterious Celtic depth to her soul while at the same time promising advanced and supple sexual accomplishment. From the field we're whisked to another village street down which a riderless bay horse, joyfully free of bridle and saddle, is galloping.

But before we can shout, 'Loose horse! Run!' we're back in New York and back in the bar. Our man is now holding a full pint and looking faintly bewildered. But, what's this? The place is empty – the swaying, honking, bellowing crowd has disappeared entirely. The final shot is of his three friends, apparently the only ones still left in a bar that had until twenty seconds ago been packed tighter than Eamonn Holmes's cummerbund, looking at him levelly from the other side of the pool table. It's a look that says, my friend, we understand. We understand that the glass of watery ale you've just purchased is about more, much more than a wincing headache, dry-mouthed nausea and crushing feelings of self-loathing tomorrow morning. It's about your roots. You're Irish; you're special. Ours is a fake existence, we have no depth, no substance. But you, you're from a place where red-haired colleens pout at you in bogs, where escaped horses are a constant traffic hazard and where people apparently park boats in the middle of fields. In that froth-capped glass of dreams is distilled an entire culture, one that has fascinated, tantalised and seduced the world for centuries with its mythology, history, literature, music and the down-home charm of its cultural heritage.

The meaning of Ireland, it seems, can be found immersed in the contents of a pint glass in the hand of a young man with great hair in a New York bar whose friends are wondering why every time he orders a pint he falls into a slack-jawed trance. Is it to deflect from the fact that he only got himself a drink rather than his round? And anyway, where has everyone gone? While our man had been transfixed by this mental slideshow of sugary Irishness, had there been a shout of, 'Uh-oh, lads, Declan's having another one of his turns,' that prompted a stampede for the exit?

We're all familiar with this romantic notion of Ireland, with its hills, its music, its bogs, its literature, its pubs that are mimicked across the world, its easy charm, its warm welcome. The image is put about by advertisers and tourist brochures and is a myth happily propagated by the likes of that Caffrey's ad (that particular ale, incidentally, dates back through the Celtic mists of time to, er, about 1993 and has never been available in the Republic of Ireland), and it's one that continues to seduce the world. It also seduced me, but back then I was permanently puckered up for such teasing one-dimensional paddywhackery. The advert served only to top up the romanticised notion I had at that time of my Irish heritage, and I lapped it up.

At that time I was living in the south London suburb of Penge. It's a place notable for the fact that Rumpole of the Bailey's name was made by a case called the Penge Bungalow Murders and that Bill Wyman was born there. And that really is all you need to know about Penge. In my mind though, I was that lantern-jawed hunkerama who would stare wistfully into my living room in the ad breaks during *Coronation Street* while I lay on the sofa balancing a Pot Noodle on my stomach. My Manhattan was Croydon, my heaving, jumping bar a dingy, old man's boozer with a sticky carpet on the other side of the railway line and any stubble I managed to squeeze out was usually seen off sharpish by a strong gust of wind, but I was hearing the call of Erin's Isle just as he was. My body may have been laid out and stationary but my mind was escaping Penge for Ireland. I dreamed of upping sticks and moving to a place where, like our bewildered New York friend, as far as I was concerned it wouldn't be so much an emigration as a homecoming *from* emigration – despite the fact that I'd barely ever set foot there in my entire life.

This wasn't a desire suddenly sparked by a criminally sentimental beer advert (so all you advertising folk can stop whooping and high-fiving each other for a start). My father's family came from Ireland and my view of the world had always been drawn towards Ireland for almost as long as I could remember. As I emerged into adulthood my coquettish glances across the Irish Sea became more lingering and during the nineties began to turn into an obsession. Every time I saw that advert I knew Ireland was the place for me and vowed that one day I would live there. Much more than that, though, I wanted to *be* Irish and for a good while set about convincing myself – and, more importantly, other people – that I was.

That Caffrey's ad was the final prod I needed to seize upon this ill-defined genetic memory and run with it, run like the wind into what I perceived to be my heritage. But what heritage? My dad didn't know much about our history beyond the fact that we came from Cork and he had only a vague idea of how many generations ago the Connellys had arrived in Britain. Family politics and ancient arguments meant that he'd never pursued it, had never questioned when we came and why we were here. Dad is English, patently so. So is my mum. I am as English as they come; I was born and raised in London of London parents. My whole life, everything I knew, was in south-east London, where I grew up in an anonymous pseudo-suburb between suburbs in a soulless hinterland largely disowned by both London and Kent. It was an undefined place; a place so 'between' that when people asked me where I was from I had trouble answering. I felt rootless, deprived of a grounding in a firm sense of place and belonging. Perhaps it's no wonder, then, that in trying to define my own place in the world I seized upon an unknown quantity of blood sloshing around in me from a country that appears to be more defined than anywhere else.

There are few places more assertively sited in the consciousness than Ireland. What other countries have their national holiday celebrated with massive parades in major cities all over the world? Do we see St David's Day greeted by thousands of people dressed as dragons marching through Manhattan brandishing leeks and rugby balls while Max Boyce belts out 'The Fly-Half Factory' from a float alongside a Hudson River dyed red? Can we go to any town in Europe and search out a Norwegian theme pub where we can drink *akevitt* and snack on *lutefisk* as Henrik Ibsen, Edvard Munch and Roald Amundsen gaze down at us from picture frames and 'Take On Me' plays over the speakers? No, yet thousands upon thousands take part in worldwide St Patrick's Day celebrations every year and there's barely a town of note left that doesn't have at least one pub called Punchy O'Toole's or some such, crammed with old Irish direction signs and bodhrans and sepia prints of Dublin in the rare oul' times. Ireland, or at least a perception of Ireland, more than any other nation holds much of the world in its cultural thrall.

It's little wonder then that a young man growing up in a place where he didn't belong – because no one belonged there; it wasn't really a place as such – grabbed at an apparently defined and tangible piece of genetic heritage and held on for dear life, and as he struggled to find his place in the world came to embrace it more and more.

Every week I read the *Irish Post*, the newspaper for the Irish community in Britain, from cover to cover, lapping up the pictures of Irish dance competitions in Coventry community centres and accounts of committee meetings from Irish associations in Huddersfield. Volumes of Joyce, Behan, Yeats and Wilde lined my shelves. A couple of them even looked like they'd been opened. I watched *The Commitments* over and over again until I could confidently separate (and indeed imitate) a northside Dublin accent from a southside one. I was knee deep in CDs by Planxty, the Saw Doctors and The Pogues. I shut myself away in my bedroom with a cheap acoustic guitar and learned every song from Christy Moore's *Live at The Point*.

The flailing and hollering might not have impressed the neighbours but somehow I scraped a living for a good while as a musician on the Irish music scene in London, belting out the classics in smoky pubs and dark, sticky-floored venues that smelt of old cigarettes and bleach. By accident I became a very occasional and way-out-of-his-depth performer – or more accurately, hanger-on – with one of Ireland's most successful bands of the day, playing to big crowds and hanging out backstage with some of the people whose CDs lined my shelves. Barely a night would pass when I wasn't in some kind of venue, be it a several-thousand-capacity sell-out or the corner of a tiny Hackney pub, flailing at strings and a-hollerin' like a banshee about the hills of Donegal, the cliffs of Dooneen, the fields of Athenry and the rocky road to Dublin, places I'd never seen and, in most cases, couldn't even point to on a map. I embraced this hard-drinking yet damp-eyed version of Ireland as much as I could from the depths of anonymous south London where, as I looked out at the scruffy, rain-swept streets of Penge by day and the faces belting out the old songs with me at night, be they whiskery, rheumy-eyed old men in Kilburn pubs or a concert hall full of bouncing students pissed on cheap stout, I dreamed of that red-haired colleen, loose horse and inexplicable boat in a field. I created an identity for myself that allowed me to hide behind a puffed-up pride in a nation that wasn't my own.

My tenuous association with the famous band – often aided by my criminally overplaying my significance: after a few pints I sometimes went from being a friend who played a little bit of mandolin on stage to practically writing all the songs – afforded an ill-deserved kudos that had people asking me about the best places to visit in Ireland, the things to see, where the best *craic* was to be found. I handed down my sage advice and wished them well. I'd go to pubs in Kilburn and Stockwell and sing songs of the old country with men in flat caps. I'd sit in suburban Irish theme pubs and tut at the artificiality of it all, complaining about how none of the pubs in Ireland were anything like this. The thing was, until hooking up with the band, I had never actually been to Ireland in my life. Aside from a pint or so of blood sloshing around somewhere inside me I had no more tangible connection to Ireland than I had to the teak forests of Borneo.

For all my passionate enthusiasm and wistfully expressed desire to return 'home', if the opportunity had arisen back then for me to actually move to Ireland, if someone had said to me, OK, here's a ticket, off you go, the chances are I would have let out a yelp and hidden under the nearest table. For one thing I couldn't seem to get out of Penge let alone out of the country, but the main reason was that despite my attempts to ingratiate myself with gritty, modern Irish reality it was merely fantasy I had in mind; the fantasy of the Caffrey's ad, the fantasy of my undefined Irish heritage and the fantasy that I would any time soon even get off the sofa, let alone move to a different country. I'd bought into the wistful, fairyland notion of Ireland, the Ireland of stone walls, fields and thatched cottages; the Ireland of country pubs, mist-shrouded mythology and flame-haired colleens, but in my heart I knew I'd never go. It was a pipe dream, an escape valve from a dreary existence. If the dream was always there then I could always hang on to it. If it became reality, then I had nothing left to dream of. If I was honest with myself my embracing of all things Irish, sincere though I felt it was at the time, was little more than a bit of wistful escapism born from a deep-set desire to belong to *something*.

As the years passed my music career experienced a swift diminuendo and other things took over, while my immersion in Irishness drained away to the occasional Guinness and the odd spin of a Christy Moore album. My mandolins and guitars moved almost imperceptibly from a spot by the front door to a spare bedroom and finally to the loft where they were left untouched for years, the dates on the backstage passes affixed to the cases receding further and further into history with each new layer of dust. Real life eclipsed daydreams, I eventually got out of Penge, and while I still acknowledged and was proud of my Irish roots, however deeply they might be buried, memories of my plastic paddy period caused me to wince with embarrassment, frequently to the point of the foetal position.

Then I met Jude, a beautiful, funny, independent, fiercely intelligent, typically dark-haired and blue-eyed girl from County Mayo in the west of Ireland who, having lived in various places around the globe, had wound up back in Dublin. Suddenly my personal compass recalibrated itself westward across the Irish Sea once again. Having tried so hard to lose my heart to Ireland all those years ago, I'd now lost it irrevocably and speedily to a remarkable girl from its rural west. After a brief courtship based on snatched weekends with a half-unpacked bag constantly in the corner of the room and fistfuls of boarding passes scattered on the floor we decided that, with her having a proper job, I would join her permanently in Dublin.

Hence late one night a decade and half after I'd last watched that Caffrey's advert I disembarked on to the rain-shiny tarmac of Dublin airport, collected my rucksack from the carousel, hoisted it on to my back, looked both ways for loose horses and walked out of the terminal building into the night-time drizzle to begin a whole new life in Ireland.

As I joined the weary shuffle of the taxi queue that snaked back and forth outside, I reflected on how my arrival wasn't really supposed to be like this. I wasn't supposed to be waiting blearily in line for a taxi behind three gabbling Polish students while the Kildare family just back from Fuerteventura behind me bumped their trolley repeatedly against my calves. Back on that Penge sofa I'd planned my arrival in my imagination and many years ago devised exactly how I would do it. A damp, shuffling taxi queue with the hybrid whiff of jet fuel and wet tarmac in my nostrils wasn't it.

Back then, my mixed-up shamrocked mind had it that any move to Ireland would be a homecoming of sorts. At some undetermined point in the nineteenth century, somewhere in County Cork, a Connelly had packed a few possessions into an old cardboard suitcase, unfurled his cap, placed it on his head, bade his family goodbye and set off for England. I didn't know when this was; I didn't even know his name. Of only one thing was I certain: that one day I'd take the Connellys back home for good.

I had the moment all planned out. I'd be on a ferry, arriving at night, standing at the prow, overcoat collar turned up against the buffeting wind as the lights of Dublin appeared on the horizon. I'd turn my face towards them, almost hearing them calling me home. I'd have a specific piece of music on my Walkman, the haunting 'O'Carolan's Farewell to Music' played on the Irish harp, and my fellow passengers would accord me the same understanding and respectful glances the bloke in the Caffrey's ad had received, recognising that here was a man who'd been away a long time but was finally coming home. I was mysterious, I was charismatic. I was the living epitome of Behan, Yeats and Cúchulainn. I was a returning prodigal. I was a complete and utter penis.

The intervening years had served to ensure the circumstances of my arrival in Ireland as a resident had a little less of the phallus about them and there was none of the ceremony, awe or knowing nods from passers-by that I'd envisaged all those years earlier. I was still slightly hungover from a wedding I'd been to the previous day and suffering that listless, slightly grumpy fatigue that flying with Ryanair seems to induce on even the shortest flights. 'O'Carolan's Farewell to Music' was about as far from my mind as my old Walkman was from the cutting edge of audio technology. I was so excited about being with Jude that I didn't even give a moment's thought to the fact that on that night, that drizzly, unremarkable summer night, the Connellys were returning to Ireland after an absence of more than a century.

In fact for the early weeks of my time in Ireland the fact that I'd emigrated didn't really register at all. There was the overriding happiness of being with Jude without the churning nausea of knowing that one of us would have to leave the country after a couple of days, the excitement of moving into a new flat, with its strange aromas and unfamiliar space, finding places to put things and snuff out the echoes that go with emptiness, the initially unfamiliar patterns of swaying leaves thrown on to the wall by a lamp outside, its new smells, creaks, clunks and squeaks. There was the novelty of a new neighbourhood – the corner shop, the walk to the bus stop, neighbours to nod at – but this was all on a parochial scale; I had no real sense of the displacement I'd foisted upon myself. I'd left everything I knew; friends, family, regular haunts, old routines, everything that had ever been familiar, and traded it for another country. OK, a country that wasn't exactly far away and that spoke the same language as me, but a country where people had different passports from me and a different currency in their pockets.

In a way, at first it was almost too easy. When our cable was connected we had all the BBC radio and television channels. The shop around the corner stocked the *Guardian*, *The Times*, the *Daily Express*, the *Star* – they were tweaked to provide Irish news coverage, but the mastheads were the same. The chocolate bars racked on the counter were the same (with, I'd come to appreciate, the honourable exceptions of the mighty Catch and the magnificent Moro). Tesco, Aldi, Currys and Lidl competed in adverts. Ikea was opening. I walked up Dublin's famous Grafton Street past Burger King, Marks & Spencer, HMV, River Island and Vodafone.

Yet, while everything was reassuringly familiar, I began to start noticing the little things that really were different. Things like, if I saw an accident, is the number for the emergency services here 999 too? The police officers wore the same fluorescent jackets, but on the back they said GARDA instead of POLICE: the *Garda Síochána*, the guardians of the peace. Dublin's pelican crossings made a space-age laser noise instead of beeping. In the

pub, you just asked for a packet of crisps and were given cheese
and onion, no questions asked. You didn't ask for a half, you
asked for a 'glass'. At six o'clock every evening the national
broadcaster RTÉ broadcast the Angelus, the minute-long ringing of a church bell and pause for reflection which means that in
Ireland the six o'clock news is known as the Six One News. In
Ireland there are two colours of lemonade: a friend's wife over
from England was baffled when asking for a vodka and lemonade in the pub to receive the reply, 'Red or white?' The post
boxes are green and there is no mail delivery on a Saturday.
Most startling of all to someone used to the NHS, the concept
of paying your GP €50 just for walking through the door was a
shock, all right.

It took a while for the realisation to finally burrow through
with an audible clank of shovels that I really was actually living
abroad. I'd emigrated; I was an immigrant. I was now a part of
Ireland's largest ethnic minority in a country whose entire population is half the size of that of my home city. As far as my
subconscious was concerned I had been largely ignoring the
chunky pile of forms marked *Leaving the United Kingdom* as much
as Her Majesty's Revenue and Customs had since I'd posted
them, but I was undeniably now a foreigner. Outwardly I was in
Ireland; inwardly, in some senses, I'd never left London. Even my
mobile phone was still a UK one; something I realised with a yell
when I finally started opening the billing statements.

I don't know whether my younger self started tugging at my
sleeve, but gradually I began to acknowledge that I was living in
a new country; a fascinating, historic, beautiful, culturally marvellous place with which I had fallen utterly in unrequited love
as a confused, rootless, young dreamer. Was I rejecting the follies
of my younger self through a knuckle-gnawing sense of embarrassment at my rampant erstwhile plastic-paddyness? Whatever

the reason, I became aware that I had to change things. I *wanted* to change things, and not just because my mobile phone bills were ruining me.

I'd never felt a sense of belonging anywhere for as long as I could remember. The identikit, identity-free suburban south-east London streets had failed to root me in any identifiable place. Yet here I was somewhere that, if the GPS of my genes was in any way accurate, gave me the best opportunity I'd ever had of putting that right. By chance, I'd arrived in the place where I'd once dreamed of living. Of all the countries in the world, I'd rolled up in this one through the beautiful accident of falling in love. It was too much of a coincidence. I had to do something about it. I had to find out if I truly belonged here.

To achieve that I needed to do two things. First of all I had to put the image of Ireland that I'd grown up with in the songs, the myths, the clichés and the dodgy beer adverts against the country itself. Find out whether the Ireland I'd fallen for all those years ago was merely one that had been inadvertently exported with the millions of Irish emigrants over the last couple of centuries, romanticised, then repackaged and rebranded into a perfectly spun image woven from the shards of the broken hearts of exiles. Their memories of home that faded slightly with each day on the building sites and with each generation, but whose warm turf fires – and pouting red-haired colleens – helped perpetuate a specific global industry of Irishness.

I'd also have to define my own Irish heritage, if such a thing even existed. For too long I'd settled for vague, woolly hints in family legends as sufficient to place me among the Irish diaspora. I had the Irish name all right, but from whom was it inherited? Who was this mysterious Cork ancestor whose name I now bore and had returned to its native country? When did he leave? And why? If I was bringing the Connelly name back to Ireland,

I'd have to find the man who'd taken it away; to complete the circle.

The impending dawn of a new year would give me the timescale: I'd give myself a calendar year to find out whether the Ireland of my imagination was anything like the real thing and I'd stop avoiding my own mythology to find out the truth behind my Irish heritage. One year to define a country and a life.

The first firework is a bit early. It's away to the right and far in the distance, an orange dandelion of lights that flares briefly and melts back into the darkness. The faint 'pock' of its detonation arrives a good couple of seconds later, barely audible over the sound of the lapping waves on either side of us.

It's a clear, cold night at the very end of the North Bull Wall, a thin, two-kilometre concrete finger stretching into the north side of Dublin Bay that separates the calm waters of the harbour from the choppier brine of the Irish Sea. We're sitting on a bench, looking back towards the coastline as Bull Island, the sandy isthmus that has built up against the harbour wall over the previous couple of centuries, stretches away to our right. Above me *Our Lady, Star of the Sea* stands atop her slender concrete tripod, her back to the bay, looking across to the city. Orion glistens in the night sky behind her. Away to our right the midriff of the Howth peninsula, lurking black against the dark blue sky, is strung with a line of pinprick orange streetlights. To the left across the water the floodlights of Dublin port are topped by the twin chimneys of Poolbeg power station, so high that the winking beacons on the top of them are almost absorbed into Orion itself. As the coldness of the bench's metal slats begins to seep through the thickness of my coat a firework goes off directly ahead of us, a fountain of bright green lights that must have been launched from the back garden of a house party in Artane.

There's another nearby, then another away to the left. Then to the right. The distant bangs begin to sound like a far-off military invasion and the horizon fills with flashes and brief puffs of bright colour. A couple of hundred yards ahead, here on the wall, there's a swoosh and a scream and a delicious moment of silent suspense before a rocket explodes with a bang that thumps our chests and scatters a cascade of red lights that illuminates our faces, before flickering and dying to leave faint trails of blue smoke against the dark.

It's New Year's Eve and it's just turned midnight. I take the hipflask from my coat pocket, unscrew the top and hand it to Jude. She takes a swig and hands it back. I raise it to my mouth and lean my head back. There's a faint sting on the lips, a slight metallic tang and the whiskey warms my throat.

'Happy New Year,' says Jude, wriggling in closer against the cold.

I look behind me to the sea where a container ship, its super-structure lit up like a fairground ride, glides into Dublin port with a silent grace. A couple of bonfires flicker into life on the island's beach. I look over to the left, following the line of the coast to where the city of Dublin lies and the country beyond. In the coming dozen months I would compare the image of Ireland I grew up with to the Ireland I now live in, the country beyond the big green leprechaun hats and fake ginger beards that hang in the window of every souvenir shop and beyond pseudo-mystical adverts for gassy beer. In addition I'd try to blow away some of the mists of myth surrounding my own Irish background and find out exactly where my Irish roots lie, when they were uprooted and by whom. How different was the image I'd built up of Ireland from the reality? Just how accurate were the songs I used to sing about the place? Was the Irishness I'd craved back then anything like the real thing? Does 'the real thing' even exist? Most of all, did I really belong here? The dawning of a new year had turned my face to the future, a fresh start for the calendar nudging me towards a sense of the fresh start I'd made.

We stand up from the bench and set off for home.

CHAPTER TWO

The Ireland I'd arrived in was about as far from any green-tinted, happy-go-lucky expectation you might have of the place as you could imagine because the nation was suffering from the mother and father of collective hangovers after the dramatic and spectacular end of the boom famous the world over as the Celtic Tiger. Over a period of around a decade from the mid-nineties Ireland became one of the fastest growing and most dynamic economies in the world. For the first time almost in its entire history Ireland had money in her pocket. Lots of money. More money than she'd ever had before. Whereas people had traditionally left Ireland throughout history, now they were actually showing up in droves seeking a slice of the action.

It couldn't last. The boom was built largely and literally on the property market and in a country as small as Ireland that's never going to be sustainable. Even I can see that, and I failed my economics A level. Twice. Huge housing estates sprang up everywhere, estates that will never be filled, not ever. It's estimated there are as many as six hundred 'ghost estates' in Ireland and at the time of writing some three hundred thousand homes stand empty. If each of those has space for, say, a family of four, then that's enough housing to accommodate a quarter of the population of Ireland. While the old image of Ireland is of derelict, roofless stone cottages dotting the countryside, now it could conceivably become one of brand new empty houses with the manufacturer's stickers still on each windowpane and grass growing through cracks in the driveway.

On a bus once in the midlands I passed a housing estate that practically typified Ireland's bust in the space of a few hundred yards: a handful of houses at one end with tended lawns and cars outside giving way to empty houses, scrubby patches of grass in front and darkness behind the windows. Next were some half-finished homes in a sea of mud, gaping holes where windows should be, and finally a few naked, skeletal chimney stacks rising futilely from foundations that support nothing but ghost houses, the evaporated financial dreams of a property developer still drifting among corridors and rooms that will never be built. The derelict cottages that spatter the Irish countryside are testament to the generations of people that left; these estates mourn the people who will never come.

As a result of this flurry of overfinanced bricks and mortar, when the global recession kicked in the toe-end of its size tens landed firmly and squarely in Ireland's knackers. The nation plummeted from being one of the world's most dynamic economies into the worst recession of any western nation since the Great Depression of the thirties. What's the capital of Ireland, people would ask? About a fiver, came the reply.

So as the year dawned it was greeted with trepidation and fear. Indeed, while the spent cartridges of the New Year fireworks were still hitting the ground, one *Irish Times* columnist wrote of 'the least anticipated year in decades'.

'On Monday the country will finally return to business as usual,' he wrote. 'We'll tiptoe back cowering a little in anticipation of the pain to come. We know we're going to be slapped in the face, but we're wondering if we're going to get kicked up the backside and kneed in the groin at the same time.'

In timing terms, it seemed that in moving to Ireland I was up there with the bloke who'd exchanged contracts on his dream home next door to the bakery in Pudding Lane in the early summer of 1666, or the Roman citizen who moved to Pompeii in AD 79 because he liked the view of the rumbly mountain. In pretty much the couple of hours it had taken me to check in for my flight in England and touch down in Dublin, Ireland had plunged from being one of the most vibrant, cash-slathered nations in the world to the many-fathomed depths of the worst recession in generations.

There was a sense of hubris in the air, like that felt by the lottery winner who'd spanked the lot in a big blowout and ended up back in the same two-up, two-down with a broken washing machine in the front garden. The nation's immediate prospects were gloomy and the signs of recession became more noticeable with each passing week. A dedicated mortgage shop at the bottom of Grafton Street was one of the first to close down and with its windows whitewashed was one of the most visible and emblematic everyday symbols of the economic decline. Across the country brand new office blocks stood empty, with the hopeful signs detailing square footage, the prime nature of the location and immediate availability sounding as hollow as someone pitching Pripyat as a funky holiday town while the Chernobyl number four reactor was still smoking.

The number of homeless people on the streets increased noticeably. Ireland had once been a major destination for EU labour (a sign on some freshly painted railings I saw outside the Irish parliament, the Dáil, once said 'wet paint' in English, Irish and Polish: by around 2006 Polish was in real terms Ireland's second language). When I first arrived in Ireland and would take the bus into town nearly every conversation you'd hear on the top deck would be in Polish. Even in the short time I'd been in the country, the buses were getting emptier and the Polish conversations were becoming the exception again. Something like half the foreign EU labour force in Ireland in 2004 would leave by the end of 2009.

I sensed too that the Irish were starting to ask questions about themselves and about their identity as the post-boom hangover took hold. Dublin in particular had in recent years become an energetic European capital, given a youthful vigour by an emerging generation of young professionals patronising its new coffee shops and working in offices in its redeveloped docklands, reading new glossy lifestyle magazines and shopping in swanky designer clothes outlets.

There was no finer illustration of this than the day Jude and I were in a coffee shop in the Southside suburb of Dún Laoghaire having just spent an agreeable time laughing ourselves silly at some of the more extravagant prices in a Celtic Tiger-era homeware shop banging out what my cockney grandmother would have called 'a load of old toot', when a boy of no more than twelve walked in. He was wearing his school uniform. Oh bless, I thought, his mum must have told him to meet her here. Bold as brass he walked straight up to the counter and asked for a 'skinny hot angel to go'. Jude and I looked at each other. Yes, we had heard right. Now I have no idea what a 'skinny hot angel' is now, let alone when I was twelve years old. I didn't go into a coffee shop until I was probably in my mid-twenties and even then expected to be taken by the elbow and marched straight out again by someone saying something terse that ended with the phrase 'the likes of you'. In fact when I was twelve I don't think I even knew that coffee came in a form other than freeze-dried brown granules. Yet since the boom in Ireland twelve-year-old

schoolboys on the Southside of Dublin are strolling about, cool
as you like, in posh coffee places asking for things that sound
more like a porn website than a beverage. I felt like accosting
him as he left and telling him he should be, I don't know, outside the Spar drinking cider out of a plastic bottle and saying
'word, blud' a lot, or something.

But that's the Southside of Dublin for you. Dead posh. The
Northside on the other hand is traditionally the rougher side of
the city. That's not to say you cross the Liffey and immediately
walk on to the set of *The Wire*, but Dublin's more notorious
estates are on the Northside. Away from the troubled parts of
the Northside however, there's a much more bohemian aspect
to the place. I live on the Northside of Dublin, in a district of
wide, leafy boulevards close to the sea. There's a village feel to
it, which is certainly something that helped me to assimilate. My
barber, Dave, a one-man operation close to the coast, provided
a perfect barometer for my assimilation in fact. Dave is the most
Northside man in the world. The walls of his small room, in
which there's space only for him, his barber's chair, and a short
bench for waiting customers, is slathered with pictures and
memorabilia from Dublin's Gaelic football team, punctuated
with the odd Blackburn Rovers scarf and an Elvis Presley clock.
Dave has a north Dublin accent so thick you could put a pea
beneath it and the princess on top and she'd still get the best
night's sleep of her life. When I first went to Dave for a haircut
I understood around one word in ten as I nodded and smiled.
But as my monthly visits progressed that became one in eight,
then six, and is now down to about one in three. He'll still
throw me occasionally though. One day he announced, 'I've got
meself a mickey extension.' My eyes looked up at his reflection
in the mirror. A what?

'A mickey extension, I've got meself a mickey extension,' he repeated, smiling enthusiastically. I was still utterly none the wiser.

He reached over and pulled a colour photograph from a shelf nearby – it was of an immaculate vintage motorcycle he'd just bought. Mickey, I realised, is Dublinese for, well, penis. Dave was telling me he'd bought himself a penis extension (later that day I saw an advert for a cable channel's forthcoming Mickey Mouse special. The phrase 'you've never had so much Mickey!' suddenly had an entirely new context).

We also have a tremendous fish and chip shop nearby. I soon learned to refer to it as the vernacular 'chipper' rather than 'chippy', but most importantly, the chipper's name is Beshoff's, purveyors of the finest fish suppers in Ireland, better, I say at risk of sacrilege, even than Harry Ramsden's in the UK. While most of Ireland's chippers were started by Italians, its most famous chain was launched by a Ukrainian immigrant named Ivan Beshov. Beshov had participated in the 1905 mutiny on the battleship *Potemkin* from where he made his way west until he landed in Ireland. He was interned in a prison camp outside Dublin on suspicion of being a German spy and on his release set up a fish and chip shop on North Strand, north of the city centre, before the Second World War. Ireland remained neutral during the war (the conflict was referred to here as 'The Emergency') and hence was spared the air attacks that flattened British cities and much of continental Europe. Despite this, in May 1941 German bombs fell on North Strand and killed more than thirty people in one of the city's poorest areas. No one has ever truly discovered what happened: the theories range from Churchill ordering British airmen to fly captured German aircraft to bomb Dublin in order to draw Ireland into the war, to German pilots getting lost and mistaking the lights of Dublin for Liverpool, but as well as destroying a huge chunk of Dublin slums the bombs reduced Ivan Beshov's chipper to rubble. He rebuilt however, and extended his chain until the anglicised Beshoff's became, as it remains, one of the best known names in Dublin and beyond. Ivan, incidentally, died in 1987 at the age of 102, insisting that he was actually 104.

Just around the corner from Beshoff's and Dave the Barber is Connolly's pub, known locally as The Sheds after the old fishing net sheds that used to stand there. It's a typical local Irish pub in that it's practically the community's living room, all dark wood and display cases full of antique bottles of long-forgotten beers and some of the produce that used to be on sale when the pub doubled as a grocery shop. The floor is black, red and white tiles, there's table service when it's not busy, and televisions show big sporting events except for the one nearest the door which is tuned permanently to the horse racing. For me Dave's barber shop serves as the daytime hub of the community; The Sheds takes over in the evenings.

For all that certain people look down on the Northside of Dublin, it's home to me and it feels like it, from the church bells calling the faithful to Mass at 9.45 every morning to a mighty fine pint of Guinness in The Sheds, from the island and its beach a short walk away to Dave's chair, the best place to find out what's really going on in the locality.

Dublin is a little like an inverted London – north Londoners look down on south Londoners, who in turn don't really care, and Southside Dubliners look down on their Northside counterparts just the same and with the same reaction.

(It's the same nationwide, incidentally. Where Britain has its north–south divide, Ireland's nearest equivalent is the division between the capital and the rest of the country. It's a dichotomy that gave the English language the phrase 'beyond the pale': 'the Pale' was a fortified lowland that surrounded Dublin and the area that was subject to English rule in the late fifteenth century and that became politically obsolete with the Tudor conquest of Ireland. Today however it remains, roughly speaking, perceived as a cultural and political barrier. Beyond the pale today are the 'culchies', a term that to many Dubliners means anyone from outside the city but is more generally accepted to mean a rural-dweller, a bit of a country bumpkin. Your culchie is never out of wellies and rarely without a ham sandwich (pronounced 'hang sangidge') and a flask of tea (pronounced 'tay'). It's a term that's been reclaimed by those it seeks to lampoon and there's now a popular Culchie Festival in Cavan which annually elects the Culchie of the Year.)

Yet even with its café culture and burgeoning class of young professionals – with new generations marching through behind them carrying their skinny hot angels – Dublin was suffering with the rest of the country. Shops and businesses were closing by the day, from boom-era start-ups to family concerns dating back to before independence. Outside Dublin whole factories and plants would close, kneecapping entire small towns with the knock-on effects of unemployment and lost income throughout the local economy. When a large global computer manufacturer announced that it would be shedding 1900 staff from its plant in Limerick, economists warned that each of those jobs underpinned four or five others in the Irish economy.

It would be a crucial year for Ireland in so many ways. Its new confidence would be shaken and its people would genuinely suffer. Could the nation go back to being one that saw net emigration again? What values, if any, would it rediscover once the hardship set in?

So, at this tender time in modern Irish history, what exactly was I trying to learn? What did I want to find? The lazy answer is 'the real Ireland', something I'm pretty sure doesn't exist, any more than there's an unequivocally 'real England' or 'real Tajikistan'. Stop half a dozen people at random across the country and their 'real Irelands' will all be quite different. No, what I wanted to find out was whether the image I'd been fed of Ireland and its people matched up to what I'd find actually living here.

The extreme version of this image struggled to be discerned through the thick layer of syrup with which it was smothered: the Ireland of stone cottages, bogs, sheep being driven along the lane, a land populated by a people couched in rural wisdom, living in thrall of fairies and who started every utterance with 'begorrah'. It's an Ireland where modernity and urbanisation never arrived, a backward rural idyll where everyone attends dances at the crossroads and spends their days sitting at the door of their cabin whittling shillelaghs. It's the 'Emerald Isle', that glistening, mythical place where old men dispatch naïve wisdom from beneath jauntily angled derbies with their teeth clamped around the stalk of a clay pipe while an old fiddle lies never far from arm's length.

Recently somebody sent me a link to a trailer for a new Hollywood film set in Ireland. An American woman had somehow landed in the west of Ireland and needed to get to Dublin fast. The main road to Dublin from wherever she'd ended up was a single lane, largely unmade and lined by low stone walls and the constant hazard of livestock herds meandering along stretches of it marshalled lazily by toothless, whiskery farmers. Now I may not have been here long but I've travelled to and from Dublin in most directions and am sure that I recall the roads being modern tarmacked affairs with a variety of vehicles heading in both directions, none of which had to be cranked with a starting handle. I've also noticed a distinct lack of bovine ambling on the highway and have even, gasp, seen white lines painted on the road surfaces. Our heroine's self-appointed chaperone was a Caffrey's Man for the new millennium, all dark floppy hair and stubble and the twinkling eyes, straw-flecked sweater and the sort of ready charm that comes from being, you know, Irish and that. He drove a beaten-up Renault 4 and spoke with an alleged Irish accent that frequently placed him in Kansas, Melbourne and Mumbai in the space of a single sentence.

Along the way they stayed in dingy bed and breakfasts whose curtains hadn't been opened in fifty years and were run by humble elderly couples who apparently hadn't been aware of the outside world since about the same time. You can just imagine the fun and larks that this odd couple thrown together by happenstance had – after all, every bed and breakfast owner in Ireland these days expects two people of different genders sharing a room to be married. Anything else would just be utterly preposterous. Apparently it can take days to get to Dublin rather than a few hours, necessitating overnight stays, but then if you take into account how the odd couple had had to travel back to the fifties it's no wonder a bit of time was added to the journey.

It's a hackneyed, condescending image of Ireland and one that is as far from the truth as you can possibly get, a time-warped fairytale of lazy stereotypes: a simple, happy-go-lucky, essentially rural Emerald Isle, an Ireland that in fact never really existed in the first place. Maybe it originated in the wistful nostalgia of the emigrant, forced by hardship or famine to a new life in a totally alien land: of course homesickness will set in and of course the memories of home will be subconsciously airbrushed. It's the stone cottages, tranquil countryside and down-home charm that remains while the starvation, degradation, poverty and disease is wiped away altogether, and that's the image that's handed down. I've even heard stories of distant American relatives, three or four generations removed from Ireland, visiting family here and rebuking their hosts for having a modern tiled roof on their house rather than thatch and even for giving their children names that are not 'Irish' enough. Apparently, actually being Irish, born in Ireland and living in Ireland falls short if you're not ticking all the right cultural boxes, as if Ireland has become a green-tinged, thatch-roofed Disneyland; a place so firmly embedded in the consciousness that anything slightly different is regarded with something between disbelief and horror.

Don't get me wrong, I'm not saying that Hollywood is responsible for every leprechaun, shamrock and reference to an 'Emerald Isle' there's ever been, quite the opposite: it's an image that was once encouraged here at the highest level. On St Patrick's Day in 1943 the then president of Ireland, Éamon de Valéra, addressed the nation on the radio and expressed his desire to see 'a people who were satisfied with frugal comfort . . . a land whose countryside would be bright with cosy homesteads, whose fields and villages would be joyous with the sounds of industry, with the romping of sturdy children, the contest of athletic youths and the laughter of comely maidens'.

But this isn't 1943. The Ireland I'd arrived in might have been licking its economic wounds but it was still a modern, confident European nation just like any other. Its sturdy children weren't romping, they were Facebooking on their iPhones and the comely maidens were laughing all right, laughing at the idea they'd be satisfied with frugal comfort when there was a sale on in Topshop. It might have missed out on the massive industrialisation of its neighbours over the previous century or two, but that didn't make Ireland a rural backwater full of amiable drunks gnawing on spuds.

Talking of drunks, there's also the reputation the Irish have for taking a drop. The Irish have always been viewed as a nation of boozers, chronically so, whether the view is expressed jovially or disapprovingly. It's a frighteningly prevalent image even in modern times: in 1999 a Florida lawyer named John Stemberger, representing the family of a woman who had died in a car crash, attempted to sue the Dollar Rent-a-Car company for leasing one of their vehicles to an Irish citizen, as the Irish are a race of known abusers of alcohol. According to Stemberger, Dollar 'knew or should have known about the unique cultural and ethnic customs existing in Ireland which involve the regular consumption of alcohol at "pubs" as a major component to [sic] Irish social life'. Dollar 'knew or should have known that [the driver] would have a high propensity to drink alcohol.' The suit was withdrawn after noisy complaints from Irish-American community groups and Stemberger was forced into an apology, but clearly, even allowing for the frequently bananas world of American litigation, the perception of the Irish as drunks was rife enough for Stemberger, a qualified lawyer, to feel that the stigmatising of an entire nation was strong enough grounds on which to pursue a case. What are you doing letting Séamus drive? He's bound to be arseholed.

When I was growing up in Britain the Irish were the butt of jokes: Paddy was a bit of a thicko, he hung around with an Englishman and a Scotsman and spent much of his time going into pubs with them where he would show up his innate idiocy by providing a suitably imbecilic punchline. The Irish were also dangerous: barely a television news bulletin would pass without footage of a rubble-strewn street, its bombed buildings still smoking, or British soldiers nervously on patrol in places with exotic names like Crossmaglen and Enniskillen. Yet at school we never learned why there was trouble in Northern Ireland. I never learned why terrifying men in balaclavas were setting off explosives in my city.

So, according to the images I was assailed with growing up,

your Irishman was a simple, friendly fellow who lived a slow and lazy life among fields, playing his fiddle and sometimes taking his clay pipe out of his mouth long enough to impart some pearl of rural wisdom while the spuds were boiling. He hung around with an Englishman and Scotsman, usually in pubs (if he managed to stay in them long enough without starting a fight and smashing up the furniture), compared to whom he generally looked a bit of an idiot truth be told, but that was probably because he was permanently roaring drunk. Oh, and he'd blow you to smithereens as soon as look at you.

As I grew older however, perceptions began to change. A new kind of Irish culture was emerging from a country that seemed to be growing in confidence. U2 became the biggest rock band in the world. Acts like Clannad, Sinéad O'Connor, The Waterboys and The Pogues proffered different musical versions of Ireland and Irishness from the ethereal to the raucous. *The Commitments* was one of the must-see films and indeed must-read books of the nineties. Bombs went off less regularly and eventually stopped going off altogether. Irish pubs, previously sticky isolated dens in the parts of north London and Birmingham where Irish communities would gather and the exclusive preserve of the emigrant, began to spring up all over Britain and beyond. There were even chains of them, meaning you could go to pretty much any city in the country and enter the same establishment with the same name. Irish pubs, or at least a version of them, became a franchise operation: the McDonald's of booze. You could buy into another culture for the price of a pint and then leave it behind as soon as you left the premises. Even the Irish football team, with its exploits in the 1990 and 1994 World Cups, helped to make Ireland cool. We laughed ourselves silly at the brilliance of *Father Ted* and when Riverdance leapt, skipped and bounded on to our television screens during the interval of the 1994 *Eurovision Song Contest* we were absolutely blown away by this extraordinary little nation.

The nineties was a time when Irishness became desirable and at that particular time nobody desired it more than me. Even I, a ham-fisted musician and nasal, croaking singer at best, rarely went short of work in Irish pubs and venues. It was into this mood of exultant shamrockery, a raucous, knowing version of Irishness that blew away a little of the sugar – or at least redesigned the icing – for the new millennium, that Caffrey's tried to tap, and the timing for me was perfect. Here was something tangible, easily identifiable and desirable and it was something I could be a part of. As a member of the Irish diaspora (so I thought) this was my culture thriving, or at least my perception of my culture. The water was lovely and I was coming on in.

I could see the water from the window. My tenuous and decidedly dodgy claim to be a member of the diaspora was largely irrelevant now: I lived in Ireland. It was home. Out there was Dublin Bay; the lights I could see through the window from the sofa were the same lights I'd once dreamed of sailing towards for my mythical great homecoming; the Wicklow mountains, snow-capped in the January chill, the very skyline I'd imagined the prow of the ferry slicing through the waves of the Irish Sea towards (I winced again at the memory: if I'd had the chance to go back and meet my younger self a sharp poke in the eye would have been worth the time travel alone).

Having never had any kind of view before beyond a garage and some dustbins, I'd spend hours staring out at the bay, as far as the horizon, watching the ferries and container ships sailing in and out, the little white sails of distant yachts, the silhouette of the mountains, squalls and storms heading in off the sea, the

kite-surfers on the strand and there, down there, if I just leaned
to the right a little, yes, I could definitely see the off-licence. I
was living in a city yet it also felt like I was living in a quiet village by the sea. In the local supermarket pasta could be found in
a section marked 'ethnic foods'. I spent the first few months
believing the local post office had closed down (it always seemed
dark and deserted) until I passed by one day and saw a man in a
white coat and hat in the window cleaving up an entire side of
beef on a butcher's block while, at the back in the gloom, I could
just make out someone sticking stamps on a parcel. People
smiled at me in the street, nodded, said hello, and I started doing
it back – if I'd tried that in north London I'd have got a faceful
of pepper spray and a roundhouse kick to the temple for my
trouble.

For all its character and history, Dublin is a city with surprisingly few genuinely memorable landmarks. The classy ironwork
of the Ha'penny Bridge graces most postcards, and the millennium needle at the heart of O'Connell Street is a fine modern
structure that can be seen from most parts of the city and may
well become its icon, but there's no Eiffel Tower, Big Ben or
Brandenburg Gate here. At the bottom of Grafton Street however, opposite Trinity College, is a statue that you'll rarely see
without tourists posing for pictures in front of it any time of the
day or night. It attracts more attention than the James Joyce
statue on North Earl Street, more than the Oscar Wilde statue in
Merrion Square and more than the life-size Phil Lynott on
Harry Street. It certainly attracts more photography than the
imposing figure of Daniel O'Connell, whose statue at the junction of the Liffey and the street that bears his name is probably
the most visible of all Dublin statues. No, the one that garners
the most attention of all, the one that's rarely seen without somebody standing in front of it, next to it or, in some cases, on it,

willing the person with the camera to hurry up because every-one's looking, is not of a great writer, politician or historical figure. It's of Molly Malone. You know, her from that song. Wheeling her wheelbarrow and hawking crustaceans through the streets of Dublin and all that.

Now, Molly Malone never existed. The song was written by a Scotsman in the nineteenth century and became a music hall staple, picked up by street performers in Dublin and popular among children. Its chorus cry of 'cockllllllles and musselllllllllls' also makes it the perfect boozy singalong. It drips with sentiment and tragedy and recalls a time long gone and tells of how Molly's voice could be heard in the streets advertising her wares long after she'd parked her wheelbarrow for the last time and headed for the great fishmongers' in the sky.

Molly became a famous figure throughout the land and beyond. Today there are pubs bearing her name in Gran Canaria, Los Angeles, Bangkok, Amsterdam, Cambodia and on Capitol Hill in Washington to name just a few. Hence it's not surprising that a statue of such a global phenomenon should go up in her honour in the city where according to the song she plied her wares, and that's what Dublin did in 1988.

Which is when things got a bit weird. People started claiming that Molly had really existed and was a known figure around seventeenth-century Dublin. It was suggested that she'd been buried in a cemetery close to Fishamble Street, a claim made around the time Dublin city was planning to bulldoze the old cemetery in the name of modern development. Which it did. In 1988 Dublin celebrated its millennium, as part of which the city announced that it had found Molly Malone, or at least tracked her down in the parish records: a Mary Malone born in the heart of Dublin in 1663 who died in 1699. Now, Mary Malone is a common name, there are hundreds in the parish records, and it was never revealed how these birth and death records had been established as the right ones, but these were solemnly offered to bring Molly from the myths of song to the reality of seventeenth-century Dublin. A whole legend developed, that Molly had sold fish by day and worked as a prostitute by night, that her daytime route took her from the Liberties to St Stephen's Green via Grafton Street, that some of her evening 'clients' were Trinity College students. Hence the statue that went up on her route in 1988 depicts Molly wheeling her cart and dressed in seventeenth-century clothing with, it must be said, her décolletage prominently displayed. Let's just say she has the goods on the barrow in more ways than one. On cold Dublin nights you pass Molly and think, hell's bells, the woman will catch her death. (Jude passed her one freezing night and saw that somebody had kindly tied a red scarf around her neck.)

It's an extraordinary, wilful blurring of myth and fact. There's no real harm done of course; the statue is a tremendous image to have on postcards and in brochures and it is probably the most photographed piece of Dublin by far, but why a whole fantastical history had to be constructed around it, why there had to be an attempt to create a fake legitimacy to the story, I'll never know.

In contrast, at the end of January I attended a real piece of history and celebrated one of the most tangible and positive aspects of Ireland and its history at the same time. And there wasn't a cockle or mussel in sight.

There's something relentlessly exciting about walking towards a stadium at night. The white glow in the sky of the floodlights, the knots of people falling into step to create one united crowd the closer you come to the stadium, the clouds of breath in the air, the smell of frying onions from the modern Molly Malones offering hot dogs and burgers of questionable provenance and potentially dubious consequences. The narrow streets become crowded, the cries of the programme sellers soar above the thunder of hundreds of footsteps, the dazzle of the floodlights ahead making the street dark and your every step feel as if you're heading into an unknown blackness. Most of all though, there's the anticipation, the nervous excitement of the encounter ahead.

For more than thirty years as a south Londoner I'd experienced this going to watch Charlton Athletic. Since my first match as an eight-year-old I'd lost count of the number of times I'd made the walk to the stadium, felt the same butterflies of anticipation and, more often than not, the eventual crushing and frustrating disappointment of yet another hapless display of slapstick in football form. Despite the guaranteed lack of genuine success the routine was familiar and reassuring, knowing I shared a collective memory and experience with those around me walking to the stadium. I belonged to that experience, I had an investment in it, and it belonged to me.

That night in January the old sensations came back as I walked through the dark and narrow streets that surround Ireland's finest sporting arena. Croke Park is one of the best stadia in the world, it sits in the heart of the community, it has an eventful and tragic history and is home to one of the most remarkable institutions of any kind you'll ever see.

I was on my way to the official celebration match to mark the 125th anniversary of the Gaelic Athletic Association, the GAA. They'd chosen a Gaelic football league match between Dublin and the reigning All-Ireland champions, Tyrone, to launch a year of events to commemorate a small gathering one day in November 1884 when a handful of like-minded men met in the billiard room of the Hayes Hotel in the town of Thurles in Tipperary and changed the course of Irish sport and indeed Irish culture and community for ever.

The late nineteenth century had seen a flourishing of interest in Irish nationalism. Poets and writers led the way as much as politicians, and organisations emerged across the country to promote Irish culture and heritage in response to the creeping Anglicisation of Ireland since the Act of Union had brought Ireland officially into the British Empire in 1801.

In sport, cricket, believe it or not, was seen as the biggest threat to traditional Irish pastimes (in Irish it was known as *iomáint ghallda* – 'foreign hurling') and in the 1880s, a period of particular upheaval in Ireland with the Irish engaging in fierce struggles with the British over land rights and freedom, two men came together to try and protect traditional Irish sports from foreign influence. Michael Cusack was a schoolteacher from Clare who'd emerged from a poor background to become one of Ireland's leading educationalists while Maurice Davin was from middle-class Tipperary, a studious and educated businessman who was one of Ireland's leading athletes (he once held the world record for throwing the hammer). Concerned at how disorganised athletics in Ireland was, he and Cusack founded the Gaelic Athletic Association. Almost as an afterthought they were involved in drawing up laws for the ancient Irish game of hurling and codified laws for a style of football that brought together the kind of traditional folk games that had become association football in Britain in the 1870s.

Where the organisation really flourished though was in organising sport on a parish level: each parish had a club. This gave local GAA clubs a real place in the community; the sports field became as much a part of the local landscape as the church: it gave the organisation a sense of belonging and led to the clubs representing their community in a very real way. It's a system that survives and flourishes to this day in a parochial manner that sport in Britain has never truly emulated.

While chiefly concerned with athletics at the outset, the football and hurling codes (and camogie, a version of hurling played by women) became by far the most popular sports under the GAA umbrella. The Association also promoted other aspects of Irish culture: the Irish language was an important part of GAA life and to this day teams must submit their team lists written in Irish to the referee before the game, or the match is forfeited.

As a result of this promotion of indigenous culture the British were suspicious of the GAA, suspecting it was a front for more political aims. There was undeniably a nationalist slant to the GAA's activities; its very nature made this almost inevitable, but it remained neutral during the civil war in the twenties and acted as an agent of reconciliation between the pro- and anti-partition forces.

There were two controversial rules of the Association that inevitably made it a political entity. It was forbidden for any GAA person to be associated with any 'foreign' sport on risk of suspension or even permanent expulsion from the organisation. Not just playing, either: you could be banned for just watching a cricket match, for example. It led to some ridiculous situations, such as that of 1938 when the President of Ireland, the Association's own patron Douglas Hyde found himself suspended from the GAA for attending an international soccer match in his capacity as president. In the sixties a Waterford player was suspended for attending a social function organised by a soccer club. Eventually the famous Rule 27 was lifted in 1971 but it would take until 2002 for rule 21 to be revoked, a rule that prevented members of the British armed forces or security services from joining the association.

These days the political side of the GAA is all but gone. The last real vestige of it ended in 2005 when the Irish Rugby

Football Union and the Football Association of Ireland approached the GAA to see if they might use Croke Park while their own stadium, Lansdowne Road, was knocked down and rebuilt. Rule 42 of the association determined that no 'foreign' games would ever be staged on GAA grounds, and the debate was fierce. Eventually it was agreed that the Irish soccer and rugby teams could share Croke Park temporarily, leading to emotional scenes in particular when the English rugby team arrived for a fixture soon after the lifting of the ban. Matches with England are always highly charged affairs, but a match against England at Croke Park was something that sent emotions through the stratosphere for reasons that will become clear later. There was much debate leading up to the game on how the British national anthem would be received when it rang out across the stadium – would it be greeted with jeers and whistles, would there be demonstrations? In the event, 'God Save the Queen' passed off with unified and dignified respect: the Irish did their talking on the pitch instead, sending England home on the wrong end of a thorough hammering.

Today the GAA boasts more than eight hundred thousand members, a huge section of a total population a little north of four million, divided between around two and a half thousand clubs. It's an organisation that really does reach down to the very grass roots of the Irish community and there are no equivalent associations anywhere in the world. It's almost like a trade union, a sports club, round table and a community group rolled into one.

The main focus of attention is the inter-county game, culminating in the All-Ireland football and hurling finals at Croke Park in September. Those days were a long way off on a chill January evening as I passed through the turnstiles, bought my programme and climbed the concrete stairs at the back of the Cusack Stand.

There are few more awe-inspiring moments than your first glimpse of the playing field when you enter a big stadium, especially for a match under floodlights. You've been pressed in with the crowds in the dark streets, you've queued, you've presented your ticket and clanked through the turnstile. You've walked along corridors and climbed stairs and finally, you emerge into the seats and the glistening silvery green of the pitch is spread before you. Its emptiness makes it special: you'll occupy a seat with just enough room for your legs but the pitch is the reason you're here, everything is kept away from the pitch. It's not called hallowed turf for nothing. The goals at each end, the markings on the field, it's a sacred space. It's a magnificent spectacle, a packed Croker on match day. That night nearly eighty thousand people were there to see Dublin play Tyrone: the Superbowl took place in the US the same night and there were more people at Dublin versus Tyrone than at America's sporting showpiece.

Croke Park is a wonderful modern stadium, but its history makes it much more than that. The stand on the other side of the field from where I was sitting is the Hogan Stand, named for one of the victims of one of sport's greatest ever outrages. On 21 November 1920, at the height of the War of Independence, Dublin were due to take on Tipperary in a football challenge match at Croke Park. Early that morning Michael Collins had sent out an assassination squad to kill a unit of British secret agents known as the Cairo Gang. Fourteen British intelligence officers died that morning, many still in their beds; a fifteenth would die later of his wounds.

That afternoon five thousand people gathered at the stadium for the game. Around ten minutes into the match British police and auxiliaries, the notoriously vicious Black and Tans, entered the stadium and began firing into the crowd. Fourteen people died that day at the stadium, twelve from gunfire and two more who were killed in the stampede that followed. Among the dead was twenty-four-year-old Tipperary player Michael Hogan who died on the pitch wearing his Tipperary jersey and after whom a new stand was later named, and continues to bear his name to this day. To my right at the end of the stadium was Hill 16, behind the goal, where Dublin fans traditionally gather. While the other three sides of the ground are all cantilevered double-decker seating, the Hill is open to the elements and for standing spectators only, earning its name because it was originally constructed from rubble left over from the 1916 Easter Rising.

There is no segregation at GAA matches so the Dublin and Tyrone fans, of whom thousands had travelled south, mingled good-naturedly all around the stadium, the Dubs in their light blue replica jerseys, Tyrone in their white shirts with red trim. The atmosphere was exhilarating: there's not the same tribal feeling as there is in English football grounds, but the noise is deafening, especially when the teams take the field. It's the moment when the anticipation reaches its height and the noise levels reach a new peak. Just under eighty thousand people are in the stadium and yet – and this is the real reason why the GAA is such an incredible organisation – the thirty players sprinting, jumping and stretching down on the field below, the heroes to young and old whose exploits are spoken about in awed tones in pubs and homes across the land and possibly will be for decades, are all amateurs. They all have day jobs. They're at the pinnacle of their sport yet they're not paid a penny. Having performed in front of a packed crowd at one of the biggest and best stadia in Europe in front of live national television cameras, some twelve hours after trudging back to the changing rooms with the noise still ringing in their ears and the triumphs and disasters still lodged in their aching thighs and thumping hearts, the players will be back at work, processing insurance claims, delivering post, whatever it is that pays the bills that Gaelic football or hurling never will.

The match is a thriller. Nobody had expected a classic as this was the first match of the new season and Dublin in particular were a team in transition, but both teams rose magnificently to the occasion. Gaelic football is a fast, skilful and muscular game. The goals – the same goals and pitch layout are used in both hurling and football – look like a cross between those used in soccer and rugby: a soccer-style goal from which the posts project upwards like a rugby goal. If you put the ball over the bar it's a point while if you lash it into the back of the net it's three points. Players can use their hands but can't carry the ball as they do in rugby, they have to bounce it and play it from their hands to their feet and back again. It's a simple game, which is the key to making it one of the most exciting sports to watch anywhere in the world.

It was a humdinger of a match. Tyrone, playing with the confidence of champions, looked to have taken the game by the scruff of the neck when they went in at half-time four points ahead after a terrific display of fast aggressive football. Dublin, traditionally one of Ireland's more successful teams but undergoing a few lean years, fought back in the second half and, in the last minute, took the lead by a point. In injury time however Tyrone hit back with three successive points to win a belter of a game by a goal and eighteen points to Dublin's goal and sixteen.

It was strange for me to watch the game as a neutral. I didn't have a dog in this scrap and I didn't have the shared history of my fellow fans, the great games, the fair-to-middling games and the forgettable ones; the great players and the absolute donkeys, the crafty veterans and the fresh-faced young hopefuls. Although Dublin was my local team I had already plighted my allegiance elsewhere, to Mayo, Jude's native county. After three decades of general disappointment punctuated by the odd memorable moment watching Charlton every week I quite relished the fresh start, the hope that I might see a bit of success at long last. I should have known, of course. Mayo are the great underachievers of the game. While renowned for playing attractive, flowing football and producing consistently excellent teams and players, they last won the All-Ireland more than half a century ago in 1951. They've reached five finals since and lost the lot, most heartbreakingly of all in 1996 when they conceded a fluke last-minute equalising point in the final against Meath and then lost the replay. Mayo people talk of the Croke Park jinx, of a football legacy soaked in heartbreak and anguish. I read a book about the history of Mayo football: it was called *House of Pain*. Here we go again then. Sigh.

That was for other Croke Park days though. On this night, after a spectacular fireworks display and light show to officially launch the 125-year celebrations, we headed down the concrete staircases and filtered back into the night, watching silhouettes of people darting between the slow moving traffic and disappearing into pubs or piling on to buses, the whole magnificent occasion bleeding back into the city.

For all Dublin's attractions, the Book of Kells, the museums, the pubs, the galleries, the bosomy statues of fictional provenance, to gain a real sense of the city and a real sense of the country, there are few experiences in Dublin – and indeed Ireland – to beat seeing a big GAA game at Croke Park. It might not appear in many tourist guides, at least not prominently, but when Croke Park is packed for a big match and the game's ebbing and flowing and the crowd gasps and roars as one, it's almost as if you can sense the heart of the city physically beating.

CHAPTER THREE

When I boarded the bus the driver looked at the destination on my ticket, clipped it and said, 'Going to see oul' Barack, eh?'

I was heading for Moneygall in County Offaly, pretty much your typical small Irish town. It sits on the main road from Dublin to Limerick at the very bottom of the county in the southern midlands. In fact, when you look at the map it's almost as if Offaly was extended to include Moneygall at the expense of Tipperary: so nipped by the border is it that the Moneygall GAA ground on the outskirts of the town is actually in Tipperary. The border is so tight that locals say you have to be born there to know what's actually where − on the map it looks a little as if Moneygall has sunk slightly and taken the county border with it. It has a couple of pubs on the main street, a smattering of shops and not a great deal else on the face of it, but on one cold and snow-sugared winter's day early in the year Moneygall was the focus of Irish (and not a little international) attention on one of the most hopeful, exciting days in recent history: the day Barack Obama was inaugurated as President of the United States.

Moneygall was festooned with Obamabilia: his face grinned from posters in every shop and pub while the Stars and Stripes hung in bunting along both sides of the main street. Now, most of the world was pretty excited by the prospect of an Obama presidency, whether it was because he represented a genuine force for change and progress or simply because unlike the last guy he looked like he could actually tie his own shoelaces, but Moneygall in the county of Offaly kicked up its heels with particular enthusiasm. The reason for this lies incongruously in an empty plot of land not far from the centre of the town; an uneven patch of long grass roped off and with a weathered 'for sale' sign banged into the mud with a mallet. Back in 1850 that piece of ground was home to the Kearney family, and one day during that year a shoemaker's son called Falmouth Kearney left the house that had once stood there, his head probably still a little muzzy from the 'American wake' of the night before, walked to the road, turned around and took a last look at the simple homestead that was all he'd ever known. Then he walked off with a determined vigour, leaving Moneygall and Ireland behind for a new life in America. Those first few steps began a journey that would end in Ross County, Ohio, where he would find work, a wife and start a family. Falmouth Kearney would never see Moneygall again.

It was a typical story, unremarkable even in that it was one repeated more than a million times over that decade as desperate people left a land devastated by famine and poverty for a new life across the sea. Currently there are millions upon millions of people around the world with the same kind of story in their family history, but in this case Falmouth Kearney's leaving Offaly and raising a family across the Atlantic led directly to his Indonesian-descended, Hawaiian-raised great-great-great-grandson becoming the first black president of the most powerful nation on Earth. And on the day that president was sworn in, I was in the small corner of County Offaly that will now remain forever Obama.

★

When a local vicar unearthed the parish records that proved the link Moneygall couldn't believe its luck. A local band, the magnificently named Hardy Drew and the Nancy Boys penned a catchy song called 'There's No One As Irish As Barack O'Bama' that was released as a single and sold by the shedload (once they'd changed their name to the more PC Corrigan Brothers). Reporters and camera crews showed up from all over the world: the route between the vicar, the plot of land and the pub became a well-trodden one. Obama himself spoke of his delight at learning that he had roots in the tiny town on the fringes of Offaly and the locals began to whisper feverishly about the prospect of a presidential visit.

There were precedents for presidents mixing with residents in Ireland. In 1984 Ronald Reagan visited the village of Ballyporeen in Tipperary, from where his great-grandfather had emigrated in the 1860s. He stayed for hours, addressing the locals from a podium in the main street and drinking in O'Farrell's pub. The pub was later renamed the Ronald Reagan Bar and, on the death of the former president in 2004, was dismantled and shipped to the Ronald Reagan Library and Museum in California and reconstructed there, complete with the original mahogany bar, signage and stools and even the very glasses from which Reagan and Nancy had drunk. You can't get a pint there any more though: it serves as a snack bar, as part of the massive complex dedicated to the former president.

But of all the American presidents with Irish roots the man who embraced them most readily was undoubtedly John F. Kennedy. Both his parents had Irish roots: the Fitzgeralds on his mother's side, hailing from County Limerick, and the Kennedys from Dunganstown, near New Ross in County Wexford. In the summer of 1963, just five months before his death, Kennedy visited Ireland and made a pilgrimage to the old family homestead (which is now open as a museum in the summer months). For such a poor and often overlooked country, Kennedy's visit made Ireland the focus of world attention and cemented strong links between Washington and Dublin that remain to this day. Four decades on from Kennedy's visit the inhabitants of Moneygall dared to dream that Barack Obama might one day rock up to their little town.

While my own visit didn't create the same kind of stir that one by Obama would – the only thing I've ever been president of was an obscure university music society of which a friend of mine was the only other member – I wasn't just heading to Moneygall for a look-see. I'd been invited to appear on Ryan Tubridy's radio show on Ireland's main national station, RTÉ Radio One. Tubridy is Ireland's leading broadcaster; his radio show pulls the highest listening figures in the country while he also hosted *Tubridy Tonight*, a Saturday-night chat show on RTÉ television. Later in the year he would take over Irish broadcasting's top job, the prestigious Friday night *Late, Late Show*, as the natural successor to its two previous hosts who'd spanned four decades, Gay Byrne and Pat Kenny. For the Obama inauguration the radio show would be broadcast live from the front bar of Ollie Hayes's pub on Moneygall's main street and for some reason I'd been asked along to talk a little bit about history and plug a book I'd just written. Now, before moving to Ireland I'd done a few radio things for the BBC in London. They would send a swanky car to pick me up to ensure I got to Broadcasting House on time and then take me home again afterwards feeling very grand and hoping all the neighbours had noticed (although asking the driver to honk the horn as we pulled up was a little bit excessive, I'll admit).

This occasion would be different though. 'OK,' the researcher had told me on the phone a few days earlier, 'this is going to

sound a little unconventional, but bear with me.' As the programme was on first thing in the morning I'd have to get to
Moneygall on the bus the day before and stay the night.
However, there was nowhere to stay in Moneygall itself, so when
I got off the bus I was to ring a woman called Bridie who would
then drive down from a small hotel a few miles up the road and
pick me up. I'd stay the night there and then in the morning
someone, as yet unspecified, would come and take me to the
pub for the programme. Either way, I was going to Moneygall.

Hence the Bus Éireann driver's reaction when he saw the
destination on my ticket. I was indeed going to see oul' Barack.
At least, sort of.

A couple of hours or so later I was the only person to alight
at Moneygall when the bus pulled in with a hiss of hydraulics
above the heavy rumble of trucks thundering past in both directions. Just as I stepped from the bus on to the pavement the
heavens opened with a vigorous and freezing winter cloudburst.
Battered by big, cold raindrops I ran into a shop doorway, pulled
out the pizza delivery menu on which I'd scribbled down the
number and called Bridie. 'Oh how are ya?' she said, sounding
delighted to hear from me. 'Did you have a good journey
down?' I did, I replied, but ooh, what terrible weather. 'Ah, yes,
well, that'll be the day that's in it,' she replied mysteriously.
Hoping she could hear me over the roar of the monsoon going
on around me I asked if it was right that she was coming to pick
me up.

'Ah, no, there's been a change of plan on that front,' she told
me. 'I've a delivery coming and I can't get away right now. Can
you see Ollie Hayes's pub from where you are?'

I couldn't see much beyond a five yard radius thanks to the
stair-rods hammering down from the heavens. Um, no, I couldn't
see Ollie Hayes's pub, I said. 'Ah, sure you will, don't worry,

you're on the right road. It's opposite another place called Hayes on the same street.' How will I know which is the right one? 'Well, that would depend which one you go into first, so.' Ah yes, true.

'If you ask at the bar for Ollie, he'll sort you out. I'll be seeing you shortly anyway, come and find me when you get here.'

As the rain slowed to a mere heavy drizzle I emerged from the doorway and looked both ways along the street where the traffic passed with the ceaseless noisy hiss of sodden tarmac. I walked along a few yards and eventually found the red and black frontage of Hayes's pub, a typical Irish bar with the name picked out in gold letters along the frontage above darkened windows and a central double door. The only thing that made Hayes's pub different from any other in Ireland that day was the enormous chrome-plated bus outside with 'OBAMA FM' plastered all over it and the slither of cables leading from it, across the pavement and in through the door. I stepped over them and went inside.

The place was festooned with American flags. There were more stars than in the entire Horsehead Nebula and enough red and white stripes to keep barbers in poles for decades. There were stickers everywhere declaiming 'Obama abú' (meaning, roughly, 'Obama! Woo! Hell, yeah!' in Irish) and at a table in the middle were two lads sitting behind two microphones and a small mixing desk, wearing headphones and playing middle of the road American rock interspersed with the odd announcement that 'you're tuned to Obama FM, broadcasting live from Moneygall in County Offaly' between tracks.

I went and stood at the bar. A middle aged man came over.

'Hello, um, I'm looking for Ollie,' I said, inexplicably raising the pitch of my voice at the end of the sentence to make it sound like a question in a way that I really hate when other people do it. He became tight-lipped, shifted his gaze from side to side, drew closer, looked me right in the eye and said conspiratorially, 'Who wants to know?'

This I hadn't expected. As an early indicator that Ireland was quite different from the friendly stereotype, this was a belter.

'Umm, I'm, er,' I stammered hopelessly, 'I'm, ah, going to be on the, er, Ryan Tubridy show here tomorrow, and, er, Bridie said . . .'

His face broke into a huge grin from which emerged the words: 'Ah, I'm only messin' wit' ya. You'll be the fella who needs a lift up the road. Help yourself to a cup of coffee at the end of the bar there and I'll be right with you.'

Relieved, I sat down on a stool, heaped coffee granules into a mug, filled it with steaming water from an urn, splashed milk over much of the bar, my groin and eventually into the cup and looked around. It was late afternoon and the pub was all but empty save for me, Ollie and the two lads with the mixing desk who looked glassy-eyed in a way that suggested they'd found themselves in the grip of some kind of existential nightmare where time was stretching beyond the limits of human comprehension. They exchanged wordless glances that narrated eloquently how they didn't go through all those years of college and work experience at radio stations to end up playing John Mellencamp records in a deserted pub on a rainy afternoon in Offaly.

That night, having been deposited at the hotel by Ollie, I sat in the bar where I was alone nearly all evening save for the television in the corner showing a documentary about the murder of a policeman in the eighties at ear-splitting volume. Bridie was behind the bar, standing on a chair stapling Barack Obama T-shirts to the ceiling. Apparently one of Nuala's daughters was going to pick me up early in the morning to take me back to the pub for the radio programme. To this day I'm not sure who

Nuala is. 'One of her daughters plays camogie for the county, you know,' I was informed. 'She's really very good.'

Later a man came in and sat at the bar with me and we bought each other whiskeys and talked about Obama and the inauguration. As we left later in the evening, he asked me how I was getting back to Moneygall in the morning. 'Nuala's daughter's giving me a lift,' I said.

'The one that plays camogie for the county?' he asked. 'She's really very good.'

It was a frosty morning when my lift arrived, a young blonde girl in a tracksuit driving a hatchback. We exchanged greetings; she was on her way to college and passing through Moneygall and hence able to drop me off en route. 'Are you the one who plays camogie for the county?' I asked. 'No,' came the reply in a firm tone that suggested this was a common question, 'that's my sister.' Which rather killed the conversation for the rest of the journey.

The pub was unrecognisable from the previous afternoon, not least because you couldn't see most of it with all the people crammed into every available space. The entire town of Moneygall appeared to be wedged into the bar where, at the same table that Obama FM had commandeered the previous day, Ryan Tubridy himself was going through notes and listening to instructions from the producer while accommodating every request for an autograph or a picture. The producer and researchers marshalled the contributors, making sure everyone knew when they were on and where they should be. I'd be on near the end of the hour-long programme with a local historian, so took up a position out of the way, by a speaker set up to relay the programme to the people gathered in the pub.

The show had everything. Barack Obama's eighth cousin Henry Healy, a Moneygall resident, came through loud and clear down the line from Washington where he was attending the inauguration. The sound of his disembodied voice in the pub caused a hubbub of excited recognition from the Moneygall folk as Henry revealed that when he told people who he was they'd said the only family resemblance they could see was alas in the ear department. He was clearly taking the new-found recognition in his stride as he also related how he'd had to turn down an invitation to join Senator Edward Kennedy at a pre-inauguration reception as he was already committed to another event. Excited glances and rocketing eyebrows were exchanged throughout the pub – imagine, a Moneygall man turning down canapés with a Kennedy.

Back in the pub a local councillor was telling Tubridy how the authority was now giving thanks that nobody had come in and bought the Kearney land from them since it was placed on the market a year or so earlier. He hoped the site would now be developed in some commemorative way and turn Moneygall into a tourist destination in the same manner as the Kennedy family homestead in Wexford, something echoed later in the show by a local businessman. He was already looking into the feasibility of building a hotel on the outskirts of the town so that if Obama ever came to visit his Irish roots he'd have somewhere to stay. He'd clearly given it a great deal of thought: it would, he said, be an establishment of 140 rooms, have a conference centre and a 'retail fuel facility' ('That's a petrol station, right?' said Tubridy). The establishment would, he revealed after a pause for maximum effect, be called the Barack Obama Hotel.

'You'll really call it that?' asked Tubridy.

'Most certainly, Ryan,' came the reply. 'I'm not important enough yet to call it after meself.'

This wasn't the first time that Offaly had been in the political spotlight recently. The Taoiseach, Brian Cowen, who had a few months earlier taken over from the charismatic and controversial Bertie Ahern, is also an Offaly native. His brother, a local councillor, was on the programme and described Cowen as 'Offaly's Barack Obama: there was the same euphoria when he took charge and the same sense of expectation'. Cowen is an old fashioned politician, in many ways the antithesis of Obama – chubby, heavy-lipped, with the sort of thick hair that looks like it has to be parted with an angle grinder and a way of wearing a suit that makes it look like he's slept in it for a week. A cartoonist's dream, unfortunately for him, in appearance he is the embodiment of one of Ireland's more popular acronyms: the BIFFO; the, ahem, Big Ignorant Fucker From Offaly (the London *Times* was a little more reticent when it published news of Cowen's accession to the top job, replacing the third word with 'fellow').

Unfortunately things weren't going well for the new man. Like Gordon Brown he'd had the misfortune of being sold a pup by his predecessor who had, it seemed, sensed the coming storm and ducked out sharpish. Local unemployment (it was revealed on the programme) had in recent months gone up by a whopping 71 per cent, and by 76 per cent in the midlands as a whole. While Cowen's accession to the top job had initially been greeted with a-whoopin' and a-hollerin' in his native county, the honeymoon was now well and truly over. That morning there could scarcely have been a greater contrast between the two Offaly-produced politicians.

Three young girls played a couple of Irish tunes on their fiddles, all furrowed brows and tongues sticking out of the sides of their mouths in concentration, and the show was nearly over. George the local historian and myself had only a few short minutes to talk about Offaly and history. George is an expert in this field, I patently am not. He gave a fascinating rundown of some of the finer points of Offaly history, one of which – that one of the signatories of the American Declaration of Independence was an Offaly man – I repeated seconds later as new information because I hadn't been listening properly. It was pretty much my only contribution before Tubridy handed back to the studio after a rousing singalong version of 'There's No One As Irish As Barack O'Bama'. There was a moment's hush, Tubridy took off his headphones and said, 'thanks everyb—' and the rest was drowned out by massive cheering applause from the Moneygallers. The presenter vanished beneath a crowd of well-wishers and autograph hunters and to his credit he didn't leave the building until the last hand had been shaken, the last picture taken and the last scrap of paper signed. I followed the departing crowds out on to the main street and walked through the chilly drizzle to find the Kearney homestead. And there it was, a scrubby patch of grassland, taped off and fronted by an estate agent's sign, on which the word 'WANKER' had been sprayed in big red letters.

I stood in the damp cold and pondered what to do next. So, this was Offaly: a county of rain, heavy traffic, unimaginative graffiti and Barack Obama. Surely there was more to it than this? I didn't know much about Offaly before I went to Moneygall. I'd barely even heard of the place before I arrived in Ireland: it isn't exactly one of the higher-profile parts of the country. It had none of the urban sophistication of Dublin, nor the dramatic scenery of the west coast. Tourists might pass through it without even realising. The Obama link might induce the curious to call in on their way through, but until the Kearney homestead is more than just a patch of ground marked with an abuse-smeared 'for sale' sign there isn't really much to see.

When I'd mentioned to friends that I was going to Offaly they'd boggled slightly as if I'd announced that I was in fact the rightful King of Hungary just off to reclaim my throne with a troop of highly trained, heavily armed gibbons. 'Why on earth are you going to Offaly?' they'd ask, and these weren't even the sort of Dublin folk whose map of Ireland features only the words 'Dublin' and 'culchies'. I was getting the impression that Offaly didn't exactly send a frisson of excitement down the spines of anyone who wasn't actually from Offaly. It seemed you went through Offaly to get to other places but didn't dawdle. It certainly didn't feature in any of the sugary images of Ireland on which I'd been raised. I'd never come across a song wistfully postulating that it was a long way to Offaly or pining for the hills of Offaly, nor had I read misty-eyed travel supplement articles about how vibrant, colourful Offaly was truly the jewel in Ireland's crown. Perhaps if there was somewhere where I might find an example of the Ireland behind the image it might be here and it might be Offaly. In Moneygall I was on the very fringe of the county; to get to its heart I would have to head to its centre and, indeed the very centre of Ireland. I looked down at the 'for sale' sign again, put my can of red spray paint back in my bag, turned on my heels and went to Birr.

Birr, despite sounding like the noise retired colonels make when they hear of some political-correctness-gone-mad outrage that prompts a letter to the *Telegraph*, is, my guidebook told me, a fine example of a well-preserved Georgian Irish town. The bus dropped me at its centre from where I could tell that as Irish towns go it was indeed well-preserved and Georgian, but I wasn't in Birr's Emmet Square on a grey, miserable, rainy afternoon in January in order merely to appreciate this. No, I was actually there partly because I wanted to see more of Offaly but mainly because I'd heard that according to some calculations Birr, and more specifically Emmet Square itself, is the exact geographical centre of Ireland. How this kind of thing is worked out I've no idea – lots of difficult sums and nifty work with a slide rule I'd imagine – and there are similar claims for both an unremarkable spot a couple of miles south of Athlone and the myth-shrouded Hill of Uisneach between Athlone and Mullingar, but some inky boffin somewhere had decreed that Emmet Square was where the Irish north, south, east and west all converged and that was good enough for me.

The bus roared off, leaving me standing in a cloud of exhaust fumes in a square otherwise entirely devoid of people. I was alone at the very centre of Ireland.

I'd presumed there'd be some kind of marker, perhaps a plaque, maybe even a monument of some kind: after all, being the dead centre of anything is surely worth commemorating even if there were other places with competing claims (maybe the location varied depending on whether the tide was in or out) but I walked all the way around the square twice and found nothing to mark this amazing if debatable geographical quirk. In the centre of the square is an austere-looking stone pillar that used to be topped by a statue of the Duke of Cumberland, erected in 1747 to commemorate the English victory at the Battle of Culloden. What this had to do with Birr I'm not entirely sure and naturally this didn't go down too well with the locals, an antipathy magnified in the late nineteenth century when a regiment of Scottish soldiers was stationed nearby and found itself marching past the man who had been responsible for horrific acts of slaughter against their people in one of the most mercilessly bloody incidents ever perpetrated in British military history. Eventually the statue, which bizarrely featured the Duke in the guise of a Roman senator swathed in a fancy toga and crowned with a wreath of laurels, was removed early in the twentieth century (ostensibly for safety reasons) and, with the coming of independence, was never replaced. The top of the plinth is now empty save for Cumberland's sandalled right foot.

Maybe the pillar was it. Maybe that was the centre and the siting of the controversial Duke's statue had been a deliberate one by the British: this is the very centre of the country and look, here's one of our most eminent psychopaths to demonstrate just how much we're in charge here lest you forget it. There was nothing on the plinth to mark it as the spot where the extremities of the island converged, and the tourist information board a few feet away made no reference to Emmet Square's apparent national centrality, but in the absence of anything more certain the crumbling, sandal-topped pillar would suffice. It even seemed faintly appropriate for the times; this monument of decaying hubristic grandeur at the heart of the nation almost a euphemism for the state of the Irish economy.

I stood there with, so it seemed, the whole of Ireland surrounding me. I was at the heart of the place, the epicentre of the entire island. On a cold, wet midweek day though, it was difficult to gain any sense of this geographical achievement. I walked over to the pillar. I did a circuit around it. I looked up and down it, trying anything to instil some kind of awe at my indefatigable centrality. I turned so I had my back to the plinth and looked down along Emmet Street, the town's main thoroughfare. And then I did a curious thing. I started moving sideways, shuffling, keeping my heels against the pillar until I reached the first corner, which I turned and kept shuffling, performing a complete circuit, taking in the whole of Ireland around me before returning to the point where I'd started. It wasn't the most soul-enriching experience, it must be said: it's hard to get a sense of being at the very heart of a country when your vista takes in a newsagent, a car park, a police station and a couple of bins, but no matter, as far as I was concerned I was at the centre of Ireland: I was the node where invisible lines of geographical trigonometry all met; ancient lines whose convergence might at that very moment have been investing in me the energy and the wisdom of the ancients. I completed my circuit and it was only then, when I'd returned to my starting point, that I noticed I wasn't alone in the square after all: a young woman sitting in a parked car eight feet away was looking at me with a mixture of curiosity and suspicion. Thinking quickly I pursed my lips, reached into my pocket, took out my notebook and scribbled unintelligible things in it, every now and then looking up and down the street while extending my arm and holding out my thumb as if I was performing some kind of important surveying work rather than just being, you know, a pillock. After a while I nodded to myself, stabbed an emphatic full stop with my pencil, flipped the book shut with a flourish and strode off purposefully on what turned out to be a roundabout route to Birr Castle.

One of the things I love most about travelling is that the most unlikely places can throw up remarkable things. Places that would on the face of it hold absolutely nothing of interest often emerge as the scene of extraordinary events or the home of extraordinary people. I have a theory that is yet to be successfully contradicted which states that wherever you go, no matter how dull or lifeless it might appear, you will find, if you look hard enough, something or someone that will make you raise an eyebrow at the very least and certainly make your visit worthwhile. Birr, it turns out, is no exception to my holistic theory of exploration and that's due in the main to the Parsons family of Birr Castle, whose history and achievements almost outdo the town itself.

It was William Parsons, the third Earl of Rosse, who really put Birr on the map. He may not be an immediately familiar name – I'd certainly never heard of him before I went to Birr – but William Parsons was a quite amazing man whose achievements and discoveries are still resonant today.

Born in 1800, he was, unusually for the aristocracy at the time, educated at home at Birr Castle. From there he went to Magdalen College, Oxford, and graduated with a first in maths. Although he was elected to parliament representing the King's County, as Offaly was bizarrely known for the duration of British rule in Ireland, it was heavenly bodies rather than government bodies that interested him most. In the pure darkness of the Offaly night, from the roof of Birr Castle the young William had a magnificent view of the slowly rotating celestial canopy, enough to inspire him to become one of the most innovative, precocious and groundbreaking astronomers in history. Frustrated that the stars looked so close from the castle roof that he could almost reach out and snatch down a cluster yet remained in reality so far away, William set about doing something about it. He began making his own telescopes. By the age of twenty-four he had become a member of the Astronomical Society and within seven years a member of the Royal Society itself. Becoming more and more ambitious, William experimented with reflecting mirrors, grinding larger and larger ones until, in 1841, he had cast two that were six feet in diameter, their scale belying the delicacy of and meticulous accuracy needed in their construction. Each was five inches thick, weighed three tons, and would form the basis of a monumental astral telescope.

Clearly the completed telescope would be far too large to accommodate indoors so William set about constructing in the castle grounds two vast semicircular stone walls a full fifty feet high, walls that would support the suspension mechanism of the telescopic tube which itself was fifty-four feet long and seven feet in diameter. By the time it was completed in 1845, Parsons' creation was easily the biggest telescope the world had ever seen. Known as the 'Leviathan of Parsonstown', it would remain unsurpassed anywhere in the world until as late as 1917. At the official unveiling – and this is one of the things that made me most disposed towards William Parsons – in order to emphasise the sheer size of the telescope he got a local Church of Ireland minister to walk the entire length of the tube wearing a top hat and holding an umbrella open above his head.

Within a few weeks the telescope had made its first significant sighting, and it wasn't the shivering silhouette of a forgotten, cold and hungry church minister in a top hat. It was a 'bright round nebula, surrounded by a halo or glory at a distance from it, and accompanied by a companion', beamed from the heavens straight to the Parsons nose – the first ever sighting of a geometric spiral nebula. Parsons was seeing further into space than anyone had ever seen before.

The coming of the Great Famine in 1845 put a stop to most of the observations as the Earl and his wife Mary became occupied with famine relief projects. In fact William was one of the few landlords to emerge from the Famine with any credit, one contemporary report opining, 'Lord Rosse is not a person to seek knowledge or enjoyment in the heavens when he ought to be employed on earth and he has devoted all his energy to relieve the present misery and provide for the future.'

When the Famine had passed and he could continue his work, William's discoveries made him hot stuff in the scientific world. He was made President of the Royal Society in 1848, received the Society's Gold Medal in 1851 and was made a commissioner of the Great Exhibition at Crystal Palace. To celebrate this he organised an elaborate fireworks display which, according to contemporary accounts, pulled in a crowd of twenty thousand to the castle grounds. (Fortunately this incendiary hootenanny didn't go the same way as one in nearby Tullamore sixty-odd years earlier, when Charles Bury marked his inheritance of the estate there by sending up a hot air balloon that snagged on a chimney, exploded and burnt down most of the town. I wonder how long it took before people realised that it wasn't part of the show and they should perhaps stop applauding and eating hot dogs.)

After a short meander through the town I arrived at the Birr Demesne, the grounds of the castle where the great telescope still sits. The current Earl and his family continue to live in the castle but the grounds and gardens are open to visitors. On a drizzly day out of season I was the only person exploring the well-appointed science museum near the entrance that is dedicated in the main to the achievements of the Parsons clan. From what I could gather about the third Earl, as well as being a pioneering astronomer and a tireless worker for the poor during the Famine, he was an immensely likeable fellow with few of the airs and graces of the landed aristocracy and none of the ruthless disregard for the tenants of his lands that characterised many of the other Anglo-Irish nobs. Portraits in the museum showed him to be a kindly looking man in images that revealed on the surface little of the relentless zeal and burning passion which he carried for astronomy and discovery throughout his life.

Even from the little I knew about him I was already growing to like William. I am hopeless when it comes to science. I find it utterly incomprehensible. I am the kind of person whose only achievement in school science lessons was absent-mindedly opening a gas tap with a lit taper in my hand and taking my eyebrows clean off. I find it hard to understand people who can be passionate about science purely because I just don't get it; to me science is a workmanlike thing devoid of beauty, something that could never inspire the awe of a great book or piece of music, but the passion that William showed for discovery and the heavens was proving me quite wrong on that score.

William wasn't the only Parsons to make a name for himself, incidentally. His eldest son Lawrence, who became the fourth Earl of Rosse, continued the family's astronomical tradition, establishing for the first time the temperature of the moon, not to mention succeeding his father as Chancellor of Ireland's leading university, Trinity College Dublin. His youngest son, Charles, invented the steam turbine engine which revolutionised the shipping industry. Charles also produced lightweight unmanned aircraft and a helicopter powered by steam turbines. It wasn't all success though: one invention that didn't catch on was a device called the auxetophone, a large, curly, metal horn that was designed to be attached to musical instruments to aid their amplification. Not only did it look unwieldy, but by all accounts the sound was pretty horrendous too. It functioned courtesy of a compressed air system which produced ear-splitting volumes, not just of the instrument itself but also a background hiss so overwhelming that it sounded like the recital was taking place directly beneath Victoria Falls.

Charles Parsons had inherited his love of steam power from William who, by 1869, had in addition to his astronomical exploits created a steam-powered automobile that would chug gently around the grounds and the town. In August of that year, the naturalist Mary Ward and her husband were visiting the Parsons and took a ride into the town with William and two of his sons, including the then fifteen-year-old Charles, in his new contraption. On my way to the castle I'd walked along part of the route they would have travelled until reaching a corner by the church. When the vehicle, 'going at an easy pace' according to a local newspaper report of the time, reached this corner and began to turn, Mary Ward fell from her seat and was fatally injured, meaning that I had stood on the site of the world's first ever automobile fatality.

It wasn't just the Parsons menfolk who had the monopoly on pioneering activities: William's wife Mary certainly didn't just beam proudly at her ingenious family while embroidering samplers. Oh, no. Mary was a noted early pioneer of photography, producing a number of wonderful pictures of life around the estate in her own darkroom and winning the first ever Silver Medal of the Photographic Society of Ireland in 1859. Quite a family, all told: imagine receiving one of those round-robin Christmas cards from them. 'This has been a relatively quiet year for the Parsons, with only four earth-shattering inventions, three national decorations for innovation, a couple of ground-breaking astral discoveries and Mary's chutney scooping the rosette at the town fete once again.'

From the museum I went through the door into the grounds in search of the Leviathan. I soon glimpsed it through the trees, but instead of sloshing over the wet grass straight towards it I followed the path that took me past the front of the castle itself towards the narrow, fast-moving river spanned by what appeared to be a miniature, whitewashed version of the Golden Gate Bridge. This was, being the Parsonses' home, something ground-breaking: the first suspension bridge to be built in Ireland. From further upstream I could hear the rushing water of the small waterfall, where the fourth Earl had set up a water wheel connected to a turbine that powered the castle and the town, giving Birr yet another claim to fame: that of being the first Irish town to be lit by electricity. Speaking as someone whose only notable achievement has been to flip and catch five beer mats in each hand simultaneously, if they hadn't been so nice I could really start to hate the Parsons.

I skirted the river along the paths, deliberately putting off the Leviathan until last. The castle's planned gardens are probably quite something when in full summer bloom, but on a wet and cold winter's day I wasn't exactly seeing them at their finest. I did, however, attain the honour of walking between the garden's three-hundred-year-old, forty-foot-high box hedges which, a little sign nearby told me, are officially the tallest hedges in the world as confirmed by the *Guinness Book of Records*. And I've walked between them. I'm thinking of having a badge made.

Finally I approached the dénouement of my drizzly wander: the Leviathan, its barrel wider than I am tall. Beautifully restored, it sits between its semicircular walls like a gargantuan cannon. As I stood there, the only person in the entire gardens, the only sound the soft staccato hiss of the rain hitting the grass around me, I tried to imagine the telescope at its opening, the walls and wooden staircases and platforms strewn with bunting, a crowd of dignitaries in their finery gathered on a dais: a forest of top hats and crinolines, a band playing, speeches from the podium praising the telescope's size and marvelling at the great discoveries that would be made thanks to its construction. Finally, the highlight of the ceremony: the church minister strolling along the length of the telescope, top hat rampant, twirling his unfurled brolly over his head and emerging at the mouth of the tube, whipping off his hat and sweeping low in an emphatic bow to polite applause and, if he'd been a real show-man, stepping off and floating gently to the ground using the brolly as a parachute.

I stood beneath the end of the barrel that was silhouetted

against the grey sky and rendered blind by a wooden cap, and
tried to picture the place at night beneath a massive clear sky
speckled with layer upon layer of stars: the Earl's assistants in
the dim glow of lanterns heaving at the pulleys that raised the
barrel with a steady metallic clanking, their shouts and instructions ringing across the castle grounds. The Earl in shirtsleeves
rolled to the elbow taking his observations and, in those days
before scientific photography, drawing the things he saw
reflected in the mirrors on to a sketchpad. I pictured him deep
in conversation with one of the regular visiting astronomers,
pointing out things on his sketches and inviting him to view
them through the telescope, sharing his discoveries and hearing
his guest's awed whispers as the secrets of the universe were laid
out for him. Here, in a small town at the very centre of Ireland,
with the castle silhouetted in front of him where as a boy he'd
jump up and try to pluck the stars from the sky, here, William
Parsons made his telescopic journeys deep into the night sky,
travelling further into the speckled darkness than anyone ever
before and coming back with news of great and beautiful
things.

I took out my notebook. Before I'd left the museum I'd
copied down a statement William had made when addressing the
British Association for the Advancement of Science in 1843 that
was superimposed on a giant picture of the man. 'The love of
truth,' he'd said, 'the pleasures which the mind feels in over-
coming difficulties; the satisfaction in contributing to the general
store of knowledge, the engrossing nature of a pursuit so exalted
as that of diving into the wonders of creation: all these are very
powerful incentives to exertion.'

Spots of rain spattered the page from the thick blanket of
grey that hid the sky. I put the notebook away and looked again
at the Leviathan, this massive Cyclops of the skies, and imagined

again those clear and endless nineteenth-century nights, the dark tube silhouetted against a curtain of brilliant stars, the place where a remarkable man dove headlong into the wonders of creation fired by the love of truth.

CHAPTER FOUR

As the Offaly countryside gave way to that of Kildare and beyond I looked out of the bus window and thought about the places I'd just seen and what lay behind them. Moneygall sprouted leaves from a branch of Barack Obama's family tree, while Birr Castle is still occupied by the Parsons family, the direct descendents of William himself. Both the Obamas and the Parsons could map their Irish heritage back to their very beginnings. I knew more about their families than I did about my own.

For all the apparent pride I'd displayed in my own Irish heritage while growing up, and in particular during my rampant plastic paddy phase, in reality I knew next to nothing about what it might actually consist of. But then I hadn't really needed to: having an Irish name and knowing that somewhere in the past there was a man also with that name who had come over to London from Ireland was enough for me to regard myself as a fully paid-up member of the diaspora. It was a facade as flimsy as the fake-aged wood panelling in my local Irish theme pub.

My dad had never talked about our Irish roots. It wasn't that we avoided the subject; it just never cropped up as a topic of conversation among the iffy school reports and fruitless entreaties

to stop slouching and pick my feet up when I walked. Dad
didn't make anything of his roots as I was growing up and nor
had his father when he was growing up. The subject never really
arose, he told me, other than that according to family lore we
apparently came from Cork and he thought he was one-quarter
Irish, with an Irish grandfather. Whether it was the city of Cork
or the wider county he didn't know and I never thought to
pursue it any further. Cork was good enough for me. Cork was
in Ireland and that was all I needed. I was a Corkman, even in
the days when I didn't even know where in Ireland Cork might
actually be. While I wondered occasionally who that ancestor
was, the one whose journey across a short stretch of sea changed
the destiny of generations, back then just the basic fact of my
Irish provenance, however woolly and ill-defined, was all I
needed. The pea-souper of time could stay opaque; I had neither
need nor particular desire to venture into it.

But the longer I lived in Ireland, the more I realised that it
wasn't enough. The more I thought about my move here the
more I felt a growing sense that I was somehow completing
something, something that had begun a very long time ago,
something that was about much more than just me seeking a
shallow endorsement for an absorbed and constructed identity.
At some stage in history, at least a century ago and possibly
more, an Irishman who shared a surname and a whole bunch of
the same genes as me had boarded a boat and watched as everything he knew shrank to the horizon and vanished behind it.
What lay behind that horizon, the stage on which he'd played
out his whole life to that point, was something that in all likelihood he never saw ever again. Knowing what I did about the
history of Irish emigration I knew that it probably wasn't a journey he'd necessarily wanted to make either. This wasn't the
fulfilling of any kind of ambition or a whimsical desire for a

change of scene. No, most likely he'd been driven out the country by poverty, hardship or famine. He may have intended to return; his journey to England might at first have been a temporary solution to an economic situation he'd assumed would improve. He'd be back, he'd see his family again, sleep in his old bed once more. But, from what I could gather, the chances are that he never went home.

I began to feel the presence of this man more and more the longer I spent in Ireland. I'd done what he in all likelihood had intended to do when he'd first stepped on the boat – I'd come back. I became increasingly aware that I was completing his journey, bringing something full circle, a multi-generational story of families and relationships and friendships and tragedies and lives and careers: all the strands that had fanned out from this man's journey I was now gathering and bringing home. The more I thought about it the more I wanted him to know that we were back. I wanted to find somewhere I could physically go to in order to tell him that his story and his journey both now had endings. To do that I would need to find him, to delve into whatever records might be available and which might hold the key in order to find out as much as I could. I had absolutely no idea who he was, not even when or where he'd lived; he was a shadow, a wispy, chimerical presence in my as yet uncharted family tree, but one woven inextricably into my genes. Although I didn't know who he was, although I didn't even know his name, I carried him with me in my very make up and in that sense I had finally brought him home. To truly finish his story I needed to find him. Returning to Ireland was almost the end of the journey but not quite. I needed to find him and hear his story.

It was an exciting prospect. Sitting on the Bull Wall as the year had turned I'd looked across Dublin and thought about how somewhere out there beyond the city there was a place that this all began. The place from which this nameless ancestor had, like Falmouth Kearney in Moneygall and like millions of others, walked away to begin a new life in a new land. I'd watched *Who Do You Think You Are?* and saw myself sitting in posh hotels next to a silver tea service while slitting open big brown envelopes full of birth certificates, parking myself in the sunshine outside coffee shops with obliging genealogists, who would hand me sheaves of newspaper cuttings detailing the startling things the people on those certificates had accomplished. I'd meet long-lost and distant relatives for emotional gatherings and reminiscence and finish up weeping outside the ruin of an old house somewhere.

I told a friend of mine who'd already traced his Irish roots – to the beautiful Dingle peninsula in County Kerry – that I was going to attempt to do the same and he said, 'No doubt you will get that moment, having traipsed up to somebody's front door, of having them stare at you quizzically as you explain that your great-great grandfather's sister married so-and-so. Then the man in the doorway smiles, opens the door and says, "Come in, you're family."'

I would love that, I thought. I would absolutely love that. What greater grounding in the country I call home could there be than doorstepping a distant relative and sharing histories over a pot of tea? What better tribute to my ancestor than the reuniting of the clan after goodness knows how many years?

I was, however, working from a standing start. In terms of concrete information I had practically nothing to go on, but if my dad was right and he was a quarter Irish then my great-grandfather was as far back as I'd need to go anyway. That shouldn't prove too hard, I thought, but a mixture of geography and ancient family disagreements, not to mention the advancing years claiming those who might have remembered something, meant that the only thing I had was the name of my paternal grandfather, who had died before I was born. I thought that the spelling of our name, being a relatively uncommon one, might be an advantage – in Eason's bookshop on O'Connell Street one day I'd leafed through a dictionary of Irish surnames and learned that our spelling can apparently be traced to a particular part of Galway – but I didn't have anything more than that and I didn't really know where to start. The people on *Who Do You Think You Are?* make it look like a straightforward and speedy process, but I suspected that in reality it was nothing of the sort unless your ancestral line happens to be featured in *Burke's Peerage*. And, last time I looked, mine isn't.

It was my cousin Michael who pushed the door ajar when he told me he and his wife Sue had done some excavating of their own and found a census reference to our great-grandfather, a George Edward Connelly who'd been born in 1873 and who at the time of the 1911 British census was living in Kensington, west London. Now if my dad was right and he was a quarter Irish then this would be the man I was looking for; this George Connelly would be the man who'd left Cork. If I could just find confirmation that he'd been born in Cork and, who knows, maybe even a more specific location than that, then we were really in business. I went online and looked up the 1911 census return Mike had found, hoping that it would list his nationality at the very least and maybe even his birthplace. Once I'd typed in his name and location the scan of the census page took an age to load until the image of the return cascaded down the screen; the original document as written by the census-taker, one day in a clutch of lives and histories all gathered on to one page in neat handwriting.

I found George on the list and looked along the page at his entry. He was thirty-nine years old in 1911, he'd been married to Marion for fourteen years and had eight children of whom two had died. He was employed as a wash-house man by a laundress, it said, and at the end of the entry was his place of birth. This could be it, I thought, the key to a mystery that, well, possibly wasn't all that mysterious, as it turned out. However, as my finger reached the relevant column I saw that my great-grandfather had not been born in Cork after all. In fact he'd not even been born in Ireland. He was born in Kensington, London. This single piece of information meant that my lifelong belief I was one-eighth Irish, the one tangible piece of Irishness I thought I had, was now shattered by two words written a century earlier: Kensington, London. I was less Irish than I'd thought.

So, where to next? Well, the internet, obviously. I resigned myself to a long session with the laptop and began rummaging, trawling the many websites that promise to provide the key to unlock your past. I tried most of them, venturing into corners of the web so dark and distant that I almost had to tie a rope around my waist and loop the other end around a door handle to avoid being lost in there forever. You really wouldn't believe just how many genealogy websites there are: the ratio of websites to actual ancestors is probably nudging one to one. Seriously, type in any combination of the words 'roots', 'family', 'ancestors', 'genealogy' and 'your' between a 'www' and a 'com' in your browser and you're sure to come up with somebody panhandling a selection of old records in return for your hard currency. As a renowned sucker I was determined to keep my credit card details firmly in my pocket for as long as I possibly could and kept searching until eventually I found a website that offered a fourteen-day free trial. The range of records it held was staggering: I'd have to give my credit card details to register and the full subscription was rumblingly expensive, the sort of fee for which you really ought to expect a trip back in time to meet your ancestors and catch up over brandy and cigars, but a couple of days of pointing and clicking and I'd surely have all I needed and would be able to cancel my subscription long before the fourteen days were up, a big chasm opened in my wallet and my bank manager was carried gibbering from her desk on a stretcher.

I made a tentative start in searching for George Edward Connelly, born 1873 in Kensington. An enormous list of options unfurled down the page: census records, birth records, marriage records, death records, military records, property records, criminal records – about everything you could think of short of long-playing records, in fact. Thousands upon thousands of possible matches fell down the screen. It was as intimidating as it was exciting and I swallow-dove into this sea of genealogy with the historical enthusiasm of a Victorian man in a stripy bathing suit trying to impress a governess at high tide on Brighton seafront.

What I needed to find most of all was something that would give me the names of George's parents and, hopefully, a reference to where his father, my great-great-grandfather, was born. I tried the 1881 census, as George, being eight years old that year, would have been living with his parents then for sure. I found the most probable match: a record from 128 Southam Street in Kensington. There were seven different families listed as living at that address so it seemed to be a tenement of some kind. I opened up the scan of the original page and found George, my great-grandfather, aged eight, in the middle of six siblings. I ran my gaze up the list and there was his mother Catherine, aged thirty-five. Above her was George's father, the man I was looking for, the man whose story I was bringing full circle by returning to Ireland to live. His name was John Connelly, he was the head of the family, thirty-seven years old, working as a 'cabman' and born in . . .

Clerkenwell.

Clerkenwell, Middlesex, it added, helpfully.

This couldn't be right. It surely couldn't be right. I rummaged further through the list of suggested matches in the 1881 census but no, this was definitely the right family, no question. John Connelly was my great-*great*-grandfather and he wasn't Irish either, at least, he certainly wasn't born there. A chill ran through me – what if there were no Irish roots at all? What if it had all been a spectacular misunderstanding? Not only had I in the past exaggerated an Irish background, it was an entirely fabricated one. I remembered Dad once telling us a preposterous-sounding story involving a man drowning in quicksand and his name being mistranscribed as Connelly when it was actually Cohen, so maybe my roots were actually Jewish rather than Irish? The tale was surely apocryphal but, as I stared at the word Clerkenwell on the screen, it was starting to look almost as likely as my having any roots in Ireland.

I exhaled emphatically. The next step would be to go back another generation to my great-great-*great*-grandfather and see if I could find out where he'd been born, but I was aware that in doing this I might be cutting things fine. Most of the truly useful or at least most comprehensive and readily available records only go back to the mid 1800s (the first UK census was taken in 1841), and this Clerkenwell John Connelly would have been born around 1844. It seemed strange to think I was running out of time when I was actually falling backwards through endless masses of it.

Then I remembered that my mother had once ordered copies of birth certificates from her side of the family from the General

Records Office in the UK. If I could track down John Connelly's birth certificate it would presumably list his parents' names and then I'd at least have a lead on the next generation back.

Sure enough, a couple of weeks later an envelope arrived from England from which I pulled out a pale green folded sheet of paper. I opened it out and smoothed it flat with my forearm. 'Registration District of St George in the East in the County of Middlesex' it said. 'Date and place of birth, third of August 1844, No 5 Jones's Rents', it said. 'John, a boy,' it said. My great-great-grandfather.

I read the next column, name and surname of father. John Connelly, it said. Further along the certificate it gave his mother's name as 'Catherine Connelly, formerly Burke'. I read on: 'occupation of father, labourer', 'Signature of informant: the X mark of John Connelly, father', it said. I set about trying to work out the implications of this new information. John Connelly, my great-great-great-grandfather, was married to a Catherine Burke – Connelly and Burke are both Irish names so there was maybe a chance that both might have come over from Ireland. This could well be the man I was seeking, the man whose journey I was bringing full circle. What I needed to do now was find out where this new John was born.

I tried the 1841 census, the earliest recorded in Britain and the one nearest to the birth date of the younger John. I scoured the records there but could find nobody who might have been my great-great-great grandparents. They didn't seem to be in England at that stage, definitely not in London and certainly not in the part of London where they'd lived at the time of John's birth. Far from foolproof and flawless though the census is, I took this as a good sign: if they weren't in England it indicated that they could well have still been in Ireland in 1841. I turned to the 1851 Census where I found a record for a 'John Connoly' that looked promising. The more I used the records the more in tune I was becoming with how to weed out mismatches and alight on the right people. Now that I knew from the 'x' on the birth certificate that John had been illiterate, I could afford to be more flexible in terms of spelling. There was his name, written by the census-taker in neat Victorian copperplate, John Connoly, aged twenty-eight, which gave him a birth date of around 1823, working as a dock labourer. There was Catherine, his wife, aged thirty. This all seemed to add up. It was time to look at the crucial column at the end of the page: 'Where born'. I'd grown so nervous about it that as soon as the page had appeared I'd placed my hand on the screen covering that column. I didn't want to just glance at it, I wanted to be fully-prepared. I breathed deeply a couple of times and slowly lifted my hand away. There, filling the space allotted to it was just one word.

Ireland.

I let out an expansive sigh and slumped back on the sofa. I laughed involuntarily. I'd solved the mystery. I'd found him. This man, John Connelly, a dock labourer living and working in the heart of the East End, was the ancestor who had left Ireland; the man whose very provenance had played such a curiously large part in my own life. My great-great-great-grandfather John was the man whose journey I was bringing full circle. Not only that, the 'ditto' in the box below showed that his wife Catherine had also been born in Ireland. Both my great-great-great-grandparents had made the journey. Maybe they'd met in London, maybe they'd travelled over together, who knows. Maybe I'd find out – now that I had their names and a location I could hopefully draw even more out from the past and fill in some of the ten-year gaps between censuses.

A few days later John and Catherine's marriage certificate arrived, another light green piece of paper that dissipated the mists of time a little more. On 29 August 1843 in the Parish Church of St Mary Whitechapel, John Connely [*sic*], a bachelor of full age, a labourer of 86 Rosemary Lane, married Catherine Burk [*sic*], a spinster of full age, also of 86 Rosemary Lane. Both signed with an x mark. As a bonus, from the certificate I learned that John's father, my great-great-great-great grandfather was also called John and was apparently a hatter. Catherine's father was listed as Patrick Burk, a licensed victualler.

Two documents, both photocopied on light green paper, had given me the answer I'd been looking for. By barely even leaving the sofa I had gained two vital and irrevocable nuggets of information. One, that I had found beyond doubt the man who had left Ireland, the man whose journey I was completing. Two, that I was exactly as Irish as Barack Obama.

CHAPTER FIVE

The bus shelter was already occupied when I got there. A beaming Korean man was standing with his young son, no more than five years old, who was resplendent in a full Buzz Lightyear outfit topped with a green and white Viking hat from which hung two green and white braids. A blonde Polish woman arrived with her son of about the same age who was wearing similar headgear and had a little shamrock painted on each cheek. Parents and offspring greeted each other. 'Happy St Patrick's Day,' said the woman in heavily accented English.

On the top deck of the bus into town were a large and noisy number of children creating a forest of waving shamrocks on springs that each wore on their head. Across the aisle from me sat a serious-looking South American man, soberly dressed, po-faced and apparently entirely immune to the festivities except for the enormous bright green felt leprechaun hat he wore on his head.

Like no other country's national celebration, St Patrick's Day is marked all across the world with parades, dinners, gigs, festivals and green-hued boozy excess. It's a public holiday in the Republic of Ireland and a bank holiday in Northern Ireland but, curiously, the only other country in the world where St

Patrick's Day is an officially sanctioned holiday is the volcanic Caribbean island of Montserrat (which has a large population of Irish descent after freed Irish slaves ended up there from nearby St Kitts and Nevis in the seventeenth century). Yet still huge swathes of the world go forty shades of green on 17 March each year. From Nova Scotia to Bangkok and Oslo to Cape Town, leprechaun hats are donned, 'Kiss Me, I'm Irish' T-shirts have Guinness spilled down them and lines of people throw their arms around each other to kick their legs out in an approxima-tion of Irish dancing. In America, where some forty-one million claim Irish ancestry, they go particularly nuts on 17 March: whole rivers are dyed green, as are beer, bagels and even build-ings. The one and a half million people who turn out to watch the parade in Manhattan is equivalent to one-third of the entire population of Ireland itself. Baseball teams from San Diego to New York adopt green uniforms on St Patrick's Day: the Washington Nationals even have a 'green hat day' on 17 September, to mark the midway point between St Patrick's Days. During his presidency Bill Clinton once said on 17 March, 'I'm feeling more and more Irish every day', although it's not clear whether that was an expression of nationality osmosis on the part of the notoriously amorous statesman or the result of repeated proximity to a visiting camogie team from Cavan.

March 17 is believed to be the date on which St Patrick handed in his pail in what's largely but not definitively accepted to be the year 460. It became a civic celebration and feast day as a result of lobbying by the Waterford-born Franciscan friar Luke Wadding in the early seventeenth century, although Patrick had been regarded as Ireland's patron saint since around the eighth century. St Patrick's Day soon caught on in a form almost exactly as we know it today: in the 1680s the English writer Thomas Dineley wrote on a visit to Ireland that, 'the seventeenth day of

March yearly is St Patrick's, an immovable feast when ye Irish of all stations and conditions wear crosses in their hats, some of pins, some of green ribbons, and the vulgar superstitiously wear sham-roges, three-leaved grass which they likewise eat to cause a sweet breath . . . very few of the zealous are found sober at night'.

The nature of Irish emigration means that St Patrick has lent his name to a celebration of Irishness around the world from the feast day's earliest times: as early as 1803 an Australian farmer wrote, 'My usual time to commence sow was the first Monday after St Patrick's Day, it requiring a few days to get my men sober.' In 1713 Jonathan Swift was in London on St Patrick's Day and observed that 'the Irish folks were disappointed that the parliament did not meet today because it was St Patrick's Day and the Mall was so full of crosses that I thought all the world was Irish'.

The first St Patrick's Day parade in the US took place in Boston in 1837, with New York's first parade taking place in 1862, staged by Irish soldiers from the British army. Ireland herself, however, was much more reticent in marking St Patrick's Day with the same ostentatious enthusiasm as her overseas brethren. What organised events there were originated, perhaps surprisingly, in the Anglo-Irish hierarchy and were focused upon Dublin Castle, the symbol and seat of British rule in Ireland. These events were usually in the form of balls, galas and formal dinners and it took until 1870 for the first St Patrick's Day cele-bration to be organised across the social strata – unfortunately for most of the revellers however, the 'People's Festival' that took place in Dublin that year was largely under the tutelage of the temperance movement. So, while there were sideshows, exhibi-tions and brass bands playing the popular Irish songs of the day, they all had to be enjoyed through a coldly sober and focused eye.

If there was one positive aspect of such enforced sobriety, it was that you got to appreciate the full wonder, without impairment, of a man calling himself Professor Corteous. In the course of his act, which lasted no more than half an hour, Professor Corteous walked a mile, ran half a mile, lifted twenty 56lb weights one after another and tossed them vast distances, jumped over 225 steeplechase hurdles and for a showstopping finale completed six flying somersaults. Now I don't know about you but I'd say that's almost worth staying off the drink to see, even on St Patrick's Day.

How you could possibly follow that I've no idea, but there were balls in the evening and for those prepared to shell out 2s 6d for what was presumably another alcohol-free jamboree, there was the Grand Ball that featured harp playing, bell ringing and a Mrs Griffin reading aloud from a book called *Gerald Barry: A Story of '98*, all of which must have really torn the roof off the joint.

Despite its apparent success, the People's Festival proved to be a one-off. While it was undoubtedly a hit it still lost money (the less pious members of the organising committee might have raised a rueful eyebrow at the total absence of bar takings) and never happened again. What became of Professor Corteous is unknown: a tour of the chat-show circuit, a range of *Keep Fit with Corteous* DVDs, a couple of motivational books (*Conquering Life's Steeplechase: 225 Ways to Achieve Your Goals*) and a slow descent into alcoholism and bankruptcy, I should think.

In the years that followed, Ireland fell further behind in the global celebration of St Patrick's Day. It was still a public holiday, not to mention a religious celebration of course, but the crucial difference was that the expats wearing their green ribbons and drinking their green beer were even in the early days celebrating an idealised, sentimental image of home, not just the country of

Ireland and its patron saint. When you actually were at home, somehow the resonance wasn't there and it was largely just a public holiday like any other.

Indeed, Dublin didn't even have any kind of significant parade on St Patrick's Day until after the Second World War, when what was billed as a celebration of Irish industry began an annual trundle up O'Connell Street. A procession of tractors, diggers and combine harvesters parading past a podium of po-faced dignitaries sounds more like something you'd see in a small town in the further reaches of the Soviet Union at the end of a five-year plan than an emphatic endorsement of Irish national pride. It was hardly something to bring the tourists flocking over in great numbers, unless those tourists were a couple of traction engine enthusiasts' societies from east Yorkshire wearing matching embroidered polo shirts and moaning that they couldn't find a decent pint of bitter anywhere.

It took until the mid-seventies for the penny to truly drop as Ireland looked at the massive crowds lining Fifth Avenue and began to realise the kind of cash they were missing out on. It was decided that Dublin should become more like New York on St Patrick's Day, with a parade that didn't list caterpillar tracks as a necessary condition of entry. However, as much as Ireland quite reasonably coveted a slice of the action taking place in its name around the world, the trouble was that New York had it all sewn up. Thousands took part and millions more watched, and what they were watching was no longer a celebration of Ireland and St Patrick but the celebration of an idea of home, a memory of something lost and idealised in the collective memory. It was an idea of Ireland that had mutated through the generations to become almost a fairytale and there wasn't a silage transporter to be seen. As the seventies became the eighties and then the nineties, Dublin found that it was trying and failing to match

New York in presenting an image of itself that was idealised and, essentially, fake. Even though Ireland had the reality, *was* the reality, it tried to emulate the myth instead. It was designed to attract tourists and to an extent it worked, but the American visitors in particular were frequently disappointed. So idealised was their view of Ireland and so idealised was their expectation of what St Patrick's Day in Dublin would be – if Manhattan put on such a show, what must it be like actually in *Dublin* – that Ireland itself could never live up to the image.

So in 1996 Dublin wised up, realised it couldn't ever compete directly with New York and introduced the St Patrick's Festival, a celebration of Ireland staged over several days in locations across the city and the country at large. Most towns and many villages have parades of some description, from the now massive hootenanny in Dublin to the parade from the Weigh Inn to the Leigh Valley pub in Dripsey, County Cork – at twenty-six yards the shortest St Patrick's Day parade in the world, fact fans – via the samba-tinged celebrations in Gort, County Galway, where a third of the population of the town is Brazilian after a deal forged by the local meat processing plant with struggling counterparts in South America that brought surplus workers to Ireland.

In the Britain I lived in during the nineties the Irish were becoming cool again and St Patrick's Day began to reflect that. There were pub promotions and targeted advertising campaigns by Guinness and other brewers. Manchester staged the first parade in Britain for many years in 1990: there were less than four hundred people participating but by the end of the decade there were fifteen thousand, and this despite the bombs that went off in the city in 1996. In 1997 Birmingham had its first St Patrick's Day parade since the IRA bombed the city centre with the loss of twenty-one lives in 1974, while in 2002 London staged its first St Patrick's Day parade. Now there are events and commemorations of some kind in towns and cities across Britain as diverse as Leeds, Milton Keynes and Woking.

It was into this reborn sense of a cool Ireland that I'd waded. By the mid-late nineties, every Irish music artiste in Britain who could cobble together an hour's worth of Pogues and Dubliners covers was pretty much naming their price when it came to St Patrick's Day and even a musical chancer like me usually had no trouble finding himself a lucrative gig somewhere (I remember going into a pub in Bromley around that time and asking if they were looking for live music for St Patrick's Day. I saw the manager's hackles rise almost visibly. 'Nope,' he said, 'this is an English pub, we don't have Irish stuff, we have English things here and we celebrate St George's Day.' 'Oh, OK,' I replied, 'when's that again?' He couldn't remember.)

It's been a public holiday in Ireland since 1903 and – get this – between 1903 and the mid-seventies part of the same parliamentary bill also ensured that the pubs of Ireland remained firmly closed all day. All. Day. On St Patrick's Day. There was in fact only one place in the whole of Ireland where a drink could be had and that was at the annual dog show at the Royal Dublin Showground, which had a long-standing special dispensation to serve alcohol. You can only imagine the mass canine borrowing that must have gone on across Dublin and beyond in the days leading up to 17 March.

Such abstinence was a distant and curious memory for most Irish people as I sat on the top deck of a bus full of waving shamrocks, next to a man trying to look inconspicuous with a massive green felt hat on his head. When we reached the centre of town, Talbot Street, leading up to O'Connell Street, was a sea of these inexplicably popular hats, as if the leprechauns had all gone on strike and were marching on Dublin *en masse*. All it needed was a man with a megaphone chanting 'What do we want? Tax-breaks for people living at the ends of rainbows! When do we want them? Now!' and a few on the fringes selling copies of *Socialist Leprechaun* and the picture would have been complete.

On every street corner there were people selling hats and scarves that had clearly been in a bin bag at the back of a cupboard since the previous year's Paddy's Day, some of which even looked as though they were first draped over a proffering arm during the 1990 World Cup. We made our way to O'Connell Street where the crowds lining the parade route were already several people deep even though it wasn't due to start for an hour. Somehow I had managed to squire a couple of tickets to the VIP grandstand, a scaffolding and tarpaulin structure dead opposite the GPO: the best seats in Dublin. Jude and I squeezed past people who may well have been there since the first milky light of dawn and took our seats. Front row. I'd never been in a VIP section for anything before. I didn't know what kinds of things went on in them. Hence I had ummed and ahhed all morning about what to wear and in the event, I found that while my tails could pass through the gap in the back of the seat my top hat wouldn't fit under it and I had nowhere to put my cane.

We sat down and looked across at the crowd gathered some twenty feet away, pressed up against the barrier. They must have been there for hours already after arriving early to bag the best view, the view I'd acquired for myself wholly undeservedly after strolling in, bold as brass, hands in pockets like I owned the place, within minutes of the parade starting. Not only that, I had a seat too. If it rained I was under cover. There was even a Portaloo not twenty feet from where I was sitting: the people opposite would have to go and find a pub or cafe and use the toilet there, losing in an instant the space they'd worked so hard and for so long to obtain. I thought about me, the most un-VI

person in the VIP section and thought about the people opposite, the people for whom the parade was truly arranged, people
who had in some cases doubtless flown across the Atlantic to be
here, whereas I'd just hopped on a number 130. I thought about
the hardships they were enduring to stand pressed against a metal
barrier for hours and compared it to me swanning in at the last
minute barely an hour after rolling out of bed and finding a seat
reserved for me. And then I thought, well, better luck next
time, suckers.

A man with a microphone moved among them, trying to
cajole them into conversation or performance over the tannoy to
distract them from leading a proletarian charge across the tarmac
and skewering all us freeloading lounge lizards with their plastic
flagpoles. A small boy in a green Stetson belted out a few lusty
bars of 'The Fields of Athenry', then the compere moved to a
woman nearby and asked where she was from. 'Wisconsin,' she
replied, to which the MC responded, 'And the lady next to
you? Oh, it's a gentleman, I'm terribly sorry, sir.'

It was clear as we sat in the unseasonably warm weather that
the parade was still a while away, so I asked Jude what St Patrick's
Day means to an Irish person in Ireland.

'Well, certainly as a child it meant a day off school, there was
Mass and then a parade, but that was it,' she said. 'I don't remember it being a massive deal; you'd get *Darby O'Gill and the Little
People* on TV but that was about it. I was involved a bit when I
was a kid because I was playing the tin whistle in a band and we
were in the parade, so you'd practise for that and usually end
up standing in the cold and rain for hours on the day but you
got crisps at the end so that was fine. I remember my granddad
would always have a sprig of shamrock in his hatband on St
Patrick's Day. Also being a good little Irish Catholic, Paddy's Day
falls right in the middle of Lent, and you had to give up sweets

for Lent. But the one day during Lent where you *could* eat sweets was Patrick's Day. That's probably got a lot to do with why people go out on the lash: it was the one day of Lent you could do something like that so get plenty into you, boy.

'It was always seen as a big drinking night when you got to university or whatever, but as for the whole being Irish thing? No, it didn't make a difference: we're Irish all the time, what's different about today? You can only "be Irish" if you've got someone to be Irish *to*. Everyone's Irish here, but I think it's only when you go abroad that you feel a need to really properly celebrate it.'

At that the President of Ireland, Mary McAleese, arrived in a limousine, flanked by garda outriders wearing sunglasses and revving their machines as if they'd just watched an entire box set of *CHiPs*, and took a seat further along from us, beaming and waving from beneath an impressive coiffure.

Once the President was all settled in there was a commotion further up O'Connell Street and the telltale window-rattling thump of approaching drums began to bounce around the buildings. There was a craning of necks as small children were hoisted on to shoulders accompanied by a mass scrabbling in bags for cameras. And that was just the President. The parade was on its way and at its head was the man it was all supposed to be about. There, wearing green robes and carrying a large gold-coloured staff, was St Patrick himself waving and beaming at the crowds and generally milking it for all he was worth. He strolled off up the street a fair distance ahead of the rest of the parade, turning this way and that, clonking his staff along the ground and waving at everyone. To his credit, he stopped short of actually high fiving people as he passed. He was so far ahead of the parade in fact that it was almost as if they were getting St Patrick out of the way early doors so the real fun could start. After all, for the last four hundred years or so at least, outside the Church, St Patrick's

Day has not really been about the man himself. In fact, ask a passer-by at random about St Patrick and they'll be able to tell you that he's the patron saint of Ireland and that he drove the snakes out of the country but I bet that's probably about the extent of it.

As the man in the green robes waved his way along the street in the direction of the Liffey I wondered who he really was; this saint who is known and celebrated all around the world and whose name is once a year taken as the dropping of the flag on a day of boozy excess, vomit-blocked pub toilets and misty-eyed global diddly-aye.

As you'd expect for someone who lived in a century numbered in single digits, we don't know very much for certain about him. Where historians have been lucky is in the fact that he left two written documents behind, the *Confession* and the *Letter to the Soldiers of Coroticus* from which some kind of timeline and biography has been established, embellished and fleshed out into a number of versions of his remarkable life, the broad gist of which goes something like this. Now, bear in mind that there are a number of theories about who Patrick might have been – one of which even suggests he was two people – so what follows can be taken as nothing more than an approximation of definitive biography that's probably along the right lines.

Patrick was born a Roman citizen in Britain in the late fourth century, possibly during the reign of Emperor Theodosius, into the landowning aristocracy. His father Calpornius was a magistrate and a Christian deacon while his grandfather Potitus, who was blessed with a name that sounds a bit like an Australian saying 'potatoes', was a priest. Historians say that these religious vocations may not have been as holy as they seemed: at that time members of the clergy benefited from tax relief which led to a flurry of holy orders being taken by the suddenly pious.

The family lived in a small town called Bannaventa Berniae whose exact location is unknown but was somewhere on the west coast of Britain, possibly in what's now Wales. He received some education in Latin and probably spoke a local dialect. In the documents he left behind Patrick says that as a youngster he was an atheist who at the age of fifteen did something extraordinarily bad; he committed some kind of crime, some kind of outrageous sin that would haunt him for the rest of his life. He doesn't specify what it was, but clearly it was something quite spectacular that happened 'on one day in my youth. Not even a day, in the space of an hour'. Many scholars have pondered whether he might have killed somebody, but while we'll never know for sure it's probably safe to say it was more serious than doing a runner from Bannaventa Berniae's leading curry house.

He wouldn't have had much time to ruminate on his indiscretion however, for within a year he had been captured by one of the raiding parties that regularly plundered the coast and taken to Ireland as a slave. Such kidnappings were a constant threat to coastal communities and a terrifying prospect: the raiders would creep into towns and villages under cover of night and take as many people as they could back to the shore where they'd left their ships. They would then cherry-pick the ones who would command the best prices in the slavery market and kill the rest, after which the select few were chained together by the neck and taken across the Irish Sea. There can't have been many worse experiences than being torn from your bed in the middle of the night by fearsome men screaming in a language you didn't understand, being route marched to the sea, seeing friends and family members butchered in front of you and then being herded on to a boat by the same murderers and taken to an unknown land for a life that came with a cast-iron, copper-bottomed guarantee of utter relentless misery. The Romans had never reached

Ireland, or at least never conquered it: evidence has been found
that some trading would have taken place, but there was no significant Roman presence there. Hence the Roman communities
on the western coast of Britain would have hummed with terrifying rumour and hearsay about the brutal, ruthless people that
occupied the mysterious, windswept, rain-lashed land across the
water. When the rumours became reality the prospect must have
been utterly terrifying.

When he arrived in Ireland Patrick was almost immediately
sold to a farmer with whom he would remain during his six
years as a slave. Tradition has it that the farm was in County
Antrim, while some historians reckon the description Patrick
gives of the place in his writing suggests somewhere further
south and west; possibly in modern County Mayo. Patrick
worked with sheep, which placed him in one of the lowest
classes of slavery (domestic slavery was seen as the mildest role
while animal husbandry was somewhere near the bottom of the
list, just above the death sentence of mining). The farm was a
small one where he looked after the sheep and hence spent
much of his time alone in the fields. It was during this time that
he seemed to undergo a profound religious conversion.

'I was like a rock stuck deep in muddy water,' he wrote, 'but
God arrived and with his power and compassion reached down
and pulled me out.'

Whatever the nature of Patrick's epiphany, he began to recall
the Bible stories he'd heard in his youth and started praying
morning and night. He also undertook periods of fasting. It was
after one of these periods that Patrick heard a voice call to him
one night: 'You have fasted well and soon will be going home.'
The following night the same voice announced: 'Your ship is
ready.' Patrick knew what this meant: he snuck off from the
farm early the following morning and made for the coast.

At the time the most likely ports where Patrick would have found a ship to take him across the sea would have been Wexford, Waterford and Cork – all a great distance from both Antrim and Mayo. It was an unspeakably dangerous journey: had he been stopped or discovered he would undoubtedly have been killed. Being of a different race to the Irish he would have been recognised as an escaped slave immediately so would have travelled at night and hidden by day. Somehow he evaded detection and reached one of the ports where he set about finding the ship that would carry him home. Eventually he managed to persuade a captain to take him across and on arriving spent a month wandering through empty country with the crew (presumably looking for cargo to take back to Ireland). Things weren't going well and, having noticed Patrick's enthusiasm for praying, eventually the captain asked him to pray for some food, a prayer that was answered almost immediately when a herd of pigs squeaked and grunted into view from around a nearby hillside.

Finally Patrick left the captain and crew and made his way home, where he must have been greeted as if risen from the dead. Nobody ever, ever escaped slavery in Ireland. After a few days' resting and presumably going through his whole repertoire of anecdotes about life as an Irish slave to the parade of family and friends that came to visit, he had a vivid dream one night in which a man named Victoricus arrived from Ireland looking for him with a bundle of letters, one of which was headed 'The Voice of the Irish'. At that Patrick heard voices calling, 'Holy servant boy, come and walk among us.' He woke up with a terrible, heavy sadness that stayed with him all day – a few pints of Caffrey's used to have the same effect on me – until another dream the following night. In this dream, Patrick heard a prayer in words he couldn't understand until the final lines, when the voice intoned, 'The one who gave you your spirit; it is he who speaks in you.' Putting both dreams together, Patrick felt he was being called back to Ireland to do religious work.

No one is entirely sure what happened next. Rather than standing on the coast and flagging down the next passing shipload of hairy-arsed raiders, Patrick would have studied to become a priest, some say in France or possibly even as far away as Italy, and before long was appointed bishop. It was only then, when he was probably in his early thirties and a fully fledged, card-carrying bishop that Patrick went back to Ireland to fulfil his destiny.

When he arrived there were already Christians there, possibly, like him, slaves kidnapped from Britain. Pope Celestine had sent Palladius there in 431, and he wouldn't have done that if there weren't already Christians in Ireland. There's a suggestion that Patrick may even have travelled as one of Palladius's assistants; after all he would have been one of very few clerics, if any, who would have known Ireland well. Whatever the circumstances of his arrival he travelled around the country for several years, mainly in the north, meeting with local kings and converting many of them to Christianity. He spent forty days fasting on the mountain now known as Croagh Patrick in Mayo, where he banished all the snakes from Ireland (some of them would return as property developers in the boom years) and ensured that centuries later people would climb the mountain in his honour, often in bare feet. Even in the days before Twitter he managed to build up a considerable following – he claimed to have converted 'thousands' to Christianity – and it was when an attack by the English king Coroticus saw many of his converts on the east coast of Ireland killed or sold into slavery that he was prompted to write the letter whose text survives to this day. It was an epistle that infuriated the Church, who regarded it as an attempt to interfere with the congregation of another bishop and recalled

Patrick from Ireland. Knowing that this would inevitably lead to his replacement, and wanting to finish his work in Ireland, Patrick instead sent them his *Confession*. In response, the Church brought up the matter of the terrible sin of his early years and went on to accuse him of corruption on a massive scale.

And that's pretty much where the trail goes cold. We don't know the outcome of Patrick's run-in with the men in the big hats, nor do we know when he died: 460 is a common estimate and 17 March a downright guess, but his legacy and legend survived in Ireland, survived for so long in fact that a man dressed as him was now wheeling around the main street of the nation's capital waving to the crowds and waggling a big golden staff, marking the day that still bears his name more than one and a half millennia after his death.

After Patrick the parade was a mixed bag, from the parping clarinets beneath the peaked caps of the band of the *Garda Síochána*, without whom no state occasion is complete, and the Artane Boys' Band in their light blue and red uniforms that make them look like they're on secondment from International Rescue to the frankly surreal sights of a giant golden inflatable pig and Herbie, the Volkswagen Beetle with a mind of its own. Perhaps the most bizarre part of the parade was that which celebrated the GAA's 125th anniversary. People in powder-blue shirts and white shorts came ambling down the road carrying and wearing an assortment of everyday objects rendered bizarre by their sheer scale. A giant hurley arrived supported by about a dozen people holding it above their heads followed by a sliotar of equivalent size. Then a float with a commentary box on top arrived, in which the legendary GAA commentator Micheál Ó Muircheartaigh was commentating on the crowd as he passed, sixty years to the day after his first commentary. Ó Muircheartaigh is a terrific character and the gems from his commentaries are numerous: 'Pat Fox out to the forty and grabs the sliotar. I bought a dog from his father last week. Fox turns and sprints for goal. The dog ran a great race last Tuesday in Limerick. Fox fires a shot, it goes to the left and wide, and the dog lost as well,' being one and, 'Anthony Lynch, the Cork corner-back, would be the last person to let you down: his people are undertakers,' being another.

A man then passed us with an enormous friendly looking dog strapped to his back, another with a giant log, behind him a man carrying three washing machines, one on top of the other, and next to him a guy with what appeared to be a giant book-case on his shoulders, complete with a desktop computer on one of the shelves. Now, either some ambitious burglars had inad-vertently strayed into the parade or these lads were representing every aspect of GAA life, from the games themselves to the vol-unteers and parents around the country who washed the kit and dealt with the admin all the way down to the grassiest of the grassroots of the organisation. Brian Dooher, the captain of the reigning All-Ireland football champions Tyrone, and Henry Shefflin, who skippered the all-conquering Kilkenny hurling team, had already been past in vintage cars, accompanied by the captains of the Cork women's football and camogie champions and followed by a parade of supporters from each county carry-ing flags, but this was a far more imaginative way of marking the place of the GAA in the community. It was curious, it was idio-syncratic, it was imaginative and it worked.

After that there were the obligatory people on stilts, bored-looking children in marching bands uncomfortably hot in their tasselled uniforms, mentally calculating how many more times they'd have to play the same tune and not liking the answer, and theatrical groups, using the biggest and most captive audience they'd ever had as an excuse to ham it up like they'd never hammed before.

Finally, after an hour or so of marching, parping, hamming and beaming, and as the cloud of exhaust fumes from the Irish VW Beetle Club dissipated into the warm spring sunshine, an anticlimactic silence descended on the street and people began to drift away to whatever revelry they had planned for the afternoon, pushing apart the crowd barriers and wading through discarded flags, hats and food detritus. We looked in vain for a pub that wasn't full to bursting and eventually shoehorned ourselves into the Stag's Head, a tremendous pub just off Dame Street. It was a curious phenomenon: the place seemed to be full of revellers, then empty, then full again, then empty, as if the pub was actually breathing people. Close to us a group of lads from Saskatchewan wearing hats and 'The leprechauns made me do it' T-shirts kept raising their glasses and raucously toasting St Patrick's Day before embarking on their next drinking game and launching into whichever filthy song occurred to them as a result. It was a scenario being acted out across the globe: the pubs and the streets were in a state of bibulous carnage and it was still only three o'clock in the afternoon.

In the evening Jude and I went to see a concert of Irish music specially staged for St Patrick's Day and designed to celebrate the Irish scattered all around the world. Now, while there were some tremendous musicians on stage it was soon clear that the whole thing was a little too rich for my palate. The singer kept making speeches about what a grand little country we are, sure, aren't we marvellous altogether, being spread all around the globe and that, and achieving all that great oul' stuff that we do, eh? He mentioned the United States and a great whooping and hollering sprang up around the auditorium. A couple of people near the back began chanting, 'U-S-A! U-S-A!' He mentioned Canada, and the fact that he'd once had such a great time in Newfoundland that he stayed for – wait for it – three more days than he'd originally planned, the big mad party monster. The Canadians in the audience loved it judging by the noise they made and that, it seemed, was the point of the exercise.

This was a sanitised celebration of the slickest kind; playing unashamedly to the tourist gallery (and dollar) and, understandably, giving them what they wanted to hear about the old homeland. The show, I deduced, was designed to be taken on tour, not staged here, but on St Patrick's Day it seemed to me Ireland, or at least Dublin, was temporarily abroad. The nation's capital was for the duration of the day New York, or Boston, or Philadelphia, or Toronto, or any other city in which the Irish had gathered in large numbers after having to leave their homeland. The city had become Not-Ireland for the day; taking on the mantle of its own image, the image forged abroad, the image I'd bought into back in London. This show was a part of that; giving the audience what they wanted and expected to hear, reinforcing their existing views and enabling them to go home content that yes, Ireland was just like they imagined, just like how their grandfather had described it when he'd got all teary-eyed and wistful after a couple of whiskeys with his other retired buddies from the police department.

The music was slick and smooth, the musicians spaced widely around the stage when I'd always thought Irish traditional music had been about togetherness, about being elbow to elbow, feeling the music coursing through each of you, taking on a life of its own through the proximity of the players, being about an energy attuned to the rhythms of Irish life. With the players strung out across the stage and on individual podia, it seemed that the real spirit of Irish music had been excised entirely. That's not to criticise the musicians at all, far from it, each was a terrific player and the musicianship was of the highest quality, but this seemed wrong to me, this set-up. It was quite passionless. As the show went on, with its background images of waves crashing against the rocky Atlantic shore flashing up on a screen above the musicians and its tributes to an Ireland I didn't really recognise, I found myself longing to be in a pub somewhere, at an impromptu session where the musicians sat bunched around a table in the corner and flung themselves at blistering reels while creamy pints accumulated on the table in front of them from appreciative listeners, condensation ran down the windows on the inside and rain on the outside and you had to shout to be heard above the music. I thought of the front bar at the Cobblestone, a little way out of Dublin town centre at Smithfield, a defiant reminder of old Dublin at the end of the revamped, redeveloped square that was three sides of new swanky apartments and shops and one side of condemned rickety buildings that looked as if a good hard sneeze would be enough to bring them crashing down. The Cobblestone staging its regular sessions where, even with the pub at its most crowded, the musicians' table is never occupied by anyone but musicians. It's dingy, it's busy and it's magnificent and as I sat in the air-conditioned auditorium watching musicians spread wide apart going through a pre-planned set of songs and tunes rehearsed to within an inch of their lives for a seated theatre audience, I realised that I was probably in the wrong place. I looked at Jude sitting next to me. She looked absolutely furious. She was practically curled in the foetal position and all but chewing on her kneecaps, nearly shaking with anger. You could practically see lightning playing around her temples. The lights came up for the interval and she leaned over to me and whispered, 'Can we go? I have to get out of here.'

We left, marching through the foyer at an almost military pace, and out into the night.

'That was a slightly sophisticated way of selling utter crap,' she said after fuming gently for a while as we walked briskly through the dark streets away from the venue. 'It was the most heartless, cold bullshit I have ever seen in my life, pandering to the worst stereotypes. It was . . . mercenary almost, it was all about pressing the right buttons in that particular audience, there was nothing real in it, it was dreadful. All that "Sure, aren't we a grand little country" bowing and scraping, saying ooh, we're nearly as good as everyone else now. It's the mindset of a different generation. My generation doesn't see itself that way any more. There's been an awful lot of that "Look at the size of us, we're up against these big countries and we do grand", when we're as good and as bad as any country of our size and better and worse than a lot of others bigger than us.

'What we saw in there represents a huge lack of confidence,' she continued, pointing back in the direction of the venue. 'It's almost an inferiority thing: thinking we have to paint everything bloody green to get a bit of attention when we're not inferior, not at all. It's just all so *fake*. I mean, I can deal with fake, the whole *Quiet Man* thing, because it's laughably fake, but this had just enough in it for people to actually take it seriously when it was the emptiest, most soulless, meaningless tripe I've ever seen. I actually found it hugely insulting, it was talking down to people, saying, "This is what being Irish is all about" and it isn't, it really, really isn't.'

I realised that a few years ago I would have watched that show and thought that it really *was* what being Irish was all about. The references to the Famine, the scattering of the Irish to all corners, the slick musicianship, the mystical images of rocky Atlantic shorelines: it was just the kind of thing I'd have swallowed whole. It was that Caffrey's ad turned into a live show and extended across an entire evening.

Somehow, naively perhaps, I'd expected St Patrick's Day in

Dublin to give me a glimpse into the Ireland behind the image. Instead, certainly in terms of the concert, it had sent me back to the Caffrey's ad. If I'd thought I'd find the reality behind the image simply by wandering around a selection of agreeable pubs on appropriate days I was clearly quite wrong. I realised that I would have to work a little harder than that. And first, I'd have to go back to school.

CHAPTER SIX

I couldn't remember exactly the last time I'd been in a classroom. It would have been at university, for sure, and I would doubtless have been shabbily dressed, utterly befuddled, struggling to understand what was going on and dreading being picked out to answer a question. So, when I attended my first Irish language evening class little had changed in the meantime other than the location.

I've always believed that a good way to gain an understanding of a nation or a culture is through its language; the tongue spoken by the people that has developed over thousands of years and provided the soundtrack to its history as well as being the basis of its literature and culture. It's a shame, then, that I am to languages what your run-of-the-mill dugong is to debating Cartesian dualism. French and German finished for me (or, more accurately, with me) at O level and, an unsuccessful university brush with Russian aside I have not since troubled the translators. A Norwegian friend of mine once taught me the phrase, '*jeg er kjempe dumm*', getting me absolutely word perfect and having me repeat it solemnly over and over again until it was – as it still is – embedded permanently in my consciousness, before she collapsed into giggles and revealed that *jeg er kjempe dumm* means 'I am incredibly stupid', but apart from that, nothing. So as I walked past Trinity College one dark and chilly evening I was hoping that the power of enthusiasm was enough to eclipse a distinct lack of natural aptitude. So far in my life this had failed to succeed with football or music so maybe languages would prove to be third time lucky. If not, at least my Norwegian phrase might come in useful. Again.

I'd signed up for a beginners' course in the Irish language, for which I was to give up two evenings a week for three hours at a time over the next six weeks. It was a big – not to mention expensive – commitment, but I was keen. Really keen. So keen, I'd even bought a new pencil case and ring binder specially. I meant business, and I meant it *as Gaelige*. By learning Irish, I thought, I would take a big step forward in understanding Ireland and Irishness. It would be a big step forward too in fitting in here; after all, don't they always say that as long as you make an effort with a language, people will always appreciate it? Even if you're no good and end up saying things like, 'Can you tell me the way to the dinosaur plinth please? I require a template.'

I'd noticed that even in the relatively short time I'd been in Ireland, inflections were already seeping into my accent. Ever since I was a child I've been a bit of an accent chameleon, absorbing idioms and local twangs with startling speed. I once spent two weeks in the Lake District as a teenager and came back sounding like a septuagenarian Cumbrian shepherd. This talent seems to have diminished a little with passing years, and Jude would helpfully point out that whenever I tried to imitate an accent from any part of Ireland my efforts were 'fierce shocking', but I'd definitely noticed new words and phrases creeping into my everyday speech. I'd begun appending 'altogether' and 'so' to sentences, for example. The word 'like' was also terminating a burgeoning number of phrases. 'Grand' was increasing in usage, in the sense of 'fine and dandy' rather than 'a thousand pounds'. My pronunciation of the name of my home city was well on the way from a cockney 'Dablin' to the more native 'Doblun' and my usual south London greeting of 'Awright?' was being tangibly nudged aside by 'Howzigoin?' or even 'What's the story?'

The word 'after' was beginning to elbow its way into sentences like 'I'm just after heading into town' and 'I'm after finishing the milk, can you pick up some on your way home?' It was when I started referring to people as 'yer man' instead of 'him' that I knew my south London accent was changing forever, mutating into a strange cockney–Irish hybrid that I christened Éirestuary English. It wasn't a conscious thing, in fact these linguistic interlopers often sounded faintly ridiculous when dispersed among my regular London vernacular in the way middle-aged men do when they try to adopt the youth speak of the day, innit bro? For all my subconscious adoption of certain words and idioms I would never completely assimilate an Irish accent; the cockney would always be there. My nasal south London twang would remain with me even if I never left Ireland nor watched an episode of *Only Fools and Horses* ever again. I'd be stuck with Éirestuary English for life.

The main reason for my developing these quirks so tangibly and quickly was Jude. Although she'd spent many of her adult years living as far afield as Australia, Italy and New Zealand, Jude's accent and speech patterns had not been diluted one iota, as I had to learn quickly from the fledgling days of our relationship. She described a friend of hers once as a 'gas man'. Good on him, I thought, that's a nice steady job. But no, a 'gas man' here isn't someone who'll turn up at your house in a boiler suit carrying a big spanner and telling you for God's sake not to light a match, instead he's a fine and entertaining fellow; great company altogether. When Jude 'gives out', it means not a distribution of items without financial recompense but that she's complaining about something. If the complaint is serious, she 'gives out stink'. If Jude is really startled by something she'll express it with the exultation, 'Jancy Mac!' The next level up being 'Janey Mackers' until the ultimate, jaw-dropping über-surprise of 'Janey Mackerooney!'

One word I inherited from Jude, and it's one that even now I can't work out how I managed without before I arrived here, is 'yoke'. Yoke is the most versatile word I've ever come across. In Ireland, and particularly rural Ireland, it means neither servitude nor even the wooden crosspiece joining two ploughing oxen. No, the magnificent word 'yoke' means 'thing, whatsit, thingummybob, oojamaflip' but in a much more agreeably flexible way. Those English words imply that you're fumbling for the right word, but in Ireland 'yoke' *is* the right word. 'Look at that yoke over there.' 'That's a great yoke, altogether.' 'Did you pick up that yoke like I asked you?' 'Oof, that's a fine big yoke.' See? Trust me, if you're not using it already, you will be before the day is out. It's been a linguistic revelation to me, that 'yoke' yoke.

But while I was absorbing Hiberno-English, as the English spoken in Ireland has come to be known, without really meaning to, my decision to throw myself fully into learning Irish was a conscious one. And I was excited.

Irish (although many people call it Gaelic and they aren't strictly wrong, most people here call it Irish to distinguish it from Scots Gaelic) is a beautiful language. To the ear it sounds lyrical, rhythmic and poetic. You can immerse yourself in Irish and feel content without having to understand a word: the playwright John Millington Synge, who eventually became fluent in Irish and spent months at a time on the Irish-speaking Aran Islands, said, 'There is no language like Irish for soothing and quieting.'

At first glance it's ubiquitous here. Every road sign and every government document in Ireland are in both English and Irish; in some parts of Ireland the signs are only in Irish. In parts of County Kerry, for example, the equivalent of British 'STOP' road signs say '*tóg go bog é*' which translates as – and I love this – an instruction to 'take it easy'. There's a dedicated Irish language national television station, TG4, that has a popular Irish language soap opera, *Ros Na Rún*, and broadcasts among other things *South Park* dubbed into Irish, and a national Irish language radio station. To the outsider, Irish certainly gives the impression of being a vibrant language, one that's seen and heard constantly across the country and across the media.

So imagine my surprise when I learned that Irish is the main language of just 3 per cent of the population. Three per cent. In Ireland, somewhere between just forty and eighty thousand people out of a population of more than four million use Irish as their main language. There are one and a half million people here who regard themselves as Irish speakers, a third of whom use the language every day, but for an indigenous and historic language it's a surprisingly low figure. In addition, most of those Irish speakers, almost all of them in fact, are on the very fringes of the island in areas collectively known as the *Gaeltacht*; places officially recognised by the government as having Irish as their first language. Mostly they cling to the Atlantic coast in Donegal, Mayo, Galway and Kerry, as well as odd inland spots such as in the West Muskerry region of West Cork, on the Ring peninsula in County Waterford and a couple of small areas of County Meath, north west of Dublin. There are also Irish-speaking areas developing in Belfast, and to a lesser extent in Dublin itself. *Gaelscoileanna*, schools that use Irish as their main language but which lie outside the *Gaeltacht* areas, are increasing in popularity in Ireland – there are more than thirty primary *gaelscoileanna* in County Dublin alone – while Irish is a compulsory subject in all

Irish schools right up to Leaving Certificate, the Irish equivalent of A levels.

So, given the apparent vibrancy of the language and its wide-spread role in education and media, I was a little surprised that when I told friends that I was taking up Irish they reacted as if I'd just announced that I was learning by heart the complete works of Sir Walter Scott in Cantonese. Why in the name of all that's holy, they responded in unison, jaws clunking to the floor in a cacophony of oral percussion, would anyone want to learn Irish? By *choice*?

A little concerned about this as the first class drew nearer, I asked Jude about her experiences with the language and why I was being regarded as such a lunatic for taking it on.

'I didn't mind it too much at school, I was lucky in that I took to it easily,' she said. 'I know a lot of people absolutely despised it though. There's a tortured attitude to it that's not really to do with the language itself so much as the way it was taught – it's not taught, or at least it wasn't in my day, as a living language that you can use: there's a lot of literature and poetry involved and it wasn't adaptable or practical. So a lot of people who would have studied it for ten years or more can't actually speak it very well. They've introduced more oral exams to the curriculum in recent years to try and get people actually speaking it, but generally there's a perception that it's not a *sexy* language. You're sup-posed to take pride in it, it's supposed to be a part of who you are, but when it comes down to it it's not a fun language like French or Spanish.'

I was hoping that by learning the language I'd get more of a grasp on Irish identity, something that would take me beyond the leprechaun hats into something real, something that wasn't constructed to support an easily digested and easily recycled ver-sion of Ireland. It wasn't like putting on a Dubliners CD or supporting the Irish soccer team or drinking in an Irish theme pub, this was something to be worked at, something that required a bit of investment on my part. Not only would I have actually learnt something constructive, I'd be gaining some kind of insight into what it actually means to be Irish. The way Jude was talking though, I was starting to worry whether I was on completely the wrong track.

'I think being able to speak the language does makes me feel more Irish,' she reassured me. 'I know a lot of people give out about it but I think we quite like having our own language: it definitely helps with our national identity because it's uniquely ours. We're part of a modern Europe where everyone has their own language and culture: it helps to defeat any notion that we're just a sideshow of the UK. On a practical level we don't like necessarily having to pass exams in it, but we're only delighted to have a language which is just as valid – and complicated – as anyone else's.'

Clearly the Irish language had messed up its PR over a long period. Instead of treating the language as something to be celebrated, a living, useful, desirable thing of which to be justifiably proud, the powers that be had opted instead for enforced drudgery: hours in the classroom hunched over ancient texts and dense slabs of grammar. There was nothing inspiring about the way the Irish language was taught, and that's something that is almost entirely responsible for its perception today. Obviously English is going to be the dominant language thanks to the long-term presence of the British in Irish history and culture for centuries. Even the most fervent proponent of the Irish language will concede that Irish will never usurp English here, but the way the language was forced upon generations of Irish schoolchildren over the decades since the establishment of the Republic has meant that a beautiful and useful tongue now needs hefty support and lobbying to maintain a place in society.

'A lot of us didn't feel any connection with the language because the way it was presented didn't tie in to our everyday lives,' said Jude. 'Look at the GAA, founded to help preserve the old sports and also the language to an extent, and it's a living, vibrant thing that whole communities become involved in. It's not something that's been put on a shelf to be admired, which is I think where the language went wrong. I know the intentions were to keep the language alive and to make sure everyone had at least a smattering, but they just ended up with a whole lot of people actively disliking it. For a country trying to get a sense of its own identity it wasn't really the way to go.'

Now, the course I'd signed up for made much of the fact that it would leave me with an ability to speak conversational Irish. The emphasis would be on speaking and not so much on writing: certainly there'd be no plodding through great hunks of old texts, which had to be a good thing. But what should I expect? I suppose what I really wanted to know was, how hard would it be?

'Irish needs a lot of repetition as it's not structured naturally,' Jude advised. 'In Italian or French, say, once you get the basics you can figure out pretty much how the rest is going to go from there. Not in Irish. I don't think it's a dreadfully difficult language and people perhaps paint it as being harder than it actually is because then they can claim that that's why none of us speak it. I think there's a slight embarrassment among some people. I mean, I should certainly be a better speaker than I am and lots of people would be the same way – how can we have got through so much education without it really sinking in? Just having the *cúpla focail*, a few words? You talk to people from outside Ireland who didn't go through our education system, people like you who will be speaking more than a lot of us can after six weeks and it's a bit embarrassing. I mean, as an English speaker you go to Italy and people won't speak English to you as they're nervous and embarrassed about their level of competence: we do that here with Irish, which is ridiculous as it's our *own language.*'

There's also the Peig factor. Mention the name Peig to most people who were forced to learn Irish at school and watch the blood drain from their faces with an almost audible gurgle. Peig's story was the set text used by just about every school when teaching Irish and the grind and slog that it took to wade through the book has meant that one of the greatest storytellers in the history of Ireland is now viewed as a linguistic pariah.

Peig Sayers was, without doubt, a remarkable woman. Born in Dunquin on the far tip of the Dingle Peninsula in County Kerry, she moved to the Blasket Islands after marrying an island native named Pádraig Ó Guithín. There she became renowned as a storyteller while at the same time living a life that could not really have been harder on one of the most remote and inhospitable islands in the northern hemisphere. Tragedy and hardship were the main features of her life until she died in 1958 leaving behind a tremendous body of work dictated to folklorists, including her autobiography, *Peig*. Alas her name will be forever associated with the hardship of Irish classes by generations of schoolchildren as *Peig* was a required Irish language text. As the Celtic Tiger took hold in particular, it also served to confirm in the eyes of a new generation of affluent Irish people that Irish was the language of poverty and misery (one reason for its original decline was that it was spoken by the poorer people, particularly in the west, who suffered most in the Famine and who were most likely to emigrate) while English was the language of commerce and the future.

'Poor old Peig,' said Jude ruefully, 'a tragic – and interesting in a social history way – old lady talking about how rough and tough her life has been; a life where everyone seems to die and kept falling off cliffs: when you're seventeen it's not the kind of thing you want to be reading, especially in a second language. In its place it's fine and I'm sure that if I read it now, or in English translation, I'd find it fascinating. She lived in some very strange times, no doubt about it, but dear God, it was awful whiny. I wanted to go on to study biotechnology: I didn't want to know how the potatoes were served on the Blaskets nearly a century ago.'

I was a little cowed by all this, but my enthusiasm held up. I was confident this new awareness that the language needed to be taught as a living thing adaptable to modern Ireland meant that my course would leave me with at least the ability to hold basic conversations in Irish. The bewilderment with which my friends would greet the news that I was learning the language had taken me aback, even though I was now aware of some of the reasons why this was the case.

Incidentally, while English rule in Ireland tried – and ultimately failed – to drive the language into extinction, it couldn't stop a number of Irish words passing into its own tongue. Keen, tory, bard, brogue and banshee are just a few examples, not to mention '*craic*'. This word, ubiquitous as it now seems, is actually a recent arrival, no more than fifty years old. It originated as 'crack' in Scotland and the north of England and it's thought it first emerged on the island when Ulster Scots began to use it in the north. Its Gaelicisation occurred in the sixties and now it's probably one of the most 'Irish' words there is; certainly the most successfully exported. No Irish theme pub – and indeed many a genuine Irish hostelry – is without its sign promising *ceol agus craic*, music and, er, craic, and yet the word is, surprisingly, a recent foreign arrival.

Talking of recent foreign arrivals, there I was pitching up at the premises that would be the nerve centre of my immersion in the Irish language. I stepped through the door and into the office where I'd gone in and paid my course fees a couple of weeks earlier and was motioned by the receptionist towards a door at the back, through which I could see a handful of people sitting beneath stark neon lights, nervously facing a whiteboard. I was sure I'd be the only foreigner: after all, why would anyone else want to learn Irish? The seats were arranged in two rows facing the board; I walked in and sat in the front row like the swot I intended to be. Next to the whiteboard was a map of Ireland with the place names given in Irish – a familiar map rendered suddenly entirely alien. *Gaillimh* instead of Galway, *Corcaigh* where Cork should be, *Cill Chainnigh* for Kilkenny, *Tiobrad Árann* for Tipperary and, most bizarrely, *Baile Átha Cliath* written over my home city.

We all sat there, united in a slight air of anxiety that we were unfamiliar with the classroom atmosphere yet curiously familiar at the same time thanks to long-dormant memories being revived from schooldays. We passed the time smiling awkwardly at each other, chewing pens and shuffling paper self-consciously, none of us thinking now was really the right time for proper introductions. Finally a young, stocky man with a shock of dark hair tumbling over his forehead bustled into the room looking faintly harassed. He was wearing a suit that, with its shirt hanging out and tie askew, looked like it had been forced on to him in a dark room, and put a folder of papers down on the table at the front with a whump. He exhaled expansively, as if relieved he'd made it at all, paused and surveyed the motley gaggle of students in front of him. He had an open, friendly face, from which he announced that his name was Eddie and he was to be our teacher. He taught Irish in a local school so knew what a commitment it was to take on this course on top of our jobs and other commitments. He conceded that three hours was a long

time but that we'd break halfway through each class for coffee
and biscuits. He looked as relieved about that as we did. We'd get
a lot done, he said: by the end of the course we'd be holding
basic conversations in Irish. My stomach actually tingled at this:
in six weeks' time I'd be having whole conversations in the language of my adopted country. Eddie called the register: there
were about a dozen of us in the end and I wasn't the only foreigner. There were two American women and a well-spoken
Englishman who was, we'd learn later, something high up at the
state broadcaster RTÉ.

With the formalities exhausted the class could begin in
earnest. Eddie paused again and held his hands together to his
lips as if in prayer, gathering his thoughts. We held our pens
poised above paper where we'd all written 'Class One' and
underlined it neatly. The air was heavy with nervous expectation.

Irish, explained Eddie, isn't easy. Especially if, like most of us,
you were starting absolutely from scratch.

There was a slight collective crashing of enthusiasm from the
bleachers, like when glaciers shed little chunks that fall into the
sea. What we'd hoped to hear was that Irish was a piece of piss
and by the end of the six weeks we'd be as comfortable with it
as with our own native tongue.

For one thing, Irish is not one homogeneous language. There
are dialects; maddeningly diverse dialects. There is Connemara
Irish, spoken in the western region of Galway. Nearby there was
Mayo Irish. Further north there was Donegal Irish, the mention
of which caused a sharp intake of breath, at least one strangled
yelp and the odd toothy crunch of shattering biro among my
classmates: Donegal Irish is famous for being almost a language
unto itself, a dialect and accent that is almost impenetrable to out-
siders. Donegal Irish terrifies most non-Donegal Irish speakers.

With Eddie hailing from County Tipperary however, what we'd be learning was Munster Irish, Munster being the southernmost of the four Irish provinces. I flicked my pen between my upper and lower teeth. I was already a bit confused by the language and I'd not even learned a word of it yet. So, while we would be learning Irish there were actually lots of different Irishes of which we would be grappling with just one. Did this mean that, having learned Munster Irish, if I went to Connemara and tried to speak it no one would understand a word I was saying? And what's this Donegal Irish all about that it has people crossing themselves and leaping into one another's arms in fright at its very mention? I'd had fantasies of wandering into a pub in the furthest reaches of Mayo where the Atlantic sprays the windows, falling easily into witty conversation in perfectly-accented Irish with someone at the bar at the conclusion of which they'd buy me a pint and ask which part of Ireland I was from. I'd chuckle self-consciously and reveal with fake modesty and mock embarrassment that I was not, in fact, from Ireland at all but from England and had merely picked up a *cúpla focail* along the way. Now it seemed that I was in danger of learning a version of Irish that nobody from outside Kerry would understand.

But Munster Irish it was to be, and before long Eddie had us working on some of the basics. We paired off, me with the American girl sitting beside me, and spoke our first ever words in Irish, parroting what Eddie had just taught us. '*Mise* Charlie,' I said awkwardly after much throat-clearing and a bit of self-conscious umming and ahhing, '*cé tusa*?' My name is Charlie, what's yours? '*Mise* Jill,' came the response, '*cé tusa*?' I paused uncertainly for a moment. '*Mise* Charlie,' I said, '*cé tusa*?' '*Mise* Jill,' said Jill after a slightly longer pause, 'erm . . . *cé tusa*?' Given that this was currently the sum total of Irish that either of us knew we had become locked into an infinitely revolving circle of nomenclative enquiry. Panic filled our eyes. We kept talking, kept giving our names to each other and casting panicky glances at Eddie, who seemed oblivious, concentrating on shuffling together some handouts. We were almost whimpering at each other after a while, and by the time Jill and I were actually starting to doubt which one of us was actually which, Eddie finally broke the spell and moved on to teach us how to say hello.

Which is when things got complicated.

There is no direct translation for 'hello' in the Irish language, something that would be the first of many idiosyncrasies in our journey through this curious tongue. In any language, probably the first thing you learn to say is hello, and there's no hello in Irish. This is true of many other words we take for granted in English, incidentally: there are no direct translations for 'yes' and 'no' either. It was this apparent lack of willing to give a straight answer that coined the word 'blarney' in fact. It may be an apocryphal story, but apparently Queen Elizabeth I was trying to get some information from the Earl of Blarney and, being a busy queen, she wanted straight answers and he was being determinedly evasive. She couldn't draw a simple yes or no out of him, partly because he didn't want to give her a straight answer but partly also because he didn't have a yes or no to give her. Later, when faced with a similarly evasive noble, Elizabeth threw up her hands and announced, 'Oh, this is just so much Blarney!'

The closest equivalent to 'hello' in Irish is the greeting, '*Dia duit*', pronounced 'deeya gwit' and meaning 'God be with you'. The response to that is '*Dia is Muire duit*', (deeya iss meera gwit), 'God and Mary be with you'. Now, to that you're officially supposed to reply, '*Dia is Muire is Pádraig duit*', 'God and Mary and Patrick be with you', and the response is, '*Dia is Muire is Pádraig is Brid duit*', 'God and Mary and Patrick and Brid be with you'.

And so it goes on, with more and more saints alternately being wished upon you and on the person you're addressing as if you're picking sides for some massive holy football match. When you consider that the Catholic Church recognises more than ten thousand saints, two particularly polite people could be stuck there for weeks just saying hello and not wanting to be the first to stop, just as Stalin's underlings didn't want to be the first to cease applauding one of his speeches. Thankfully though, we learned that most greeting exchanges settle for the basic serve-and-return of God and Mary being with you.

From there we progressed to '*conas atá tú*', meaning 'how are you?' There is a whole bunch of replies: I won't go into all of them, but the best, the most utterly boomps-a-daisy response of the lot, is '*tá mé ar mhuin na muice*', (taw meh air vwin na micker), which means, wait for it, 'I'm on the pig's back'. This, apparently, is a very good thing, an expression that you're in the finest of form, living an easy, contented life and being generally on top of the world as well as on top of a pig. The reason why being astride a porker has emerged as the best way to convey this is lost in the history of Irish etymology – where it's probably best left – but it worked for me. I started using it all the time, even when people weren't even asking how I was.

By then, it was coffee time – '*Buíchoas le Dia*,' said Eddie, 'Thanks be to God' – and while we certainly needed it, the hour and a half had flown by. It's amazing how invigorating finding out people's names and asking after their health can be. We fell upon the supermarket brand custard creams and asked after each other's health with such joyous enthusiasm that if the poor old pig had been in the room it would at that point have been heavily burdened by biscuit munching linguists.

The rest of that first session saw no let-up in our scholarship. By the time Eddie let us back out into the Dublin night we'd all lost our Irish language innocence. Our cherry *as Gaelige* had been popped. As we said goodbye to each other (*'slán!'*) and melted into the dark, rainy streets calling out that we were on the pig's back, we were different people, people who could now name colours with the best of them. We could even ask people if they had things and impart to them what things we had too, as long as those things were a car, a book, a pen, a belt, a coat or a jumper. We were a crack unit, highly trained in basic Irish phrases; a bond had been established. We would go into verb declensions for each other, go side-by-side over the top in the syntax wars and be there for each other whenever we fell from the pig's back.

The six weeks passed remarkably quickly. Eddie was a brilliant, inspiring teacher and my classmates were a terrifically friendly bunch who ensured that I looked forward to each session even though I was far from taking to the language like the proverbial quacking *lacha* to *uisce*. I did my best, though. Whenever I could I watched the evening news in Irish on TG4 and could pick out the odd word or short phrase, especially if the item involved people introducing themselves, establishing their general state of health or featured inquests regarding the ownership of a jumper.

I looked at the course leaflet: there was the next beginners' level after this one, then two intermediate courses, a short advanced course and finally the chance to spend a week in the *Gaeltacht* speaking nothing but Irish, all in the space of a year. In the coffee break during one class a small group of us, including Liz, a civil servant from Boston, Alan, a chirpy middle-aged man from Meath who worked for An Post and who would emerge as the swot of the class, and Ann, a young primary school teacher from Fermanagh, all vowed our intention to make it all the way through to the *Gaeltacht* where we'd be yapping away in Irish like a house party at Peig Sayers' place only with more jokes and jumper talk.

At the end of the course, even though it was hardly any time at all until the next level began, we had an emotional parting in the downstairs bar of the Stag's Head. It was a busy Thursday night and we crammed into a corner as a traditional Irish folk band fired up at the other end of the packed room. Eddie told us he'd been impressed at how far we'd all got in such a relatively short space of time. At the end of the class he'd given everyone a certificate, only a photocopied piece of paper put together with a bit of basic clip art (and clearly done in a hurry too: the exclamation mark that followed *comhghairdeas* – congratulations – was on the next line), but in Irish it said that we had completed the first beginners' course. Eddie had filled in our names translated into Irish too, with mine being Searlus o'Conghaile. I liked the sound of that. Searlus o'Conghaile. It had a ring of authenticity to it that 'Charlie' lacked. I didn't like to admit it, and don't tell anyone, but I felt more pride in receiving that certificate that I'd felt in anything I'd done for a very, very long time indeed. I'd passed no test, I'd just turned up to classes and engaged in faltering, uncertain conversation that generally involved me falling into every possible linguistic trap like the world's most hapless stooge, but I was proud of myself and of my classmates.

I had a chat at the bar with Jill: although we'd all spent thirty-six hours in each other's company over the previous weeks this was the first time we'd really had the chance to find anything out about each other. Jill was from Evanston, Illinois, just outside Chicago. She'd lived in San Francisco for four years and Cambridge, Massachusetts, for two years before arriving in Ireland five years earlier.

'After grad school I worked for a year in Chicago at a job that I hated,' she told me. 'I nearly died when I realised that a full year had passed there; my future life of being old, like forty, and still having that job and an overweight husband and horrible kids flashed before me, so I bought myself a one way ticket to Ireland for my twenty-eighth birthday. Ireland was actually inviting immigrants then, so I managed to charm my way in. I had visited once before, so illusions of leprechauns saying "begorrah" had already been shattered. I'd seen films like *The Commitments* and realised they couldn't possibly represent modern day Ireland: I mean who rides horses in the middle of cities? In reality I didn't think through my move all that well and did it with surprising nonchalance; I probably wouldn't have the nerve now to do what I did then.'

I asked what she liked about the place.

'I have no idea what I like about Ireland, but I love it and regard it as my second home after Chicago. On the other hand, Ireland at the height of the Celtic Tiger was like an awkward teen with raging puberty hormones. It was like I imagine New York City was in the mid-eighties. I mean, velvet ropes in Dublin? Get over yourself. I've been to every county now except for some of those silly ones in the middle that no one goes to, not even An Post. And why are there so many Irish who have never been to the North? I mean, I get *why*-why, but really, why?'

So why learn Irish?

'I thought it would be a nod to my adopted homeland,' she said. 'I think it's kinda sad that it's fading into oblivion. Also I like a challenge. Oh, and I heard that there'd be a nice biscuit selection. I've enjoyed the language, very much so even though it's convoluted and most people outside Ireland don't even know that it exists. It's a bit like knowing a secret language, one that only pasty people can speak.'

As we clutched our pints, cheeks flushed with delighted

achievement, and shouted conversation into each other's ears above the flying jigs and reels from the far end of the room I realised that I was finally starting to feel like I belonged here. As far as I was concerned, that certificate, that cheap, photocopied certificate with its dangling exclamation mark and my name biroed on to it in Irish represented more than just finishing a course. It was a step forward to belonging. Even if I stayed in Ireland for the rest of my life my cockney accent would reveal me as a foreigner every time I opened my mouth. At least now that I had a little *Gaelige* I had evidence that I'd made a tangible effort to get to grips with the country I call home. I was already looking forward to the next level of the course: I'd crack this beautiful, maddening, lilting, confusing language, or my name wasn't Searlus o'Conghaile.

It was totally out of character for a born procrastinator and someone who would invariably be found doing his homework on the bus to school, but I managed to keep my Irish going. I'd leaf through my notes, trying to follow the news on TG4, pointing at things in the kitchen and barking their names triumphantly at Jude like a man just home after coming out of a twenty-five year coma. As I grew in confidence I began to appreciate the nuances, rhythms and beauties of the language more and more. In the past if we'd heard an Irish language speaker on the television at home, Jude would sometimes say, 'They've got lovely Irish' and I'd nod solemnly in agreement while thinking, 'Er, have they?' Now when watching the Irish news broadcasts on TG4, as I tried to discipline myself to do most nights, I began to hear it for myself. Just hearing the language was important but, Dublin being Dublin, I wasn't going to hear much of it here. One night as I walked past the Abbey Theatre a young man with a holdall over his shoulder asked me directions to Grafton Street. I pointed him in the right direction and, as he headed off, he nodded at me

and said '*Go raibh míle maith agat*', thanks very much. I was
stunned. It was the first time I'd heard Irish spoken in Dublin outside Eddie's classroom. I stopped and turned, watching him
hurrying across the road and off in the direction of O'Connell
Street. I'd missed a perfect opportunity for a bit of practice. Never
mind the fact that the lad had obviously just got off the bus from
somewhere way out west and was in a hurry to get to wherever
he was going, I had things to tell him: that I was feeling on the
pig's back and that I had a jumper. Did he have a jumper?

In addition, being part of the class had reassured me that I
wasn't alone being an outsider in Dublin. In a way, we all were:
Liz was from Boston and Jill from Chicago (although both had
been in Ireland far longer than I had); Alan lived way out in
Meath somewhere and didn't arrive home from each class until
well after midnight. There was Ann, the schoolteacher from
Northern Ireland who had to obtain an Irish qualification in
order to teach in schools in the Republic. We were all of different backgrounds and ages, and all of us were learning Irish for
wholly different reasons, but once the door closed at 6.30 every
Tuesday and Thursday night, we were bonded together and
when the second course began we were delighted to be reunited.

Some of the classes were intense – during particularly brain-
busting sessions, whenever I blinked it was as if there was the
sound of a ringing till and the words NO SALE appeared in my
eyes – and sometimes the quirky irregularities and idiosyncrasies
would have us throwing down our pencils in frustration, but
most of all it was clear that all of us were thoroughly enjoying
being there. Sometimes after a particularly hard session we'd
walk out feeling like some kind of survivors' support group –
only others who'd been through the eleven irregular Irish verbs
could truly know what it was like – but we all, without exception, looked forward to the next class.

During the coffee break for one class I caught up with Ann. From a village near Enniskillen, she'd been in Dublin a little longer than I had.

'I got my first teaching job in Liverpool and taught there for four years,' she told me, 'but then I wanted to move back home. I had a few friends from university who were in Dublin and I happened to be down here one weekend and a friend's mum saw this job advertised in the paper. Within days of her showing it to me I'd got the job and here I am now. It's because of the job that I have to learn Irish because you have to be qualified to degree level to teach in the Republic; you have to reach the same level in the language as if you were doing a teaching degree here. It's going to take me seven years altogether, but I'm already teaching the younger kids some basic words and phrases. I didn't learn Irish at school because in Northern Ireland the Protestant schools don't teach Irish, it was only taught in the Catholic schools. It's a shame because I would have liked to have learned it: it's a part of our island's culture and when I trained to be a teacher, not having Irish limited where I could teach and even where I could study to be a teacher.

'Does the language go hand-in-hand with being Irish? I think it does but I've only really noticed that since I've been down here; I didn't really think about it growing up in Northern Ireland. I think people should have a little bit of the language at least. It's a great language, beautiful. Friends back home are amazed that I'm doing it, they say things like it must be torture for you, but I'm glad that I'm doing it, it'll be worth it in the end.'

With Ann being from the north it was the first time I'd considered the language in a political context. It seemed odd to me that people could find a language offensive by its very nature.

'There are a few people that I know back in Enniskillen who

would be quite anti-Irish,' she said. 'They see themselves as British through and through and would think it's awful that I'm learning Irish. My parents were very liberal when I was growing up and encouraged us to mix with both sides of the community, but some people up there see things from a completely different point of view. Irish is certainly becoming more popular now among the Catholic community there and only recently the first Irish-speaking primary school in Fermanagh opened. Some of the signage is being written in English and Irish now as well which is causing a bit of friction. Martin McGuinness wants to get all the road signs in both Irish and English and there's opposition to that. It's a shame it has to be that way, that the language becomes political, and I can't see that changing to be honest, as it all just continues being handed down from one generation to another. I grew up more in the countryside where the divide wasn't as rigid and visible as in the towns and cities, but even there you socialised pretty much with your own: the Protestants in one place, the Catholics in another.'

Ann had definitely noticed progress in recent years though.

'I was only about ten or eleven when the bomb went off in Enniskillen, so I don't really remember it that well. I think it was the Omagh bomb when everyone thought they'd had enough, so many innocent people dying. That's when people knew it was time for change, that things couldn't go on like that any more.'

Not long before we spoke, two soldiers had been shot dead and four people injured in a gun attack claimed by the Real IRA at the Massereene Barracks in County Antrim. On both sides of the border and on both sides of the community there was anger and revulsion, a raw, deeply felt reaction that no, this was not going to start happening again, not after all this time when real progress was being made. There was still friction and division, obviously, but with political progress being made there was a feeling that if the shootings had been intended to reopen old divisions then they'd had the opposite effect. The revulsion and anger spanned geography, politics and religion. The Irish language is never going to resolve any differences by itself but it was a shame that people could actually be set against a native tongue just because of where it comes from, especially one that's so rich, diverse and beautiful.

Our numbers had dwindled when we stepped up from the beginners' to the intermediate course, but the class numbers themselves had increased massively. There were so many takers – Irish people with a grounding in Irish from school, it seemed – that the classes were split into two. We also had a different teacher as Eddie's gift for opening up the language in such an accessible way meant that he was given a new bunch of novices to teach about jumpers and pigs' backs.

For all my dedication and enthusiasm however, it turned out that this step was one too far for me. Our new teacher, a native Irish speaker from Connemara, gave most of the class in Irish. With it being his first language he was obviously utterly fluent and our hardy knot of near-novices in the corner soon realised that we were playing with the big boys. The teacher would chat away in beautiful Irish but I realised that I was just hearing a noise; most of the time I couldn't even make out individual words. Our new classmates were also way ahead of us. Ann was holding her own and Alan, the star pupil from our Eddie classes, was best equipped to keep up, but those of us who weren't Irish looked at each other with panic in our eyes. My confidence took a hammering and when put on the spot with a question I'd go to pieces: most of the time I didn't have clue what I was even being asked, let alone able to formulate an answer. I fell swiftly from the pig's back and landed with a loud spludge in the mud of mortified confusion.

After a couple of weeks I realised that I'd stopped looking forward to classes. I'd begun to look for reasons not to go. I was utterly out of my depth. The moment of truth came when the teacher was asking people about the last book they'd read and picked me out from where I was trying to hide in the back row. I had to have the question explained to me in English and there was just no way I could come up with an answer. Put on the spot, I couldn't even remember what the last book I'd read actually was, let alone translate its title and talk about its contents in Irish as everyone else seemed to be doing without a second thought. I opened and closed my mouth in guppy fashion a few times and in the end, conscious of the need to say something, anything, I blurted out something like 'My book, the one I wrote.' Oh God, I thought, oh God please tell me I didn't say that. The teacher asked me questions in Irish about it that I didn't understand so he had to ask them again in English. I stammered and spluttered, ummed and ahhhed, and couldn't answer in Irish; not a hope. I ended up having to give answers in English that he'd translate into Irish and I'd repeat. So, not only did I manage to show myself up as an utter soup-for-brains in front of the entire class, not only did I take up practically twenty minutes of the lesson with this excruciating dialogue, I'd also managed to convince everyone that I was an arrogant, self-serving cocksocket into the bargain.

I had never felt like such an outsider since I'd arrived in the country. I'd just made myself look like a puffed-up buffoon and the language that I'd fallen in love with and thought I'd made great strides in learning, was now a foreign language to me in a foreign country. That night it became a series of incomprehensible sounds again, as if the language itself was telling me I didn't belong, I'd never belong. Who was I to learn this beautiful, historic language that wasn't mine? I wasn't Searlus o'Conghaile, nowhere near, I was Charlie Connelly from London and always would be.

Confidence shattered, self-esteem battered, I stopped going to classes. It wasn't the teacher's fault by any means, he was a terrific teacher and wonderful Irish speaker; I was just way, way out of my depth. Most of the people in the class had grown up with Irish, had learned it at school, had heard it spoken – they were brushing up what they already knew. I was holding them back and I was being left behind. I was like a skater who'd mastered doing a couple of wobbly circuits at Streatham Ice Rink and been shoved straight on to the ice at the national trials as the opening snare drum triplets of Ravel's *Bolero* were playing over the speakers.

It was months later when Jude and I were watching a film on TG4 and the words *Fan Linn* appeared on screen to signify a commercial break. 'You know what that means, don't you?' she asked. Umm, end of part one? 'It literally means "stay with us".'

After the ads, the words *Seo Linn* announced the recommencement of the film. 'That,' said Jude, 'literally means something like, "ah, here you are with us".'

It beat 'end of part one' and 'part two' and was just the kind of wonderful playful wordage that had made me fall for Irish in the first place.

'That's what I love about Irish,' said Jude, 'the way it curls around the language, the way the meanings open out of the words like a fern: it makes language beautiful that way.

'In Irish nobody likes to know how it actually is,' she chuckled, 'we like to hear how it might be. I guess it might go back to talking your way out of poverty, the storyteller putting a shine on things, making dark things beautiful with intonation, loops, curls and spark.'

I thought of the *tóg go bog é* signs in Kerry, the phrases I'd learned and the way they fitted together because they sounded beautiful and I began to love the language again. I'd felt like a failure, but all that had happened was I'd got out of my depth. Phrases began to pop back into my mind, my curiosity returned and most of all my love for the subtleties, nuances and rhythms of a captivating, beautiful tongue returned.

I started thinking about the language and thinking in the language. I remembered the first phrase I'd had to utter in that ill-fated intermediate level course when we all introduced ourselves to each other. *Is as Londain mé, ach tá mé í mo chonaí í mBaile Átha Cliath.* I am from London, but I live in Dublin. Or, more literally, 'I am out of London but I am, in my living, in the town of the hurdle ford.'

I'd never master the language, but I at least felt that I understood it a little and, by extension, understood a little more about the country I call home. My next job was to find out more about the town of the hurdle ford; about the city that I call home.

CHAPTER SEVEN

I was becoming much more used to living in a country whose entire population was half that of the city in which I grew up. When I'd first arrived in Dublin, Jude had worried that I'd be bored; that it wouldn't have the facilities, entertainment potential and downright twenty-four-hour hedonism I'd known in London. I don't know what kind of party-loving, too-fast-to-live cultural vacuum cleaner she imagined was arriving to share her life but I wasn't worried at all. Yes, London is a big and lively city, one of the biggest and liveliest in fact, but wherever it is you live you don't go everywhere and do everything. It's what you make of the place, the routes and routines you establish and the friends you make that counts.

Living somewhere is largely about routines and I was establishing my own in Dublin. Before I moved here I hardly knew the city and, like most people from outside Ireland, was familiar with only a couple of places associated with Dublin. I'd heard of Grafton Street and like most people knew of Temple Bar as the destination of stag parties, hen weekends and tourists, but that was about it. I did also know, incidentally, that there was an area of Dublin called Stoneybatter, a terrific name in its own right, thanks to an incident from my musician days. I'd been playing inexpert tongue-out-of-the-side-of-my-mouth mandolin with a country rock band and we were filming a video in a vast, dark old Irish pub in Hackney. Paul the guitarist was a Geordie and had already upbraided the director for her suggestion that we all smile by pointing out that 'this is coontry rock, not fooken' Boy-zerrrn' when the landlord of the pub said he'd been let down by his band that night and would we step in? The singer asked what the fee was and received the reply forty quid between us and four dinners. Paul spied a poster on the wall that revealed the missing group's name to be Stoneybatter. 'How man,' he said, nodding at the poster, 'ah bet Sterney fooken' battah were gettin' more than forty quid an' four dinnahs.' So stunned by their name was I that I contributed nothing to the discussion in which an agreeable amount of free pints was negotiated on top of the food and cash and we went on to play to a massive room speckled with about half a dozen baffled Stoneybatter fans. The curious deep-fried geology of their name became marked indelibly in my memory, and it would be years before I'd learn of its Northside Dublin derivation.

So, Grafton Street, Temple Bar and Stoneybatter were all I had before I arrived. The first two were familiar to pretty much any weekend visitor to the city, the third I will always hear in a thick Geordie accent with its syllables bisected by an expletive.

The first difference I noticed was the obvious one of scale. There's only one centre and it's easily accessible from anywhere. If you mention a pub to someone, nine times out of ten they'll know it or at least know of it. The more friends I made in Dublin the more I noticed how often you'd just bump into them in the street. The central node of the city is O'Connell Street, the wide, almost Parisian boulevard – so wide that the bridge at its southern end that crosses the Liffey is actually wider than it is long – that has over the last twenty-five years or so been transformed from the boarded-up haunt of drug addicts to a livelier thoroughfare more befitting a major and historic European capital. Although it features some of Dublin's most sumptuous architecture in the General Post Office, Clery's department store and the Gresham Hotel it's not perfect by any means, but the revival of the economy during the boom years certainly smartened it up, its revival rubber-stamped by the erection of the Spire at its centre (some pointed out the irony of placing a giant needle on a street previously known for its drug addicts). Its wide pavements give it an easy, relaxed feel even at its busiest, a kind of Oxford Street meets the Champs-Elysées.

The bus route from Clontarf into the city centre drops me a stone's throw from O'Connell Street and it's not until you emerge on to its wide pavement, having passed the Bonavox hearing aid shop from which the U2 frontman took his nickname, that you feel you've arrived in town. On a sunny but chilly Easter morning I strolled past the statue of James Joyce leaning on his walking stick and successfully negotiated the revolving door of the Café Kylemore for a fry. The breakfast fry – the term is never appended by the word 'up' here, incidentally – is an Irish institution and the Kylemore offers a particularly good one. The staple ingredients of a good fry are eggs, bacon (or 'rashers' as they're more specifically known here), sausages and pudding, both black and white. There's also the breakfast roll which, as the name suggests, inserts the fry into a large bread roll. So woven into Irish culinary culture is the breakfast roll that a song celebrating its delights reached number one in the Irish charts a few years ago, and when the contract was awarded recently to build service stations on Ireland's arterial routes there was a specific clause insisting that the breakfast roll should be a staple of any menu therein. At the Kylemore however it's a fry for me every time.

Years ago in London I had an Irish girlfriend for a short while, a nurse from Cavan who shared a house with some other nurses that backed on to the Central Line in Ealing, and it was she who first introduced me to the proper breakfast fry. With her housemates she'd go misty-eyed over the things she missed about Ireland as the sausages sizzled and the tube trains clattered past outside the window: Chef sauce (HP didn't cut it, not even close), Tayto crisps, red lemonade; things that sounded impossibly, wonderfully exotic to me, blinded as I was by the shamrocks in my eyes. They'd somehow sourced Barry's teabags from home, presumably in a parcel lovingly assembled by someone's mammy, and they drank it like it was nectar. I pretended that it was the most amazing tea I'd ever tasted, not realising that it was the taste of home rather than the leaves themselves that made Barry's tea so special between the magnolia walls of this draughty, soulless dormitory of a semi-detached house in west London.

The Cavan nurse would shortly pack her teabags and move to America with her housemates, leaving me to parrot my lamentations for Chef sauce and Tayto crisps to anyone who'd listen, even though I'd never tasted them in my life.

I mopped up the last blobs of Chef sauce with my white pudding and sat looking out of the window between James Joyce and the Millennium Spire at the dignified classical frontage of the GPO, on top of which the Irish tricolour was reluctantly nudged and teased from its pole by the spring breeze.

It was one of those bitingly chilly April mornings where the sun shows commendable enthusiasm by sparkling vigorously with a pale yellow light but there's no discernible difference between the temperature in sun or shade. Between my empty grease-blobbed plate and the columns of the GPO, O'Connell Street went about its normal business, people hurried to work, mooched along with shopping bags, groups of cagouled young language students gathered in groups trying to make sense of a city map while a man with a dirt-smeared face and wearing a grubby fleece circulated among the crowds seeking spare change in an empty cardboard coffee cup. A Dublin morning passed before me at a time of year that resonates more than most in Ireland, and passed before the place most associated with events that triggered the creation of the Republic of Ireland.

To most people in Britain 1916 doesn't have huge significance. It was midway through the First World War – the almighty waste of life that was the Battle of the Somme would take up most of the second half of the year – but as a date in its own right in Britain it doesn't exactly resonate in the way, say, 1066 or 1805 do. In Ireland, however, it represents the most significant turning point in the past eight centuries, albeit that significance only became clear in hindsight. 1916 was the year when a small group of idealists and revolutionaries staged an unsuccessful rebellion as a result of which, in the words of W. B. Yeats, 'all changed, changed utterly'.

The Easter Rising of 1916 was as brilliant as it was harebrained, as heroic as it was shambolic. Conceived and commanded by a curious mixture of poets, radicals, schoolteachers, an ageing tobacconist and a man who had once played the uilleann pipes for the Pope, it commenced in confusion with no popular support, little in the way of equipment, almost failed to happen at all and left much of central Dublin a smoking pile of rubble when it did. All for no apparent gain. Yet as it turned out, the rising – and crucially the idiotic British response to it – proved to be the catalyst for the creation of what is now the Republic of Ireland.

Like most people growing up in Britain I was almost entirely ignorant of the Easter Rising. Although it happened in the capital city of our nearest neighbours, involved my own country, and featured the only instance of uniformed armies fighting it out in the streets of a British or Irish city in centuries, I grew up almost completely oblivious, yet the Easter Rising is utterly crucial to an understanding of Ireland and crucial to an understanding of Ireland's relationship with Britain. The Easter Rising certainly didn't feature in my vision of Ireland when I was vigorously attempting to make myself Irish. I don't think I was even aware of it. I'd probably heard it referred to in a Wolfe Tones song playing on a pub jukebox in Archway or something, but I had about as much of a clue as to what it was as I had of the inner workings of the Large Hadron Collider.

It's only in recent years that the Easter Rising has been given full acknowledgement in Ireland. The rebellion's knock-on effect was the partition of Ireland into the Irish Free State and Northern Ireland, which then led to a vicious and tragic civil war between those who supported the treaty of partition (on signing which Michael Collins said, accurately as it turned out, that he'd just signed his death warrant) as a step towards full independence for the whole island of Ireland, and those who were anti-treaty and saw partition as a betrayal. There's a certain sense of shame and embarrassment hanging around the civil war here; that having gained independence after centuries of English rule, if not for the whole island at least for most of it, Irishman was shooting at Irishman and, in some cases, brother was shooting at brother. It was a truly horrendous period of Irish history whose pain remains fresh today and for a good while the 1916 rising was associated with it: for a long time it was acknowledged without great reverence. While the fiftieth anniversary of the Rising was marked officially in 1966, the commencement of the Troubles in the north brought with it renewed problems. The Rising was known erroneously at the time as the Sinn Féin rebellion, even though the party had no direct official link to the events of 1916 (the press and authorities had assumed Sinn Féin

was behind it and the association stuck). With Sinn Féin being
the political wing of the Provisional IRA, to express admiration
for the 1916 rebels was feared by some to be seen as tacit support
for the IRA.

Today however the Rising has grown in the popular consciousness to a level similar to that of, say, the Battle of Hastings
to an English person, or Bannockburn to a Scot. The faces of the
rebel leaders peer out of picture frames in pubs and a facsimile of
the Proclamation of the Irish Republic, distributed around
Dublin and read out loud by one of the leaders, Patrick Pearse,
outside the General Post Office at the start of the rebellion, can
be bought in most souvenir shops alongside the cuddly leprechauns and Guinness key rings.

The GPO became the heart of the rising and remains the
focus of both commemoration and the perception of the rebellion in the consciousness of the Irish people. It's a beautiful
building dating back to 1818 of clean, classical lines fronted by a
portico and six Ionic columns, atop which stand statues of
Mercury, Fidelity and Hibernia. At the time of the rebellion the
GPO had just undergone an expensive, lengthy refurbishment
and reopened barely six weeks before the rebels surged in on an
unseasonably hot Easter Monday in 1916 and took the place over
as part of a strategic commandeering of buildings across the city.
When the Irish soldiers jogged through the doors the post office
was busy and at first nobody took much notice. The GPO
workers themselves carried on tearing sheets of stamps and serving customers as the rebels scrambled over the counters with
pistols drawn. It took one of the leaders, James Connolly, firing
a shot into the ceiling before people realised that they were
probably better off buying their postal orders somewhere else.
Once the rebels had barricaded themselves into the GPO the
young poet, schoolteacher and leading light of the rebellion

Patrick Pearse went outside and read aloud the proclamation of the Irish Republic that was being pasted up around the city as he spoke. A few people listened – Pearse, a notably gifted public speaker, apparently looked pale and nervous – a smattering of whom applauded politely, but still there was little inkling among the crowds going about their business on O'Connell Street that anything significant was going on.

Even for those who saw Pearse it must have been hard to grasp what was actually happening: it was a day much like the one in which I was regarding the GPO from the Kylemore: the shops were all open, crowds of people were streaming in and out of them and the sun shone out of a cloudless blue sky. Yet here was a pale and sweating man in military fatigues telling them an Irish Republic had just been established. Right there. In the post office.

The crowds began to realise something really was amiss soon after a tricolour and a green flag embroidered with the words 'Irish Republic' had been hoisted over the building. A troop of British mounted lancers had got wind that something untoward was happening at the GPO and came galloping down O'Connell Street to investigate, whereupon rebel soldiers in the post office and in Clery's department store and the Imperial Hotel opposite opened fire and killed four of them, practically on the doorstep of where I now sat. What had seemed to be a bit of an inconvenience for anyone needing a parcel weighed had become something far more serious. The rebellion was on and people were dying.

The GPO remains a focus for protest to this day: as I crossed the road from the café I could see a table set up outside ranged with leaflets and petitions protesting against the Iraq War. Another one farther along the frontage proffered graphic pictures of laboratory animals and anti-vivisection literature. I walked through the doors and into the airy, spacious galleried hall of the post office with its elegant curving dark wooden counters and polished brass grilles. Even at its busiest the GPO still has an almost reverential feel to it; it never seems to get truly noisy despite the masses of people inside the vast, echoing, three-storey-high interior. All but the facade of the building was destroyed as the British gradually reclaimed the city in the week following the storming of the GPO and other strategically valuable Dublin locations, and the rebels inside had to contend with constant shelling for days. As a result of the damage the interior is now completely different to how it would have been in 1916, but it's not just the changed floorplan that makes it hard to picture what it must have been like in there with James Connolly, Patrick Pearse, a young Michael Collins and the rest, it's the hushed elegance and serene dignity of the room. It's in stark contrast to the smashing of windows and the clattering and scraping as barricades were erected, the barking of orders given and taken by people who in all likelihood could barely believe this was happening at all, fuelled by a nervous, frightened excitement, an adrenalin rush that would last a week.

After the fatal venture up the street by the lancers there had been an uneasy stand-off as the rebels waited for the inevitable British assault. Outside, Dubliners helped themselves to the contents of most of the shops on O'Connell Street. Clery's department store opposite, still a Dublin institution, was filleted with particular skill and enthusiasm as poor Dubliners made off with fur coats and fancy jewellery. While the rebels holed up behind the barricaded windows of the GPO, across the street folk struggled off in the direction of home with armchairs, table lamps and armfuls of clothes. At one point a priest stopped a boy heading away from O'Connell Street struggling to hang on to a clutch of patent leather boots. He demanded to know where the boy had got them. 'Clery's, Father,' he replied, 'but you'd best hurry, they're nearly all gone.' One group of rebels who had occupied the upper floors of the Tower pub on Henry Street around the corner from the GPO was startled to discover looters in the ground floor bar dishing out booze to a delighted – and thirsty – clientele. One man was seen emerging from a shop with a set of golf clubs and golf balls and proceeding to drive a succession of lusty shots down O'Connell Street towards the Liffey. A woman made slow progress in attempting to manoeuvre an upright piano on to a handcart. Crowds of people gathered at the barricades to watch what was going on despite the danger. Many bystanders were killed but there remained almost a party atmosphere, especially on the Monday evening when crowds well-refreshed from the Easter races at Leopardstown returned to learn of the excitement and watch what was going on.

By Thursday much of the street was on fire as a result of British shelling as the rebel outposts were, despite courageous resistance, overpowered one by one. James Connolly had been crippled by a sniper's bullet that had shattered his ankle. The flames were reaching the GPO: water sprayed on the barricades turned to steam and conditions in the building were becoming unbearable. The women and prisoners were released, then Pearse gathered the men together as fires roared and shells and bullets continued to rain down on the beleaguered building. He gave the order to evacuate and, when they'd given a heartfelt rendition of 'The Soldier's Song', now the Irish national anthem, prepared to leave via the Henry Street exit.

I walked around the corner of the GPO to Henry Street, now a busy pedestrianised shopping thoroughfare, fought off a charity panhandler who was under the hilarious impression that a combination of clipboard, bib and a wacky manner were going to have me handing over my bank details on the street, and looked down into the crowds heading in and out of shops to top up their phone credit or buy shampoo. I found the door from which the rebels fled the burning GPO and tried to imagine Pearse standing there in uniform, pointing the way with his swordstick through the mayhem of flames and machine-gun fire. Of the first thirty or so rebels to make a break for it only a dozen made it across, the rest killed by the gun battery set up at the far end of the street. I passed the door and turned right into Moore Street. It was here that the rebel leaders holed up, apparently at number sixteen, a fishmonger's. Moore Street is a Dublin institution: there's been a street market here for centuries and as I turned the corner it was lined as ever with stalls selling fruit, vegetables and flowers, flanked by shops offering to unlock mobile phones and others selling Asian and Eastern European foods and spices. It's always a noisy, colourful place, scruffily magnificent, almost a Dublin time capsule that was overlooked by the boom years.

By the time the rebel leadership arrived at 16 Moore Street the rebellion was nearly over and the leaders knew it. Their hopes that if they'd held out long enough in Dublin the rest of the country would rise up in support had come to nothing. As they regrouped in the Moore Street house, civilians trying to escape the mayhem were being killed in the road outside in full view of Pearse, Connolly and the rest. Even as they bashed their way through the internal walls of the houses along Moore Street one volunteer was killed as the rifle he was using to break down a door went off. Everything that could go wrong was pretty much going wrong. The rebels bedded down for a night whose soundtrack would be the roar of flames, the rattle of machine-gun fire and the boom of explosions. Gangrene had set into Connolly's ankle and he was in terrible pain as he lay on a stretcher in the corner.

By noon on the Saturday, day six of the Rising, the GPO was totally burned out, and when Pearse saw the bodies of three elderly men lying dead in the street still clutching the makeshift white flag they'd been carrying he realised that surrender was the only course of action left. He and his colleagues may have been prepared to sacrifice their lives for their cause but ordinary citizens weren't meant to die. Those three old men that lay on the pavement outside with their little flag still moving in the breeze, they hadn't signed up for anything.

Today the eighteenth-century shop front from where Pearse looked tearfully at the bodies is, like nearly all the shops in that row, shuttered permanently closed. Above the shutters is the stencilled name 'Just 4 Kids', presumably the last business to operate in the condemned building. Above that, in huge white letters is the name 'Plunket' on a background of peeling red paint and above that, between the two windows from which Pearse observed the tragic scene below, hangs a drab-looking old wreath to which a bright green and white ribbon has been tied. In front of the building a weary-sounding stallholder was telling an old man that no, he couldn't come back and pay tomorrow.

Thinking that the British wouldn't shoot a woman, Pearse handed a nurse named Elizabeth O'Farrell a white flag and a Red Cross armband and instructed her to go outside and surrender. She was called forward to a barricade at the top of Moore Street where it joins Parnell Street and told the British soldiers there that Pearse wanted to meet with the commander of the British forces. Brigadier Lowe arrived soon afterwards and told Nurse O'Farrell to tell Pearse that he'd accept only an unconditional surrender.

I walked up to the junction of busy Parnell Street, where the barricade had been. On the corner, by Patrick Conway's pub with its faded red paint and black shutters, is the spot where

Pearse handed over his sword, pistol and, appropriately given Moore Street's greengrocery tradition, a bag of provisions containing two onions to the Brigadier; a surrender of weaponry and vegetables that signified the end of the Easter Rising.

It was what happened after the surrender that changed the direction of Irish history as much if not more than the Rising itself. The British were not exactly happy that they'd had their nose tweaked so emphatically by a bunch of teachers, actors and poets and set about their reprisals with ruthless vigour. Nearly three and a half thousand people were rounded up and arrested in the days following the rebellion. Of the 579 who were charged most were sent to prison or to labour camps in Britain.

Then the executions began. Fifteen of the rebellion's leaders were shot within days, including the seven signatories of the Proclamation. There was official disquiet at the carrying out of the executions right up to the British Prime Minister Herbert Asquith, who told General Sir John Maxwell, who had overseen them, that they 'would sow the seeds of lasting trouble in Ireland'.

The stonebreakers' yard at Kilmainham Gaol, where the executions took place, is a quiet spot. It's long and narrow and flanked by high, grey walls. A plaque on the wall lists the dead men while the Irish tricolour flies from a pole above. At one end is a small black cross in the ground, marking the spot where all but one of the rebels was executed. There's another black cross at the opposite end: James Connolly was shot there, his smashed, gangrenous ankle meaning that he faced the firing squad sitting in a chair wheeled in through a gate at that end of the yard.

When word of the executions emerged the tide of public opinion turned quickly and decisively. Within two years of the rebellion Sinn Féin had won a 70 per cent majority at the general election, announced that it would not be taking its seats at Westminster and instead set up the first Dáil Éireann, the Irish parliament, under the terms of the 1916 proclamation. This led to the War of Independence and eventually to the Anglo-Irish Treaty of 1921 that divided the island in the way that remains to this day and in a way that would dominate the news in Britain for decades to come.

When I was growing up in England barely a day went by without Northern Ireland being in the news, yet at school we were never taught why. Standing on what looked like any other street corner with its uneven paving stones next to a shuttered old pub on the spot where the rebellion ended I realised that here, right here, as Pearse handed over his sword, a chain of events began that led to the creation and promulgation of the country I now call home.

I was fascinated by the Easter Rising: for me it was as if in the great museum of history a tarpaulin had been pulled from a major exhibit of which I'd not been previously aware. What made it even more captivating were some of the smaller, quirkier details of the rebellion. The platoon of armed rebel soldiers who boarded a tram on the outskirts of Dublin and asked the conductor for 'fifty-nine twopenny fares' to O'Connell Street, for example. The fact that the world's first radio broadcast, a Morse code message announcing the declaration of the Republic, was made by rebels from the occupied School of Wireless Telegraphy opposite the GPO. One of the rebels involved in sending the message was Arthur Shields, who went on to become a noted actor in Hollywood, playing a priest in *The Quiet Man* among other things. Bizarrely he also appeared in *How Green Was My Valley* alongside an English actor with the stage name John Loder, who was the son and aide-de-camp of Brigadier Lowe, next to whom Loder had been standing when Pearse surrendered. By far my favourite aspect of the Rising however is the fact that while the British and rebel forces emptied guns at each other relentlessly from buildings on two sides of St Stephen's Green for several days, both sides would cease fire twice daily to allow the Green's park keeper to leave his cottage and feed the ducks on the pond.

It's impossible to identify a 'real Dublin' as like every city it's an aggregate of many things to many people. Should places be seen as less important or somehow less real because they're popular with tourists? A walk through the grounds of Trinity College and a squint at the Book of Kells is as much a part of Dublin as sitting in the stands at Dalymount Park watching Bohemians play, or the monthly horse fair at Smithfield when the modern redeveloped square echoes to the sound of hooves as small children in sportswear gallop up and down the cobbles astride their steeds, or sitting next to the statue of Patrick Kavanagh on his bench by the canal, or taking afternoon tea in Bewley's café on Grafton Street, or watching tourists being turfed off the manicured bits of St Stephen's Green by the parkies just when they've got all comfy: they're all part of the collage that makes up a city, some parts of which I seek out or have been introduced to, parts with which I am now familiar; the slices of city that make up *my* Dublin.

I didn't really have a preconceived image of the city when I arrived. The name Dublin to me conjured up, if anything, James Joyce and *The Commitments*, which made me realise how much the image we have of Ireland, its cottages, leprechauns and so on, is an essentially rural one (I wondered what urban leprechauns would be like. Were they like foxes? Sleek and clean and bright-eyed in the countryside but scrawny, mangy and constantly scavenging in overturned dustbins in the city?). It also made me realise how different Dublin was from the rest of the country;

how I needed, for all its comforts and attractions, to escape the city more if I was to challenge the preconceptions of Ireland that I'd gained outside the country. So, not long after Easter, I got up very early one morning and caught the bus to Limerick.

CHAPTER EIGHT

It being an early start at the bus station I wasn't exactly on top of my game. As I lifted the coffee to my mouth I made, in sporting terms, a schoolboy error by taking my eye off the ball. I'd underestimated the distance 'twixt cup and lip and made a solitary but crucial slip, depositing a dollop of hot brown liquid on to my shirt in a breastbone location that would prove impossible to hide for the rest of the day. Sod it. I looked down and noticed how the dollop was the size and shape of a giant monkey nut. There was something else, though. I looked at it again. It did look a bit like . . . no, it couldn't. But then, well, yes, maybe it did. The coffee stain, I couldn't deny, definitely looked a bit like the baby Jesus in swaddling clothes.

Only a few weeks earlier Jude and I had been watching the news on television. As had become customary it concerned the latest job losses, factory closures, tight-lipped politicians with document folders under their arms scurrying past camera crews and all kinds of experts grimly analysing the latest gloomy economic forecasts by effectively shrugging their shoulders and saying, 'We're screwed.'

'Tell you what,' said Jude as another group of laid-off workers trudged disconsolately past the camera, 'it won't be long before the statues start moving again.'

There hadn't been a decent Marian apparition in Ireland for a good fifteen years; the length of the boom, in fact. It seemed Ireland's years of bounty and plenty meant that either they'd stopped happening altogether or people were too busy filling bathtubs with cash and frolicking in them to notice. Yet, just weeks after Jude's prediction, the media was full of the Holy Tree Stump of Rathkeale. People were travelling from miles around, from as far as Cork and Sligo, to a small town west of Limerick city on the road to Killarney to see what was apparently a manifestation of the Virgin Mary in the stump of a newly felled tree located in the grounds of the Holy Mary Parish Church.

The story went that some workmen were felling old trees in the corner of the churchyard when, as Noel White, the chairman of the Rathkeale Community Council Graveyard Committee told the media, 'one of the lads said, look, our Blessed Lady is in the tree. One of the other lads looked over and actually knelt down and blessed himself, he got such a shock. It was the perfect shape of the figure of Our Lady holding the baby.'

As the word spread and people started lighting candles and leaving devotions at the stump, the local priest, Father Willie Russell, tried to instigate an arboreality check. 'There's nothing there,' he said, possibly in a higher-pitched voice than he would have liked, 'it's just a tree. You can't worship a tree.'

The pictures were inconclusive. The tree had been cut down leaving a stump whose open face, the part of the stump left bare by the chainsaw, did, at a push, look a little like the outline of a person. Someone had hung a set of rosary beads around the 'neck' to emphasise this anthropomorphism and if you tried hard you could see how it did look a little bit like the traditional pictorial representations of Mary, at least in outline. But most of all – well, to my eye – most of all it looked like a tree stump. The nation was divided into a minority of those who believed that this really was a visitation from the Holy Mother herself and those who thought that as a thrusting modern nation – albeit one going through a little bit of a hard time – we were really over this sort of thing. I mean, we have frappuccinos and focaccias now, surely the worship of inanimate objects was behind us?

The last major Marian mayhem in Ireland occurred in 1985 in the sputumistically named village of Ballinspittle in County Cork. One evening in summer a woman and her two daughters were walking past a Marian shrine set on an incline four metres above the road and saw the statue come alive. 'It was as if she was breathing or sighing,' said the mother afterwards, 'her chest was going up and down and the others saw her hands move.' The crowds converged upon Cork: over the next eight weeks more than a quarter of a million people showed up with many claiming they also saw the statue move: a member of the *Garda Síochána* said he saw the statue vibrate so much that he feared it would fall over. A few weeks earlier in Kerry thirty schoolchildren had apparently seen a statue beckoning to them: in all, in 1985, there were nearly fifty reports of Marian apparitions across the country. 1985 was a year when Ireland was in particularly dire economic straits.

It's not just an Irish phenomenon of course. Around the world the Virgin Mary has appeared in some pretty unexpected places. In 1996 she apparently turned up in the windows of a finance building in Clearwater, Florida: the rainbow-coloured outline of a person in a hooded robe remained there for years until somebody came along with some half bricks and broke three of the enormous panes that made up the image. Scientists claimed that the apparition had been formed by a chemical reaction on the surface of the glass but that didn't stop people travelling vast distances to see it and insisting that it was the Holy Mother herself. In 2005 Mary appeared on the wall of an underpass in north

Chicago, leading to all kinds of devotions and offerings being left there despite the city claiming that it was just a water stain on the concrete. A year later, workers at a California chocolate factory were startled to see that some excess chocolate from a machine had solidified into the form of a hooded figure that they took to be Mary, while in Coogee, Australia, devotees flocked to a pathway on the coast where, when viewed from a certain angle at a certain distance, a line of fence posts did, indeed, look like a tiny figure of Mary. My favourite however wasn't the famous pretzel or the pebble that a New Zealander once tried to hawk on the internet for fifty grand. No, for me the number-one Marian apparition is the holy toasted cheese sandwich on which Mary appeared to a woman in the US who, having kept it in a glass case packed with cotton wool for a decade, sold it for $28,000 on eBay a few years ago. Its religious authenticity was endorsed, as far as the owner was concerned, by the facts that a) the toast had never gone mouldy and b) one night she won $70,000 in a casino. The holy cheese toastie could have chosen to intervene in the Middle East or have a crack at sorting out global warming, but it was apparently too busy ensuring that a ball on a roulette wheel landed in the right place to buy someone a new car and get their kitchen redecorated. Them's the breaks, world.

I did consider whether the swaddling-stain coffee incident might have been some kind of warning in case I was intending to giggle up my sleeve at devoutly held beliefs, but that certainly wasn't my intention. I don't have much in the way of religious faith – most of my faith reserves have been sucked up over the years by the false idols in the shirts of Charlton Athletic – but I certainly respect those who do. I was however utterly intrigued by the idea that people could see religious manifestation in a tree stump, which is why I was standing at Busáras at the crack of dawn spilling coffee down my front.

Two of us stood waiting for the Limerick bus, an old lady and me. We looked out at the drizzle together. 'It's a miserable day altogether,' she said. 'It is that,' I replied. She looked at me. 'Did you know you've spilled something down your front, there?'

The driver arrived, a young man in mirror sunglasses with his hair carefully slicked back. He let himself on to the bus, reaching behind a flap to open the door with a proprietary hiss and closing it quickly lest we snuck up behind him and bundled on before he was ready for us.

'Oh no,' said my companion, 'not him. He's a miserable fecker, that one.'

Miserable fecker he may have been, and he may have had reason to be, but you can't say he didn't try and cheer himself up. Unfortunately for us he chose to do this by playing Shakin' Stevens's greatest hits. Repeatedly. Throughout the entire journey. We nosed through the Dublin traffic as Shaky wondered whether Julie loved him truly. We left the city behind as he pondered upon the provenance of an old piano playing hot behind a green door. And we thundered through towns and villages as Shaky sang, appropriately in the circumstances, of how heaven must have sent someone down, down for them to give him a thrill, causing his heart to start beating like a train on a track.

I took this religious reference as further evidence, along with the caffeine Jesus that I now wore over my heart, that I was being celestially warned. When a couple with a baby got on, sat behind me and began playing music through a mobile phone for the next hour, the pre-emptive divine retribution was complete.

When we got to Rathkeale the bus doors hissed closed behind me and the vehicle vroomed away leaving only the faint strains of 'I'll Be Satisfied' hanging in the air. I hoped I would be. But I wasn't sure in what way. Did I want the stump to be a genuine

Marian apparition? Or did I want it to be just a tree stump? I realised that I was now juggling three Irelands: the image I'd obtained while outside its borders – the old-fashioned Ireland of holy foliage; the misery-lit of Peig Sayers and the stocking of pasta in the 'ethnic foods' section of my local supermarket; and the modern Ireland, the everyday one in which I lived, with its Tesco home deliveries, high-speed broadband, vacuous daytime television shows and skinny lattes. All of them overlapped to some extent, but what was I hoping for today? Why had I just endured four hours of Shakin' Stevens in order to go and see the detritus of a recently felled tree in a small town in the wilds of Limerick?

I'd expected a small procession of pious Mrs Doyles to disembark after me, but the only other person to alight at Rathkeale was an elderly woman with a determined look on her face matched by a determined stride. As seemed to happen every time I went outside, within seconds of the bus departing the rain started, the kind of essentially Irish, torrential, utterly drenching rain that sweeps in suddenly apparently from nowhere. I fumbled in my bag for my waterproof jacket and, after a short and undignified scrimmage with a stubborn sleeve, pulled it over my shoulders and zipped up against the tempest. The old woman was clearly more experienced in these things than me: I looked up to see that she'd not only surrounded herself with a turquoise rain cape but had also got herself beneath a transparent rain bonnet that tied under her chin. I sloshed away after her up the road, turned left at the junction, overtook the caped crusader and made my way to the massive church on the top of the hill that dominates Rathkeale.

When I got to the top of the steps the churchyard was away to the left, which I assumed was where I'd find the holy stump. I made my way through puddles dented by the chubby raindrops, pushed open the gate and went inside. The cemetery was tightly packed with graves and I didn't know where to begin. I'd thought there might be crowds, hastily erected direction signs, maybe a hot dog stand, but there was nobody else around. Above the slashing sound of the rain I heard the gate squeak and then slam closed again: behind me the turquoise vision of the old woman from the bus hoved into the cemetery, cape flying in the wind like Margaret Rutherford in *Blithe Spirit*. Her determined gait had led me to believe that she knew what she was doing so I tried to slow my pace down the steep slope of the cemetery and let her overtake. Instead I skidded on a patch of mud that caused both my feet to shoot forward but left my head where it was in the pose of a rubbish limbo dancer. I straightened up with the help of an inelegant wheeling of the arms but the momentum of my forward lurch succeeded only in sending me galloping downhill over the slippy wet grass with a 'whooooaaaaa' noise that it took me a second to realise was actually emanating from me. I splashed along the pathway, heading for a giant puddle against the far wall. Instinctively I threw out an arm, hooked it around a tree and ended up wrapped tightly around it like a drunk clinging to a lamppost.

'Are you all right?' asked the old woman when she'd caught me up.

'Ah, er, yes, I think so,' I said, brushing something non-existent off the trunk in a manner that I hoped suggested this had been my intention all along. 'Do you know where this tree stump is?'

'No, I thought you did?'

'Oh, er, no, I just assumed that it would be in the graveyard.'

'Oh, I followed you in because I assumed you knew where you were going.'

'Ah, right, um, no, I don't know where I'm going.'

We set off together back towards the gate. Cold water seeped into my socks. The bottom half of my jeans were wet through and heavy. We arrived back at the church and walked around it. A small, flatbed lorry was parked in the corner of the yard with three men sitting in the cab, the rat-a-tat sound of the rain pinging off its roof and off the oil drums in the back sounding like a gun battle between two steel bands. The old woman knocked on the window and asked where the holy tree was. The man nearest us wiped the condensation from the inside of the window so we could see him properly and jerked his thumb towards the far side of the van. We walked around the vehicle. And there it was.

The holy tree stump of Rathkeale.

The corner of the churchyard was a featureless sandy sea of puddled orangey-brown mud strafed by raindrops. Close to the wall with nothing else around it or near it was an orangey hunk of wood about three feet high. Facing us was a flat surface as if the chainsaw had gone straight downwards through it rather than in the traditional vaguely horizontal direction you'd usually associate with tree-felling. The stump had been entirely stripped of bark, leaving a light swirly-textured surface all around. About a foot above the ground it seemed a small shelf had been cut into the stump. And that was it.

We walked gingerly through the mud towards it and stood there, watched from the cab of the lorry by the three workmen. It didn't look much like the Virgin Mary to me, or at least no more than it looked like Barbapapa or Munch's *Scream*. If you turned your head to the perpendicular, it looked from a certain angle a little bit like Snoopy. We stood in silence for a few moments, the only sound the rain hitting the ground and the patter of it hitting my waterproof. As we regarded the stump the rain eased and stopped as suddenly as it had begun, leaving a freshness in the newly rinsed air that made every little sound more acute now it was no longer dulled by the downpour. I turned to my companion.

'Do you think that's the Virgin Mary?' I asked.

After a moment's pause she made an elaborate dip of her head, like a dog sneezing, and announced, 'I have no opinion either way.' With that, she produced a camcorder from beneath her rain cape, put it to her eye and began circling the stump, filming every knot and grain from close range.

With the cessation of the rain a few people began to climb out of cars parked in the road outside and make their way gingerly towards the stump. They came through a gate next to which was affixed a sign that read, 'Adoration: 10 a.m. Tuesday to 9.30 a.m. Thursday.' Beside that was attached a handwritten sign reading 'No dogs. No smoking. No litter. Please respect the church grounds.' A couple of families stood at the stump and it soon became obvious that nobody was really sure what to do. Should it be treated as a religious icon, or as a quirky bit of sightseeing? Eventually a man with a moustache pulled a camera from his jacket pocket and indicated to his two young children that they should stand either side of the stump. They both obeyed but weren't sure whether they were meant to smile or look reverent. They plumped for something in between: a kind of faint beatific smile with their hands clasped in front of them, heads dipped slightly forward.

I trudged back to the lorry where two of the men were standing wearing their hi-vis vests while their colleague affixed a yellow 'trip hazard' sign to a lamp post a few feet away. Even the Holy Mother has to comply with health and safety.

'You know,' said one with a twinkle in his eye, 'if you look at it from the far side you can see Santa Claus; he has the beard and everything.'

'It doesn't look all that great in the rain, does it?' I said.

'Well, everyone's been stripping the bark and hacking bits off it,' he said before opening the door of the cab and reaching inside. 'Here's what it looked like at the start.' He handed me an A4-sized photograph run off on a laser printer and sheathed inside a clear document wallet. 'That was taken just after the tree came down.'

With the bark still attached it did indeed look a little more like a cowled figure. The devoted who'd hacked off pieces of bark and chunks of wood as relics had stripped the stump of what made it special. It was now just the stunted remnant of an old tree stuck in the muddy corner of a churchyard. Collectively they'd achieved what the person who smashed the windows of the financial centre in Florida had done: they'd destroyed the purported manifestation almost entirely. Desecrated it, if you like. If there was any kind of spiritual magic in what had happened here, magic that was enough to have grown men falling to their knees and blessing themselves in front of a tree stump, it was long gone now.

There'd been a petition to keep the stump in place rather than, as had been the original plan, dispose of it, signed by two thousand people, some of whom you'd assume had been among those chipping bits off the thing and ensuring that even if it had looked a bit like the Virgin Mary to start with it now just looked like a misshapen lump of old wood.

'I've seen a few people coming through that gate hoping to be absolved of all their sins,' said one of the men after a short silence. 'I'd say they've been sorely disappointed.'

The 'trip hazard' sign on the lamp post next to us slid down the pole and landed on top of the casing for the wiring with a slight metallic ding.

A woman in a pristine white trouser suit appeared, coiffed with an extraordinary bouffant that made James Brown's look like a crewcut. Resplendent in immaculate white trousers, white blouse, white jacket and white shoes she gingerly approached the corner of the yard where the stump lurked. She paused at the edge of the muddy expanse, slipped out of her shoes, picked them up and began a slow, barefoot and teetering progress across the swamp like a novice tightrope walker.

The council man became suddenly agitated.

'Missus, missus!' he called out. 'There's broken glass over there, broken glass!'

'I'll risk it,' she replied with a chuckle and a shrug that asked, if you wouldn't do it for Our Lady, who would you do it for? Like most people when she arrived at the stump she wasn't sure what to do. She stood and looked at it for a while, bouffant completely undisturbed by the wind, then turned around and tiptoed back again. Not a spot of mud had blemished her clothes.

A trio of young women walked towards the man from the council. He put up his hands, palms outwards in a defensive gesture. 'Don't touch me, ladies,' he said, 'you'll only get pregnant. Ever since this happened, everyone who touches me gets pregnant. It's divine intervention.'

There was a chorus of giggles and a couple of 'ah go on witchas' and the odd 'would ya go'way'.

I realised that there wasn't really much else to see. The weather might have had something to do with it, but there was no feeling of spirituality about any of this. Even the people who might have believed didn't really know what to do in front of the stump other than take a few lacklustre photographs and splash back to their cars. I squelched away from the scene as it began to rain again, leaving around half a dozen people gathered under golf umbrellas being regarded with kindly amusement by the council workers leaning by their truck. As I got to the corner of the church I turned around for one last look. For the first time I noticed the life-size statue of Christ in the churchyard not far from the stump. He had his back to the scene, his robes gathered up in his hands in front of his chest. His eyes were cast down.

I trotted down the steps and out of the gate, past the handwritten sign, 'No dogs. No smoking. No litter. Please respect the church grounds', and headed for the bus stop.

CHAPTER NINE

Once I'd got back from Limerick, dried out, thrown my shirt into the washing machine and vowed never to listen to another Shakin' Stevens record as long as I lived, I returned to the task of tracing my Irish heritage and fleshing out what I'd found so far.

I'd been trying to put together what fragments I could of John Connelly's life, a life that it seemed had lain forgotten and undisturbed for more than a century. On the face of it there was nothing remarkable or notable about John Connelly; he made no great discoveries and left behind no great works of literature or art: he couldn't even write his own name. But his was a life that I realised represented much more than an obscure family's obscure history; it represented a history of Ireland itself. It was a tale of hideous poverty and extreme hardship but it was a tale of survival and courage. It was a story like many millions of others, of those for whom Ireland was a cradle and the world became a cemetery.

John Connelly wasn't famous. As far as I could tell he left nothing behind beyond the written results of a handful of cursory conversations with census-takers and municipal registrars. The only mark he left was the spidery 'x' on the marriage and birth certificates. There would be no newspaper cuttings, no bundle of letters, not even a photograph to remember him by. His time on earth was nasty, brutish, short and caused not a ripple in the pool of history, yet John Connelly was also everyone who ever left Ireland, everyone who boarded a ship or an aeroplane and departed a land that could no longer keep them. His was a journey of millions. John Connelly was Ireland, the warts-and-all Ireland, someone who'd lived the truth behind the sugary depictions.

From the census returns and marriage certificate I worked out that he was probably born around 1824. The ages given on the censuses varied wildly – in two censuses ten years apart Catherine went from being two years older than John to being two years younger, while a brother, Timothy, appeared on two consecutive censuses and appeared to age only four years in the intervening decade – and I soon learned that not everything on the census could be taken as exact. Indeed, there's every chance that John and Catherine may not have even known exactly how old they were, particularly as the years advanced, let alone been giving the census-takers copper-bottomed information.

John spent his whole life outside Ireland in a small area of Whitechapel, living at various addresses all a relatively short distance from each other. It's impossible to say for sure why he settled and stayed there: maybe he knew people from home who already lived in the area, maybe he just got off the boat at Wapping, found lodgings nearby, secured a bit of work locally and never moved on. From what I would learn about the place in John's time, he certainly wasn't living there through choice. In every census his profession was given as 'dock labourer', save for one that listed him as a 'ship scraper': a particularly grim sounding occupation that involved scouring the hulls of ships of barnacles, weeds and other filthy detritus picked up at sea and on the way up the filthy, polluted Thames. Most of the addresses I found for him were slum tenements or boarding houses and most of their other inhabitants were also Irish: the community tended to nest together, some would have come with the address of a relative already there, others knowing that there were people from their locality there (most of John's nearest neighbours also came from Cork, or, as one census-taker noted in the spelling he heard in the man's accent, 'Cark'), yet more just gravitated there because they knew that's where the Irish gathered. There were single references to several children that would not be repeated and who had presumably died. It certainly seemed as though my great-great-great-grandfather was not a man of means and he did not have an easy life.

Census references to Catherine ceased in 1861. After searching records for the following decade I managed to obtain a copy of her death certificate, which showed she died of acute tuberculosis in the Middlesex Hospital two days before Christmas 1867. Her age was given as forty-one. As for John, census entries for him ended in 1881, which enabled me to track down his death certificate. He died in February 1890, also of tuberculosis, in the Princes Street Workhouse Infirmary in St George-in-the-East, a stone's throw from the docks and the river where he'd spent just about all his working life. His age on the certificate was given as sixty-five, which even as an approximation I thought wasn't a bad innings for a man who endured such a hard life in one of the poorest parts of the poorest part of London.

So, I at least had the basic facts of his life. I knew very roughly when and where he was born. I knew when, where and who he'd married. I knew the names of several children, one of whom survived to become my great-great-grandfather. Given that he wasn't on the 1841 UK census and married in Whitechapel in 1843 I could also narrow down a period of roughly two years within which he would have left Ireland for

England. I knew where he'd worked, where he'd lived and ultimately when, where and how he'd died. It sounds like a lot; it sounds like a pretty full account of a life, but in reality I knew very little. I didn't know the person behind the facts. What did he look like? Did I look like him? Was I anything like him? What made him laugh? Of what did he dream? In spite of all the hardship, the poverty, the harshness of slum life, was he ever happy? What made him happy? Who were his friends? What did he sound like? Did he ever lose his Cork accent? Did he have the big nose with which all Connelly men of my acquaintance seem to have been afflicted?

Short of recovering *The Secret Diary of John Connelly as Dictated to Someone Who Could Write* from behind an old Whitechapel eave somewhere, I would never know any of this. The best I could do was find out the kind of life he'd lived to at least gain an idea of the man. At the heart of everything was his emigration, the event that made his story that of Ireland and which led to the perception we have of the nation today. That's where I would begin.

While there has been migration between Ireland and Britain since medieval times, the nineteenth century was when things really took off. It's estimated that around eight million people left Ireland for pastures new between 1801 and 1921. Most of these would have crossed the Atlantic to Canada or the United States, but a huge number also made the short trip across the Irish Sea. The bulk of these people would have left as a result of the Great Famine: where around a million people left Ireland in the thirty years between 1815 and 1845, in the six years following that, years which encompassed the Famine, one and a half million emigrated. There was also a well established seasonal migration that continued right up to the sixties and was particularly strong in Connacht and Ulster where men would go to England for the summer months and work on the farms. In human terms, Ireland had the leakiest shores of any nation in the world.

John and Catherine, it seemed, had got out before the Famine took hold. The 1841 British Census took place on 6 June and neither of them is on it. They were married in Whitechapel on 29 August 1843 so obviously arrived between those dates. While passenger lists were kept for transatlantic emigration, meaning people with Irish-American ancestors can establish the date and the name of the ship on which their ancestors left, the boats that crossed the Irish Sea were less formal: you just bought a ticket and climbed aboard the first boat you could. Migrants travelling from Cork to Britain would at that time have arrived either in Bristol, South Wales or London (most of the Irish in London at this time would have come from Cork or Kerry) and most, it seemed, stayed put in the port of entry at which they arrived, which is presumably how John and Catherine came to be and remain in the English capital. But why would they have gone in the first place?

I was already learning that in John's time the Connellys would have been among the poorest of the poor, which back then was, at the risk of sounding like Bananarama, really saying something. For one thing, they didn't go to America. To a great extent, migration to Britain was the option for those who couldn't afford to cross the Atlantic. When you consider that people went to America as a result of poverty at home and that conditions on the ships were so awful that the high mortality rates lent them the nickname 'coffin ships', you can appreciate that to be too poor for that crossing meant you really were suffering excruciating hardship. County Cork in the first half of the nineteenth century was dominated by agriculture. Farm labourers would lease a hut and a tiny piece of land for their own subsistence while working for a pittance for the local farmer and landowner.

It was practically feudal and, as modernisation made agriculture less and less labour intensive, it became increasingly difficult to find work – by 1835 barely a third of Cork's agricultural labourers were in employment. Even Cork city, once a prosperous port and textile town, was in decline: its prime status as an exporter to southern Europe of goods like butter, beef, pork and tallow fell away dramatically after the Napoleonic Wars and its brewing and shipbuilding industries also began to dry up. Add to that the large numbers of unemployed men streaming into the city from the countryside in the vain hope of work and you can start to see why so many left – there was simply no other option short of starvation.

The empirical evidence I was gathering suggested to me that John may well have been one of those men from the countryside, driven out of Ireland by relentless and seemingly endless poverty and desperation. A Royal Commission report of 1836 into the condition of agricultural labourers in Ireland gave me an idea of the kind of life he was facing in Cork.

'A great proportion of them are insufficiently provided at any time with the commonest necessaries of life,' it said. 'Their habitations are wretched hovels, several of a family sleep together on straw or upon bare ground, sometimes with a blanket and sometimes without so much to cover them. Their food commonly consists of dry potatoes and with these they are sometimes so scantily supplied as to be obliged to limit themselves to one spare meal in the day.'

While that sounded faintly reminiscent of my own experiences at university in the early nineties, it was becoming clearer to me that John was probably from somewhere where life had become utterly untenable in rural Cork. From his marriage certificate I knew that his father was also called John, something that suggested John himself was the eldest son, probably of several siblings, and if born around 1824 would have been in his teens by the time he left. Could it be that there were too many mouths to feed? Was it discussed and decided that John would have to go for the sake of the rest of the family? With no work available and only a finite amount of space to grow their own food, was he given little choice but to sacrifice everything he knew in order that the number of Connellys be reduced to a more manageable subsistence level? Was he, in effect, sent away?

Two more factors persuaded me that this might have been the case. Although the Great Famine wouldn't start until 1845, there was a partial failure of the potato crop in 1842 that caused a spike in the numbers emigrating from Cork that year. Did rotten, stinking specimens coming out of the ground at the Connelly homestead make John's decision for him? Was a pathetic, tiny, diseased potato patch somewhere in rural Cork the catalyst for generations of Connellys being born in London rather than Ireland?

The second thing that might have clinched John's departure came in the nature of the boats leaving Cork in 1842. While the transatlantic ships departed from the deep-water port of Cobh a few miles east of Cork, the shorter hops were made by ships that left the quaysides of the city itself. The St George Steam Packet Company provided nearly all the ships crossing the Irish Sea at that time but in 1842 the City of Dublin Steam Packet Company placed two of its ships on the Cork to London route, sparking a price war that meant crossings could be had for as little as a shilling.

I could never be 100 per cent certain, but this combination of factors strongly suggested to me that John was the eldest male child of a very poor rural family, a family that couldn't support itself in the prevailing economic conditions. When the potato harvest of 1842 fell short of subsistence level the family was

faced with the very real prospect of starvation. John either vol-
unteered or it was decided for him that he would leave and seek
work abroad. Unable to afford the passage to America, England
would be the only option and, given the price war between the
two steam packet lines at the time, London represented the
cheapest destination. One day in 1842, then, John would have
gathered up what few possessions he had, bade farewell to his
family and set off for Cork city on foot. From there he would
have handed over a shilling for his ticket, boarded a ship at the
quay, seen the final ropes binding him to his homeland detached
from the quayside, felt the ship move gently away from shore and
sailed towards the sunset and the unknown.

The crossing itself would have been nothing like what we'd
expect today. There would be no duty free shops full of clinking
bottles of whiskey or lasagne and chips in the canteen. I found a
description of a crossing from Ireland to Britain from 1854,
twelve years after John's journey but probably still fairly repre-
sentative of his experience on board. It talked of passengers
packed into every available deck space, often with cattle right
alongside.

The account spoke of people 'huddled together in a most
disgraceful manner; and as they have not been used to sea passages they get sick and perfectly helpless and covered with the
dirt and filth of each other'. It spoke about the sea washing over
the decks, drenching everyone and 'it was only by great exertions
that some of these people were not carried overboard'. It was not
uncommon for people to freeze to death on cold and wet crossings in which the passengers were 'exposed on deck without any
covering belonging to the ship and the covering they had of
their own was very scanty'.

The crossing to London took three days, three days of standing room only, out in the open, in all weathers and in all

conditions, clinging on to anything you could. I tried to imagine John arriving at the port of London, wet through and still weak and shaking from the seasickness, and wondered what his first impressions were of his new home. It would have been quite unlike anything he'd seen before in the fields and hills of Cork: a bustling, dirty, noisy, busy place where you couldn't see the horizon for warehouses, ships and office-buildings. The welcome he received would not have been warm either: the Irish were seen as an uncivilised, feckless and lazy race who would drive wage levels down and disrupt the morality of England. According to Thomas Carlyle, writing three years before John arrived, my great-great-great-grandfather would have been 'in his rags and laughing savagery. He is there to undertake all work that can be done by mere strength of hand and back for wages that will purchase him potatoes . . . He lodges to his mind in any pighutch or doghutch, roosts in outhouses; and wears a suit of tatters'. The 'Saxon', according to Carlyle, scored over John because although 'he too may be ignorant he has not sunk from decent manhood to squalid apehood'. Carlyle had also written, 'Heaven disowns it, Earth is against it; Ireland will be burnt into a black, unpeopled field of ashes . . . The time has come when the Irish population must be improved a little or exterminated.'

You might have expected Friedrich Engels to be broadly sympathetic to the travails of the desperate, poverty stricken Irish immigrant forced out of his own land to a great extent by the dark and encroaching shadow of capitalism. But no. In 1844, the co-author of *The Communist Manifesto* said of my great-great-great grandfather and those like him, 'these people have grown up without civilisation, accustomed from youth to every privation: rough, intemperate, and improvident, bringing all their brutal habits with them among a class of the English population which has, in truth, little inducement to cultivate education and

morality . . . For work which requires long training or pertina-
cious application the dissolute, unsteady, drunken Irishman is on
too low a plane.'

While I'm sure John was under no illusions that life in
London, whether intended to be short- or long-term, was going
to be a long trip on the gravy train, he must have been taken
aback by the squalor that confronted him as he set off from the
quayside in search of lodgings and work. Whitechapel, the part
of London where he would spend the rest of his days, was deep
in the heart of some of London's worst slums and the contemporary accounts are appalling.

'Whitechapel,' wrote Hollingshead, in his *Ragged London* of
1861, 'may not be the worst of the many districts in this quarter,
but it is undoubtedly bad enough. Taking the broad road from
Aldgate Church to Old Whitechapel Church you may pass on
either side about twenty narrow avenues, leading to thousands of
closely-packed nests, full to overflowing with dirt, misery, and rags.
The residents are thieves, costermongers, stallkeepers, professional
beggars, rag-dealers, brokers, and small tradesmen.'

In 1842, the year I'm almost certain John arrived, the
Whitechapel coroner wrote about a visit he made to Rosemary
Lane, where John and Catherine would be living at the time of
their marriage the following year.

'I have this day been engaged in an inquiry into some of the
deaths in Hairbrain Court, Rosemary Lane, and have myself
viewed this evening the dead bodies of no fewer than three persons,' he wrote. 'I have been witness also to the most agonising
and appalling situation of others in a dying state in the same
locality who were found by me to be in a state of distress and
misery which could not but be most afflicting to my mind being
surrounded by the most foetid and unwholesome vapours from
privies and bad drainage, and filthiness, and much overcrowded;

and allow me to say, in such a state as I could scarcely have deemed it possible to have existed.'

Another description, from 1854, gives an idea of what life would have been like at 86 Rosemary Lane. It's an address that sounds like it should have a neatly kept front garden with at least one hydrangea, an umbrella stand in the porch and a little brick hut to keep the wheelie bins out of sight.

'The following is an account of part of a house of ten rooms in this neighbourhood, Rosemary Lane, let to the poor Irish.' wrote George Gibson. 'One of these rooms, kept by Daniel Jones, contained five beds, as they were called, but which in fact were nothing but bundles of rags. In bed number one, Daniel Jones, the keeper, his wife, and three children. In bed number two, Cornelius Toomey and John and Peter Shea, in the same bed. In bed number three, John Sullivan and his wife. In bed number four, Cornelius Haggerty, his wife, boy 13, and girl 11. In bed five, Patrick Kelly and wife: in all, sixteen persons in one room. At the time of Sergeant Price's visit the greater portion of these persons were in a state almost of nudity, huddled in this manner together. In many streets adjoining are places overpopulated and very unwholesome; indeed, Whitechapel church may be considered to be the centre of an immense mass of poverty, vice, and crime. Whitechapel is on the north and south divided by many streets and narrow courts, which are inhabited by very poor people: Jews, costermongers, dock labourers and thieves and the great extent of destitution is alarming.'

John worked all his life in the London docks. It would have been dangerous, backbreaking work and, given that most dock work was on a casual basis, was without any kind of job security. It was work for the desperate, those unable to find employment elsewhere, those with no skills and no education. It was probably the hardest life in London and among the hardest in England.

Turning up at the dock gates in the morning hoping to be picked for work, and if you got it, putting in long hours of lifting and humping and grunting and sweating and straining in abject conditions, from the fetid, sweltering holds of summer to the freezing, rain-lashed decks and wharves of winter. When times were really hard there were more casuals – men unemployed from other industries – turning up at the docks for the limited number of labour tickets, far more men than could be accommodated with work, and things would turn nasty. Ben Tillett, a dockworker at the time, remembered these fearsome mornings in a harrowing memoir. 'Coats, flesh and even ears were torn off,' he wrote. 'The strong literally threw themselves over the heads of their fellows and battled through the kicking, punching, cursing crowds to the rail of the cage which held them like rats: mad human rats who saw food in the ticket.'

In the 1880s, the *Lancet* estimated that 'in the course of five years' work more than half the dockworkers got wounded or otherwise seriously injured', and talked of lives 'needlessly squandered; men are ruptured, their spines injured, their bones broken and their skulls fractured so as to get ships unloaded a little quicker and a little cheaper'. To think men like my great-great-great-grandfather were fighting each other for the privilege of risking their lives for a few pence a day in order to ward off starvation and keep some kind of roof over the heads in a filthy, dank, rat-infested tenement.

The status of the casual dock labourer was probably best summed up by a rhyme popular around John's time:

Rattle his bones over the stones,
He's only a docky whom nobody owns.

By the 1881 census John was in his mid-fifties and living in a lodging house in St George-in-the-East (the area he'd lived in since arriving in London and one confirmed by the poverty examiner Charles Booth as the poorest parish in the East End – the slummiest of the slums). He was still a labourer, having somehow survived the deprivation and maiming potential of the docks for nearly forty years. A widower, he was still extraordinarily poor. St George's Chambers, the lodging house in which he lived, was one of many such institutions designed to house the poorest of the poor in something approaching decent conditions. They came under police supervision, bed linen was changed weekly and the place was well-ventilated. Charles Dickens' *London Encyclopedia* of the late 1880s was a big fan. 'There are few things more striking . . . than the comparative sweetness of these dormitories, even when crowded with tramps and thieves of the lowest class,' it said. 'About the best sample of this kind of establishment extant will be found at St George's Chambers, St George's Street, London docks, a thorough poor man's hotel where a comfortable bed with use of sitting-room, cooking apparatus and fire, and laundry accommodation, soap included, can be had for 4d a night.'

It was probably one of the luckiest breaks John ever had: a bed in a doss house full of tramps and thieves where at least the sheets were changed once a week.

Eventually in 1890 the years of squalor and the damp of the riverside caught up with John and tuberculosis claimed him in the St George-in-the-East workhouse infirmary, the same condition that had killed his wife nearly a quarter of a century earlier. To reach his mid-sixties, considering the kind of life he'd lived, was, as far as I was concerned, an extraordinary achievement in itself. He'd arrived as a teenager and died an old man a stone's throw from where he'd first stepped off the boat. At the time of his death Jack the Ripper was stalking the same streets and the previous year the Great Dock Strike had set in motion an improvement in the working conditions that he'd endured for nearly fifty years.

The physical hardships of his life must have been almost unbearable. One can only wonder at the injuries he might have sustained among the ships, wharves and warehouses, the accidents and deaths he might have seen, the constant threat that a loose cable, or an unnoticed open hatch to a deep empty hold might cause an injury that would ruin your ability to work or even kill you outright. The grief of losing a wife and several children before their time, the disease and squalor that could take you as well: the mental implications of John's life alone are just incomprehensible today. I wondered how often he'd thought of home. In his last days in the infirmary as he coughed his way towards a drawn-out, agonising end I wondered whether he'd pictured the place he'd left, the family he'd left behind decades earlier and never saw again. Somewhere in County Cork was a shack, a road and a bunch of fields, a village and maybe a town that he knew, views he remembered, smells, routines, faces, sounds.

As I pictured an old man wheezing in a draughty workhouse hospital, I knew that even more than ever I'd need to find that place, to go back to the spot he'd remembered for all those years, go back and tell him he was vindicated: the hardships and degradation he'd suffered, the life on the very bottom rung of the ladder, it had all been worth it. Bizarrely, my search for Irish roots had taken me to within a few short miles from where I'd grown up: now I needed to find the place where it all started.

All I had to go on was the fact his father was also called John and was listed as a hatter on the marriage certificate. This was even less than I'd started with when tracking down John himself. To make matters worse, for a nation that attracts more amateur genealogists from around the world than any other, Ireland has a dreadful dearth of records. During the civil war of the early twenties the Four Courts in Dublin was shelled and it and the surrounding buildings caught fire, leading to the destruction of just about every written record the nation possessed. Every census was destroyed bar 1901 and 1911 as well as many church, birth and death records. All the Irish genealogist has to go on are individual parish records and a few property surveys. Into this I was taking next to no information other than that I was looking for a John Connelly from Cork, Ireland's biggest county, born any time between about 1790 and 1805.

My best hope was the genealogy service at the National Archive in Dublin, where I consulted a lovely lady called Helen – who turned out to be one of Ireland's leading family history experts and is the world's only 'genealogy butler', offering an in-house service to guests at Dublin's highly salubrious Shelbourne Hotel – about what I might be able to do. The hatter thing seemed to be the way forward, she told me, and suggested that such a specialised artisanal occupation would most likely have been based in a large town, and in Cork that would most likely be Cork city itself. Hmm, perhaps my rural theory was wide of the mark. Helen pointed me towards a couple of trade directories from the 1820s and also advised me to search some property records from the city at the time. I didn't find a hatter named John Connelly anywhere, but did find a couple of people of the same name in the property records. Helen helped me to find the relevant parish records on microfiche, pointed me towards one of the reading machines and left me to it. The idea was to scroll through the years in which John might have been born in the hope of finding a baptismal record. In terms of unearthing an Irish record for John that might help me find exactly where the Connellys came from I was, if not exactly in the Last Chance Saloon, then certainly in the Limited Options Kebab House.

Once I'd finally loaded the roll of film into the reader – a long process that involved the reel unravelling and bouncing on to the ground at least once, several whispered inventive swearwords and a little bit of whimpering – I settled into the chair, adjusted the focus, cranked the handle and watched as the first scanned pages glided into view from east to west. The internet it wasn't. As I spooled through the first set of records I realised that this would be a long slog. There was, of course, no kind of search facility, no short cuts at all. Normally in this kind of situation I'd be tapping words into search engines between poking people on Facebook and updating Twitter, but here I had to examine each entry in the parish register individually, and this being the early nineteenth century, they were all handwritten in various inks and styles and spread over the pages in inconsistent, idiosyncratic and generally blobby fashion. For two hours I spooled through years of records, years of marriages and baptisms, and not one John Connelly did I find. Not a Connelly or a Connolly or a Connely or any variant of same. I'd drawn a complete blank, literally, in fact, when the final page passed through and the projected image in front of me went white for the final time. The notebook I'd opened at the start and which I'd hoped would by now contain a date and at least a hint of an address, not to mention a mother's name as well as a father's, also remained defiantly unsullied.

I truly thought I'd reached the end of the line. There was nowhere else I could go: I'd found the only likely references, checked them out and learned they weren't the right people. I may have actually found the man who started all this more than 160 years earlier, but I wouldn't find the piece of ground from which the story began. There'd be no ending, no completing the circle. I felt rootlessly dejected.

I stumbled out into the street, still seeing spidery Victorian handwriting passing in front of my eyes as if I was viewing the world through the prism of the opening credits of a Sunday night BBC costume drama, put my hands in my pockets and walked slowly back through the city. Strange as it may sound, Dublin now looked different. All the while I'd known there was a piece of ground somewhere in this country that I could find and visit, I thought I could belong here. Now that it seemed that I'd never find that place I suddenly felt like a total outsider again, like someone who'd just arrived and who had no connection with Ireland. The Georgian buildings looked foreign again, the Irish names on the road signs suddenly making me feel even more alien even though I now spoke a bit of the language. I didn't know what to do. All the times I'd cheered the Irish football team, all the songs I'd sung and played, the immersion in the Irish community in Britain, this curious affinity I'd felt with a nation that wasn't mine, it had all, I began to realise, hinged on the possibility of finding that one place where the whole thing was rooted. Now that I was no further forward than when I used to tell people my family was from Cork, it was as if the flimsy structure of my sense of self was crumbling to the point of collapse.

I walked aimlessly for a while and then decided there was only one thing for it. I'd go for a pint. I started heading for Neary's off Grafton Street, one of my favourite city centre pubs, where I'd weigh up what to do next. Or at least stare vacantly into space for a while with a Guinness in front of me. And then, walking past the National Library, I passed a man going in the other direction who looked faintly familiar. The briefest spark of recognition shook me out of my despondence for a moment and I looked back. The curly hair, the gait, the roll-up cigarette between his fingers. It couldn't be.

'Rob . . . ?' I called hesitantly.

He turned around and picked earphones from his ears. For a moment he looked at me blankly. Then he laughed, said, 'Bloody hell!' and walked back towards me.

I didn't do very well in my A levels. It wasn't surprising really, as I didn't do any work. You'd think if you were sitting an English literature A level, for example, actually reading the books might help.

I went to the local sixth form college to retake them. Not because I particularly wanted to, rather that, with no idea at all what I wanted to do with my lazy excuse for a life, this option allowed me to put any kind of decision off for another year. In my first English class I sat next to Rob, who'd been working in a bank for a while but had jacked it in and decided to do a couple of A levels. On the other side of me was Duncan, who that term would make our classroom reading of *Death of a Salesman* unforgettable to this day by reading the part of Willie Loman in an immaculate Clint Eastwood voice.

The three of us soon came to see the classes as an unavoidable hindrance to spending the entire day in The Artichoke, around the corner, talking about anything but college work. We went our separate ways after the retakes – Duncan would go on to become a successful professional actor – and gradually lost touch during the passing years. The last time I'd seen Rob, the best part of two decades earlier, the three of us had had a lost weekend at the Southampton house he'd been living in at the time that was so awful it would actually fall down a couple of weeks after he moved out.

Now we exchanged handshakes and claps on the upper arm, both declaiming the diminutive size of the world and asking the kind of questions whose answers were expected to distil nearly twenty years into a couple of sentences. Rob had moved to Dublin some fifteen years earlier and now had a couple of kids.

It was bizarre: having just abandoned one part of my past, here, by sheer chance, was another turning up.

I asked Rob what he was doing now.

'I'm a professional genealogist,' he replied and sucked hard on his cigarette.

CHAPTER TEN

Before I could catch up with Rob properly I first had to head west towards the Atlantic shore where Connemara presented me with a bit of conundrum. On the one hand it seemed to represent the kind of stereotype I was trying to get beyond: the old stone cottages, the rocky fields, the quaint villages with their pubs and flat-capped, whiskery characters dispensing wit and wisdom between gappy teeth. I was fairly confident that it was where that Caffrey's ad had been filmed. Yet at the same time, for all it had been claimed by agents of conspicuous heritage, Connemara seemed to stand for an authenticity, a near-timeless isolation borne of the fact that it's probably the most isolated part of the Irish mainland: with the Atlantic on one side, Galway Bay to the south, Lough Corrib to the east and the Maumturk and Twelve Pin mountains to the north, the region seems almost cut off from the rest of the country and left to its own devices. Time passes slower there. I planned to disappear into Connemara between two weddings in the west of Ireland to discover what the great travel writer H. V. Morton meant when he came back from a visit there claiming that he now knew where the world ended. But first I had to get out of Dublin.

★

It was a blustery September morning at the office of a car hire company not far from the city centre. After I'd handed over my licence and the girl behind the chest-high counter had clattered away at her keyboard below me, I accepted a key from which swung a clunky plastic tag and followed her finger as she pointed towards the four door saloon car outside the window.

I went outside and checked the car against the little diagram on the yellow sheet that showed the dinks, dings and scratches already on the vehicle. 'There are a couple of things marked already,' said the girl as she handed me the sheet. She wasn't wrong. On the paper several x's and circles peppered the passenger side of the car like some vigorously contested freeform jazz version of noughts and crosses. When I looked at the car itself it seemed to have been recently broadsided by a Gatling gun that had emptied its entire magazine into it shortly before the collision. Still, although it had been in the wars – possibly literally – it was a far swankier vehicle than I was used to and while gallantly leaving Jude to put all our bags in the boot I sat at what appeared to be the controls of an intergalactic starfighter.

Now, I'm familiar with cars designed for idiots; cars that were constructed at a time when they had dials and levers and the odd clunky switch; when windows had handles that went round and round in direct relation to the vertical movements of the pane. In short, cars aimed at stupid people like me. This car didn't so much have a dashboard as a mission control. There were digital displays everywhere, screens and diagrams, things that flashed and things that changed colour, a dashboard so complicated that I thought it must be linked to a vast windowless room somewhere, where rows of men in ties and shirtsleeves chewed biros in front of computer terminals while my befuddled and slightly frightened phizog loomed at them from a giant screen covering an entire wall. Most discombobulating of all, the steering wheel (thank goodness, there was a steering wheel) had a volume control on it. Wow, I thought, all the years I've been driving and not once can I say the loudness of my steering had ever concerned me.

Jude climbed into the passenger seat and closed the door. I turned the key to start the engine and a blast of searingly loud pop music nearly blew her back out on to the pavement. Now, on the kind of cars I was used to you'd turn a little round knob until it clicked and the radio would go off. This one didn't seem to have a dial. In fact I had trouble locating the radio at all. For what seemed like several ear-splitting minutes I prodded and poked at various things, in hindsight mostly the dashboard casing. The windscreen wipers would start and stop. The windows would go up and down. My seat started moving inexorably forward until I thought I'd have the manufacturer's name from the steering wheel permanently imprinted in reverse on my sternum, at which point it began retreating and the windscreen washers came on instead. Finally, as the first trickles of blood from my ears reached my collar, while I was bent double and tugging desperately at the clutch and throttle pedals, my elbow must have knocked against something that turned out to be the correct button because the car lapsed into a sudden silence save for the low throb of the idling engine and the ringing in our ears.

I pulled off a three-point turn in the customary manner of the unfamiliar car – all screaming revs and undignified lurches – and before long we were heading along the south bank of the Liffey, nosing past Heuston Station and leaving Dublin behind to bisect the country's midriff for Galway.

At around lunchtime the bed and breakfast on the outskirts of the city of Galway into which we'd booked appeared to our left. A friendly grey-haired man answered the door, but he appeared distracted slightly; as if we'd arrived just after he'd had some bad news. When he'd checked us in, given us the room key and the lowdown on breakfast times, he paused, looked at us levelly and said, 'Did you hear that a man lost his life in the bay this morning?'

Galway is all about the sea. While it's a popular and lively town, its atmosphere rejuvenated annually by a large student population, the city is defined by its historic and contemporary relationship with the Atlantic Ocean and when the sea claims one of its people the whole city is affected.

The man, a sixty-seven-year-old named Johnny Sheain Jeaic MacDonncha, who was one of the most experienced seamen along the entire west coast, had been sailing a *gleoiteog*, a small version of the Galway hooker, west to a regatta in Connemara when it capsized and sank. His brother survived, winched aboard a coastguard helicopter, but it was too late to save Johnny. Johnny had been involved in a number of sea rescues and searches himself, including an occasion in 2000 when a Spanish fishing vessel hit the Skerd rocks and twelve sailors were lost. He died five years almost to the day after four colleagues were drowned when their vessel hit rocks on the same route he had been taking that morning. It was a tragic story, the kind of story that defined the west coast of Ireland and its people and not the last of its kind that I'd hear before I headed east again.

The Galway wedding was in the Claddagh, close to the centre of Galway city and an ancient fishing village that dates back further than the fifth century. It was well known as being an independent community in itself, with its own hierarchy and customs, and is best known for the famous Claddagh Ring. It was traditionally a poor area and remained so right up until the thirties when the ancient thatched cottages were deemed dangerous and insanitary and replaced by modern housing. Today the Claddagh boasts some of the most expensive house prices in Galway.

The wedding was my first in Ireland, and was one of the few times I've really felt like an outsider here. The Catholic ceremony was so familiar to everyone else in the church that the calls and responses were murmured and spoken with a warm familiarity from which I was excluded. The people in the church that day had been raised on Mass *en masse* for as long as they could remember; there were thousands upon thousands of church hours combining in that service, a bond that spanned generations, genders and geography, a bond from which I was excluded entirely. Not in an unwelcoming way, not at all, but I felt like the person at, say, their first football match who doesn't know the songs. It was, I realised, one of very few times when my background betrayed my foreignness.

At one stage the priest invited everyone to kneel. He said this at a moment when I had my head buried in the order of service, a document the size of a sitcom screenplay. When I looked up again everyone had dropped to the kneeling mats in front of them, even elderly people and folk who looked as though they might need a block and tackle to get them upright again. I was, I realised, the only one in the entire place whose posterior still graced pew. Dropping to my knees then would, I thought, have just drawn attention to myself, so I compromised by sliding my bottom quietly forward until I was on the edge of the seat and hunching forward a little until my earlobes touched my shirt collar.

Thankfully the rain held off for the nuptials, but the following day dawned grey, miserable and soggy which, after a raucous night at a spectacular Galway wedding, mirrored exactly how I felt. I scuttled from the door of the guesthouse to the car, scrambled into the driver's seat, pointed the bonnet west and headed on to the road for Connemara. A few miles up the road I suddenly realised what was nagging at me, turned the car around and went back for Jude and the luggage.

It was a filthy day and a filthy drive, the rain lashing in torrents on the windscreen, the kind of rain that has you leaning forward almost with your chin on the steering wheel in an attempt to see where you're going. On the map it wasn't far; indeed Connemara itself starts almost as soon as you leave Galway city, but the reality of roads in the far west of Ireland plus the fact we were heading for one of the region's furthest peninsulas made it a long and, in this weather, utterly dispiriting journey. Connemara's fantastically rugged scenery was entirely hidden behind the grey mist and dark, low clouds and the short-sighted filter of the rainy windscreen that even the enthusiastic *gwersh-gwersh* of the wipers did little to alleviate. Finally, at a distant point on the long road from Clifden to Claddaghduff Jude exclaimed, 'I think that's it,' as we passed a blurry grey outline at the edge of the road. I turned around, drove back, missed the turn again and at the third attempt managed to nose the car between the gateposts of the cottage that would be home until the next wedding came around. We dashed between car and cottage a few times with holdalls and carrier bags before putting the kettle on and pausing to take in the chilly unfamiliarity of our temporary home.

With the weather, global recession and an exchange rate that made things hugely expensive for Brits it had been a grim summer for Irish tourism. The visitors' book revealed that we were the cottage's first occupants for several weeks and where previous years had seen visitors from Italy, Germany and beyond this year had seen only a smattering of entries, all but one from within Ireland.

Hence there was a cold and slightly damp mustiness to the place. Fortunately however some kind soul had dropped by earlier in the day and lit a turf fire in the stove, the orange glow and peaty smell of which is always cosily reminiscent of home even to someone like me who grew up in south-east London with central heating and a vase of dried flowers where the fire-place should be. We then realised we had no turf or briquettes with us and the fire wouldn't be on much longer, so Jude stealth-ily crept to where next door had a load piled up against the wall and stole some. She's a true country girl, all right.

There's always that strange sense that you're somewhere you shouldn't be when you stay in a cottage, especially when you arrive. When we'd put away our provisions, taken our baggage into the bedroom and popped our toothbrushes into the mug in the bathroom, we sat down in front of the fire with a cup of tea with me still worrying that we'd hear the front door open, the stamp of mud being removed from heavy boots and see a man in a flat cap who'd walk in carrying a shotgun and a couple of dead rabbits, stop in his tracks and ask us what the hell we were doing in his house.

When we climbed into bed that night, an unfamiliar, cold bed with strange creaks, twangs and noises, the storm still blew hard outside, rattling at the windowpanes and making the unfamiliar building click and groan and creak in the darkness. And what darkness it was: proper, countryside, remote, blanketing Connemara darkness, not the weak, streetlight-hued, insipid city darkness we were used to. When the wind finally dropped deep into the night, the silence was as much of a blanket as the dark. It was deafeningly quiet. I slept better than I had in weeks.

The next morning I backed the car gingerly into the narrow road, performed a nine-point back and forth vehicular shuffle to have it pointing in the right direction, and set off for Cleggan, where we'd catch a boat out to the island of Inishbofin, one of the westernmost outposts of Ireland.

We passed through Claddaghduff, the nearest village to the cottage, where on the left between the road and the inlet was the church, a sprightly looking building glinting in the morning sunshine. The sea behind it was calm and twinkling that day, but on 28 October 1927 it was a quite different prospect. In the late afternoon people had gathered as usual in the church for Sunday Mass. The parish church cast a wide net and people had travelled in from all over for the service, hoping the light drizzle would have stopped by the time it came for the journey home. Instead, as Mass progressed the drizzle turned almost in an instant into a massive storm: rain hurled itself from a suddenly dark sky and the wind roared in from the sea, ripping slates from the church roof and rendering the voice of the priest almost inaudible. From the back of the church came a bang, and the parishioners looked round to see that the doors had been blown wide open, the wind flinging rain and leaves into the body of the church and snuffing out the candles.

Standing just inside the door was a young fisherman from Rossadilisk, a small village on the other side of the headland next to Cleggan, named Michael Laffey, clad in his oilskins from which water dripped on to the church floor. People gestured at him to close the doors but he just stood there, looking towards the altar, until a woman nearby got up from her pew and pulled the doors closed herself, complaining, 'Isn't it a wonder you didn't close the door, Michael?'

But when they looked back Michael Laffey was gone. At the moment he'd been seen by several people standing in the church he was actually out at sea, drowning in the storm with fifteen other local men, tearing the very heart out of the little community huddled on this remote western peninsula and leaving a wound whose pain is still felt today.

The storm had whipped up into a fatal fury out of nothing:

the afternoon had been calm with a bit of light rain when four boats set out from Rossadilisk and five from Inishbofin. There'd been nothing to suggest anything out of the ordinary until a retired doctor living in a farmhouse not far from Cleggan village heard a storm warning on the home made radio he'd built. He ran outside, found a farmhand and told him to take his horse and ride to Rossadilisk and advise the fishermen of the impending maelstrom. Alas the rider arrived too late: the boats were already out in the bay and out of contact. Out of nowhere the storm tore at the land and whipped what had been a calm sea into a foaming, seething mass of mountainous waves. The little fishing vessels stood no chance. The boat carrying Michael Laffey smashed into rocks barely two hundred yards from the safety of the shore and all six men on board were lost, including the skipper John Cloonan and his son Michael. Two other boats were dashed against rocks at Cleggan Head with the loss of ten further lives, including Martin Murray, father of ten, John Murray, father of seven and Mark O'Toole, also a father of seven.

In one of the boats three brothers from the Lacey family all died. The only Cleggan boat to come home that night was that of Festy Feeney, who managed to stay afloat until, by the only stroke of good fortune on the entire peninsula that night, his boat was carried in by a freak wave and deposited on the beach at Sellerna Bay. Of the twenty men who'd set out from Rossadilisk that day, only four came home.

Of the five Inishbofin boats, two were lost with nine men: eighteen more children lost fathers. Only one of the bodies was recovered; that of Michael O'Toole who was found tied to the wreckage of his boat when it washed up. Twenty-four-year-old Martin McHale, one of the men from the lost boats, almost made it to one of the other Inishbofin vessels but, when he was almost within touching distance of rescue was pulled back, sucked under and never seen again. The man on the boat reaching out to him, stretching every sinew and coming within inches of clasping his hand before it and the terrified face beyond disappeared beneath the surface for ever, was his brother, Peter.

The effect a disaster like that can have on a small, remote community is incalculable. Breadwinners, husbands, fathers, sons, snatched away without warning and without mercy. As well as the fathers lost in the disaster several of the men were responsible for the upkeep of elderly parents. In Cleggan and Inishbofin there was barely a person unaffected directly by the Atlantic taking the communities' best men and breaking grief upon their shores. The sorrow was limitless: the first five bodies found lay overnight in simple pine coffins in the dim, flickering candlelight of the Cleggan village hall, a hall that at the time of the disaster was being set up for a ceilidh. After the men had been identified the coffins were transferred to the church at Claddaghduff, following which four were buried together on Omey Island and the other taken by boat to Inishbofin for burial.

When we got to Cleggan I parked the car by the quayside and walked back up to the village to buy tickets for the ferry. On the right as you leave the harbour is a stone Celtic cross dedicated to the victims of the disaster with fresh flowers planted in a bed in front of it. The names of the twenty-five men are engraved in white on a black marble tablet affixed to the low stone wall. After buying the ferry tickets at the village shop we killed time before departure with a cup of tea in Oliver's Bar, overlooking the harbour. Framed on the walls were yellowing newspaper accounts of the disaster. Through the window a couple of modern fishing boats swayed in the harbour, boats whose crews would pass the memorial every time they put out to sea and every time they came back. The roar of the storm and the cries of the drowning still hang in the air here, more than eighty years on.

At the quayside the ferry, which runs every day throughout the year, a service instigated in the thirties with a boat paid for by money donated by the public in memory of the disaster, was tucked around the corner. On the quayside were boxes of supplies destined for the island's shops and pubs: bananas, cauliflowers, onions, apples and potatoes. Several slabs of beer cans were passed aboard and finally a crate of brandy and a bag of mail. Then the small clutch of folk heading over to the island this blustery day late in the tourist season walked gingerly along the gangway, stepped down into the passenger saloon low in the boat's belly and settled in for the five-mile journey. As soon as we left the shelter of the harbour it was clear the swell was a considerable one: this wasn't some gentle crossing of an estuary; we were out in the North Atlantic itself. Great silver-grey bars of water moved gracefully towards the shore, the little red and white ferry going nose up and pointing at the grey sky, then plunging down into the trough before riding the next wave immediately behind. The boat had looked quite big back at the harbour but out here it was like a child's plastic toy, the throaty churning of the engine sounding pathetic against the power of the ocean pushing relentlessly at it and toying with its hull. Every now and then the ferry would hit the next wave hard and the whole boat would shudder, every rivet seeming to rattle in its hole, waves of reverberation passing through every iron plate. Great swathes of water would slap against the windows and a couple of German tourists descended into the cabin from where they'd been out on deck, where they'd got absolutely sopping wet. They smiled and chuckled sheepishly, sitting down on the bucket seats and brushing off some of the excess drops. In the furthest corner a large man distracted himself from the bumpy ride by plugging in a pair of earphones, tightly closing his eyes and singing loudly and tunelessly along to Destiny's Child.

After half an hour or so the dark, craggy silhouette of Inishbofin appeared through the salt-crusted portholes and before long the ferry was being moored at the island's quay. If I'd wanted to get an idea of just how remote the island was, then the jarring, undulating crossing at the mercy of the cold, grey ocean was all the confirmation I'd needed, as my slightly wobbly walk along the quay proved.

Inishbofin wasn't at its best that day. It was the very end of the tourist season, from which the island's 180 or so inhabitants (at its peak in the pre-Famine years the combined populations of Inishbofin and its little neighbouring island Inishturk were more than 1600. Inishturk's last few inhabitants transferred to the mainland in 1961) make much of their income. The island's little heritage centre was padlocked shut and the community centre had no signs of life other than two men digging a deep hole outside it. We walked around the village, passing a mixture of modern houses and ancient, dilapidated cottages. One in par-ticular had seen its roof fall in: although the windows had been piled with stones you could still see, through the gaps, the thatch undulating over the internal walls, as if protecting the dignity of the interior with a smothering shroud.

The weather didn't help to show off Inishbofin either. The sky was as grey and forbidding as the sea as we looked across from the top of the island, the cold wind buffeting our hair and clothes. There were no colours save for two curious round towers painted brilliant white, one close to the shore, the other higher up the hill behind it. It took me a while to work out what they were for: at first I thought they might be some kind of grain store, but then I looked out to sea and realised they were for ships entering the harbour. If you lined up the two towers straight ahead of you, you were on a safe passage free of sub-merged hazards.

I'll confess that I wondered how we were going to fill the hours on the island. We'd done a circuit of the village. Twice. With the heritage centre closed there was nothing to visit. There was only so much stock to inspect in the shop, particularly as we'd accompanied a good proportion of it on the ferry over. Across the harbour, at the end of one of the pincers of this crab-shaped section of the island that made the harbour such a haven, there was the forbidding ruin of the Cromwellian fort, but there was no easy way across to it: the tide was in and one thing that made it such an effective fort was that there was no purpose-built access: the way round to it was rocky, inhospitable, treacherous and long.

In 1651, as Oliver Cromwell slashed and slaughtered his way across Ireland, Inishbofin became one of the last strongholds of the Catholic resistance. It was eventually overcome by Cromwell's forces, who then built up the old castle that stood on the headland into a star-shaped fort. Its main use was as a holding camp for captured Catholic clergy who were being transported to Barbados. The fort fell out of use early in the eighteenth century but stands as a dignified, dark presence, still cowing those arriving at the island to make an immediate mental note to behave themselves.

It began to drizzle, so we headed for what's arguably the most remarkable aspect of the island: the Inishbofin Hotel and Marine Spa, a modern, white luxury hotel that sits up against the hillside at the eastern end of the harbour. While incongruous, it's certainly not obtrusive but by its very presence it hoists eyebrows and engenders exchanges of quizzical looks. It's a rectangular, modern building with an impressive glass frontage, the kind of place you know before you enter is going to have dishes of pebbles in its fireplaces and grey slate surfaces wherever there's a place to put them. This could only have happened in Celtic

Tiger Ireland: putting a massive luxury hotel on a rocky outcrop five miles into the Atlantic, five miles from what's already one of the remotest parts of the country, an island served by a plucky little ferry, an island with a population that could almost be entirely accommodated in the hotel. Undoubtedly it had provided significant employment, something of vital importance to such a fragile local economy dependent on external factors for survival, but, even allowing for the fact this was the end of a summer of poor weather and deep recession, the place looked deserted and that couldn't be a good sign.

It's an immaculate establishment, from the turbo-powered hand dryers in the toilets to the photographic prints of island life in the old days: it's not a chain hotel, built out of a flat-pack with an identikit interior where once you were through the door you wouldn't be able to tell if you were on Inishbofin or in Market Harborough. The glass front commands a view across the harbour and out to sea: almost all Inishbofin life is spread in front of you, but, sitting there dawdling over a pot of coffee, it was impossible to see how it could possibly keep going. There is talk of building a landing strip on the island, but even then, who's going to be on the plane?

As I played idly with one of the pebbles in a dish on the slate shelf next to me, I found myself worrying about Inishbofin. The derelict cottage, the heritage centre closed up for the winter as early as September, not to be open until, they hoped, the first ferryload of tourists in the late spring. There'd hardly been a soul around as we'd done our circuits of the village. How could a community like this survive in the modern age? Less than two hundred people on the furthest fringe of Europe, stuck in a recession and with a monument to the excess of the boom years parked at the end of the harbour with its halogen spotlights, spa treatments and paninis on the lunch menu. Tourism seemed to be the lifeblood of the place these days, but with tourism figures for Ireland dropping and the triple blow that summer of global recession, an exchange rate that kept the Brits away and god-awful weather, there seemed to be a sense of resignation hanging over the island.

The drizzle stopped, the coffee pot was drained, we hopped off our high stools and headed back out through the doors, walked up the slope and on to the road heading to the eastern end of the island, pausing to look down into the rows of identical empty rooms, beds immaculately made, sheets tightly tucked in, sheets that may not be pulled back in earnest until three whole seasons had turned.

As we walked along the road that gently sloped downwards towards the eastern end of the island, we journeyed back centuries in time. From the sleek, pebbles-in-dishes Irish present we were walking back through Inishbofin's past, through the days when the islanders had a reputation as wreckers luring ships to their doom on the rocks, and the days when the great pirate queen Grace O'Malley, who once went to London and met Elizabeth I and, apparently, got on great with her, purportedly had a castle on the promontory opposite the fort. Suddenly a violent squall blew up at our backs, flinging rain from behind in strong gusts of wind that soon had our jeans sticking to the backs of our legs yet left our fronts bone dry, a tempest that for-tunately blew itself out as quickly as it had begun. The rainstorm gave the rocky fields a chilled freshness, rinsing the air and bring-ing every detail, from the moss-splashed greys of the stone wall at the side of the road to the black rocks on the top of the hill beyond that almost glowed blue in the afternoon light, into sharp focus.

After a short while I found what I'd come to see, set back from the road. It was the old island graveyard, and in its corner the roofless outline of a ruined chapel that dated back to the fourteenth century. This part of the island goes back even further than that, however, as it was here that Inishbofin's first recorded settler, St Colman, arrived with a small band of followers in 665 and built a small monastery.

The former Abbot of Lindisfarne had spent thirty-seven years as a monk on the Scottish island of Iona, so was steeped in learning from the two holiest places in Britain. Colman's northern branch of Christianity clashed with the Romanesque one spreading up through the south of England over the date of Easter, a disagreement that prompted the famous Synod of Whitby in 664. Colman, alas, was on the losing side, but instead of accepting the ruling of the King of Northumbria – who had convened the Synod after he and his Kentish wife found themselves giving each other chocolate eggs on different days – he hopped it, first back to Iona and then on to Inishbofin where he built his monastery. There's nothing left now, although there are stones in the graveyard that are old enough to have been part of it, and the monastery itself was trashed by Sir John D'Arcy, Edward II's Lord Justice of Ireland in the 1330s, but the ancient graveyard and ruined chapel remain as a permanent reminder of the beginnings of life on the island.

I picked my way carefully through the cemetery: the rain had left the stones and long grass treacherously slippery. Even though the small plot is full to bursting it's still in use: among the weathered and illegible stones are modern graves, tidy family plots with black marble headstones and neatly spread green gravel. I also bumped against several small stones in the grass, unmarked chunks that represented the graves of people too poor for a proper headstone. Eventually I reached the chapel in the far corner, ducked through the old doorway and into the main body of the building. It was clearly a small chapel; you'd fit no more than twenty or so people in at a squeeze. There was an altar of sorts at one end, but it appeared to be of far more recent provenance than the fourteenth century, an old tombstone raised on breezeblocks. The altar was beneath a tall, slim window, through whose glassless opening I could see beyond the few grazing sheep and the coastline to the uninhabited hunk of Davillaun island rising out of the grey sea and, in the far distance, the hazy monochrome outline of the Maumturk mountains over on the mainland. I stood looking out in the wind and, among the dark stones and the ancient dead of Inishbofin beneath the grey sky, I felt a little gloomy. I thought of the little cottage back on the mainland on the road to Claddaghduff and I missed the warming hiss and quiet thundering of the burning turf in the stove and the parasol of stars overhead in the night sky. Inishbofin seemed fed up, stoop-shouldered, a little grumpy even, resigned to a long hard winter and maybe a long hard summer after that. There was still a good while till the ferry left and the thought of its bright red hull shone perkily in the dank grey of the old cemetery on the far end of a remote island on the very fringe of everything. I hoped it would come soon.

Then something caught my eye. Down to my right on a heap of old stones that covered the floor of the chapel was a small splash of colour. Colour was something I'd not seen much of on the island other than the greys of the stone walls, sea and sky and the dark greens of the grass. Yet there, on the ground among some long grass bent flat by the rain was an unexpected spatter of brightness. Some wild yellow flowers peeped from beneath a stone, next to what appeared to be some orange roses. Half a dozen of them, enmeshed in the grass to such an extent that I couldn't tell whether they'd been laid there or were actually growing. Then shadows appeared on the ground, faint at first but then stronger and stronger, mimicking the shapes of the stones in whose image they'd been cast. I felt a warming sensation on my back. The sun had come out and what a difference it made. It warmed colours from the stones and from the hillside. As the clouds passed over I watched through the chapel window as it warmed a bright blue from the grey sea. Inishbofin was changing in front of my eyes and it looked wonderful. I ducked through the old arched doorway of the chapel and picked my way through the nettles and across the cemetery again. On the road the sun glinted off the puddles and the island visibly came to life, as if those few flowers had been a springtime in themselves and we were passing into summer. I passed the hotel again and carried on to the harbour front. The sun sparkled on the water and even the locked heritage centre suddenly looked charming and jaunty. I decided to celebrate my Inishbofin epiphany in the best way I knew how: by not passing a pub if it was open and there was time to kill. I pushed open the door and walked into a sprawling, wood-panelled bar whose walls were covered with maritime prints and memorabilia and curling photographs of grinning regulars, their faces white with overexposed flashguns. There was nobody else in the place.

Jude and I stood there politely for a minute. Nothing. I moved a bit, making a definite scraping sound with my waterproof coat. Still nothing. I sniffed. No sign of anyone, not a sound anywhere in the pub. I cleared my throat and heard movement: a man emerged from a doorway. I looked away, and looked back again, doing that thing where you have to kind of pretend you just happened to be standing at the bar taking in the view and weren't concerned at all as to whether anyone was serving or not.

'Oh,' I said, 'hello. Um, two pints of Guinness, please.'

Without a word the man took a pint glass from beneath the counter, placed it under the mouth of the Guinness tap, flipped the tap down and watched intently as the brown liquid eased into the glass with a faint hissing sound. When it was two-thirds full he snapped off the tap and placed the glass on the bar as the liquid at the bottom emerged black from the gradual but frantic work of the brown bubbles between it and the creamy head forming at the top. He repeated the process in another glass. As the slow, delicious transformation took place between us, I stood there, still not having rid myself of that British thing of waiting at the bar until your drink arrives. In Ireland, especially if the place isn't busy, you can order a Guinness, go over to a table, take your coat off, chuck it on the seat, unfurl your newspaper and take a slow wander back via diverting pictures on the wall while your Guinness is still settling. In many places, they'll even say, 'Take a seat and I'll drop it over to you.' But no, I continued to stand there waiting and the man behind the bar continued to say nothing.

I looked at some photographs behind him. One appeared to be . . . no, it couldn't be. This was Inishbofin, not Austin, Texas. It did look like . . . no, the picture, in which the man with the laughing eyes, thin white beard and red handkerchief tied around his head was clearly taken here, and what would *he* have being doing in a harbour-side pub on a remote island off a remote part of Ireland.

It did look a hell of a lot like him though.

'That's not . . .' I said haltingly. 'Is that . . . Willie Nelson?'

The barman turned around briefly and looked at the picture, then back at our pints which had divided firmly and decisively into black and cream camps with a sharp meniscus separating the two. He popped the first one under the tap and flicked it on again.

'Yep,' he said.

'Wow!' I said.

Silence. He placed the pint on the bar in front of me and did the same with the second.

'Was it taken here?'

'Yep.'

He took the ten euro note from my hand and turned to the till.

'He played a concert here once,' he said into the cash drawer while flicking out the coins of my change with the fingers of his right hand and catching them in his left.

'Wow,' I said again.

He handed me my change.

'Been a busy year?' I asked, changing the subject. And for the first time he became animated.

'No, it's been a disaster,' he said. 'Just a disaster. It's rained here every day, *every day*, since the beginning of August. A catastrophe of a summer.'

'Oh,' I said, aware that nothing I could say would provide any consolation nor hope for a gilded future. I settled on, 'Sorry to hear that.'

He smiled at me, nodded, shrugged and returned to that mythical, mysterious part of every pub which they call 'out the back'.

We sat by the large plate glass window behind the pool table where the sun shone through at its warmest. We had a view right along the harbour and the place had been transformed by the sunshine. The sheds suddenly had a perkiness where before their angled roofs had been like stooped shoulders. The jumble of lobster pots against a wall looked almost like a carrion of bells in joyous peal. As if scripted, two small children ran around the corner, laughing and chasing each other.

As the last suds of my pint slid low in the glass I saw the red hull of the ferry chug around the corner. We walked back to the

quay, hopped up the gangplank out of the warmth and into the
cool of the cabin. The engines fired and we headed out of the
harbour and back towards Cleggan. The sea was bright blue and
calm and I went out to the stern of the boat, looking along the
white avenue of our wake and back to the island. It stood out
green against the blue of the sea, a few fluffy white clouds hung
affectionately over it beneath a clear blue sky. I'd been wrong
about Inishbofin. It's seen its fair share of setback and disaster,
from the lives lost that terrible night in 1927 to the two
American students who a few years ago had walked out to the
Stacks at the western tip of the island at low tide, been cut off
and swept away to their deaths, all of whom had memorials at
the island's church. Inishbofin has survived all sorts, from
Cromwell to the Famine, vandalising medieval chief justices to
dissenting monks, and it's still here, constantly reinventing itself,
constantly surviving. There's no better illustration than the ten-
minute walk from the tourism zeitgeist of the hotel to the
ancient, ruined chapel in the graveyard, with its yellow and
orange flowers bringing light and colour to the gloom.

The spa hotel might have seemed like a crazy idea to some but
they went for it. It's a triumph of belief, just another change in
the continuing development of the island's history. It may have
been a rotten summer for Inishbofin's tourism but I had a sense
that this was a temporary setback; that the island had faced and
conquered bigger challenges than this over the centuries. The
hotel exemplified a new beginning: it had been built in the
boom years but when the sunshine reflected back off its white
walls and flashed off its glass frontage I had an inexplicable feeling – maybe based on nothing more than the sun coming out –
that the worst was over for Inishbofin, and hopefully for Ireland
too. There were better times around the corner. It was the kind
of optimism that led to the hotel being built in the first place on

this little island that serves as almost a microcosm of the country itself, stuck out on the very edge of Europe, surviving all sorts, from biblical weather to invaders and plunderers, to always bounce back, to always win.

The German tourists who'd been soaked on the choppy journey over were standing nearby. Indicating the calm sea and blue sky the man smiled at me with a hint of embarrassment and said, 'I think it will be OK now.'

I smiled back, nodded, looked over at Inishbofin and said yes, yes I think it will be OK.

CHAPTER ELEVEN

On the last day of the Connemara jaunt we loaded the fire with turf and settled down in front of the little television set to witness one of the most compelling dates in the Irish calendar; the All-Ireland hurling final between two of hurling's traditionally greatest teams: Kilkenny and Tipperary.

There is no finer spectator sport in the world than hurling. Not one. I say this as someone who spent many years writing about sport for a living and to show I mean business I am prepared to fight anyone who disagrees, shirts off, in a pub car park of their choosing. Hurling is fast, it's incredibly exciting and has the headiest mixture of delicate skill and physical toughness of any sport you will see. Even a run-of-the-mill hurling match will leave you exhilarated at the final whistle. It's the perfect spectator sport. It combines the hand–eye co-ordination of cricket, golf and hockey, the positional play and running of football, the physical nature of rugby and the sustained stamina of top-class distance running. There's even a bit of the old egg and spoon race thrown in as well.

Hurling is similar to Gaelic football in that it's fifteen-a-side, played on the same field with the same rugby-cum-soccer goalposts. The scoring system is the same too, a point for every shot over the bar and three for every one that ends up in the back of the net. The difference is that each player carries a stick, or hurley, and the ball is a small, light, hard one called a sliotar, kind of a cross between a tennis ball and a cricket ball.

Hurling is one of the oldest sports in the world. There's a history and a heritage to hurling that goes right back to the misty darkness of Irish mythology that means when All-Ireland final day comes around the occasion at Croke Park is more than a sporting fixture, more than the climax of a sporting season: it's a celebration of Irishness with roots that go way beyond recorded history.

All-Ireland final day, in football and hurling, also has a pageantry about it that many modern sporting occasions lack. The match remains the most important thing, the only focus: there are no overt sponsors trying to persuade you that the day is really about them and their products rather than the climax of months of sweat, toil, passion and skill, no caterwauling reality show pop stars, nobody trying to hijack the occasion for their own ends – it's one of the greatest sporting occasions in the world because on the day it remains purely about the sport.

Croke Park is filled to capacity; there are more than eighty thousand in the magnificent stadium and the air crackles with anticipation and excitement. Before the game starts both sides parade around the pitch behind the Artane Boys' Band, two lines snaking around the field, hurleys in hand and determined, focused expressions. When the band departs you can sense the release in the players, that the formalities are dispensed with and until the final whistle blows it's now just about the hurling. It's always just about the hurling.

The final saw Kilkenny going for their fourth All-Ireland title in a row. The Cats, in their dark-yellow and black stripes are arguably the greatest sporting side in the world at the moment.

They are almost superhuman. Kilkenny have won more All-Ireland titles than anyone else and have a seemingly relentless production line of brilliant hurlers. They combine physical ability and almost flawless technique with a mental strength that I've never seen in any team in any sport. They are unflappable; they can make the cybermen look like quivering emotional wrecks prone to flights of irrational whimsy. Earlier in the season Kilkenny had played Galway, a rising force in hurling mainly thanks to their brilliant forward, Joe Canning. In the dying minutes Canning had almost single-handedly ensured that Galway surged ahead to open considerable lead. Other teams in Kilkenny's position, not used to being behind, not used to facing defeat, might have crumbled, panicked even. You might have seen dissent in the ranks, players gesturing at each other, apportioning blame, seen passes finding the crowd rather than a team-mate. Not Kilkenny. While the Galwegians pumped their fists, bellowed and exhorted each other to greater efforts, Kilkenny calmly carried on playing their normal game, clocking up points almost undiscernibly with metronome regularity until, before you'd barely realised it, they had pulled ahead of Galway and won the game.

This is not to say Kilkenny are boring to watch – quite the opposite. They are a joy: their fluidity of movement and invention is almost telepathic: when Kilkenny are at their very best there is no finer team to watch in the world. They take the game beyond sport into a different realm that's more than pumping muscles and the simplicity of scoring. Their players can switch positions as quickly as breathing: they're like the legendary Dutch 'total football' side of the seventies, only they win things too.

Tipperary is traditionally one of the strongest hurling counties. Hurling has over the years become dominated by a triumvirate of Kilkenny, Tipperary and Cork which, if you examine the map of Ireland, demonstrates how the game is most associated with the south of the country. Cork ran Kilkenny close for much of the last decade, but a curious propensity of the Cork hurlers to go on strike combined with the retirement of key players meant they had faded slightly. Emerging counties like Galway, Waterford and Clare have meant that while the big three have yet to be totally subsumed into a general hurling melting pot, the game is currently at its highest point in history in terms of quality and popularity.

Tipp had had a good season and there was a sense that they could give Kilkenny a good game in this final. Such is Kilkenny's dominance that media pundits found themselves discussing whether Kilkenny were a fading force until somebody pointed out that they were basing this theory on the fact that Kilkenny were this season beating people by merely big margins instead of massive ones. Tipperary were a terrific team, no doubt, but few people outside the county expected them to actually come between Kilkenny and their fourth title in a row.

The referee held the sliotar ready. Two players from each side waited for it to drop, the Tipp players in their traditional blue shirt with a yellow band across the midriff jostling for position with their Kilkenny opponents: the anticipation reached the peak of its crescendo with an expectant roar from the stands, the referee dropped the sliotar, the slashing of hurleys in its pursuit began and the All-Ireland final was underway.

Nobody can pinpoint when hurling first appeared in Ireland. Irish mythology says that when the Fir Bolg fought the Tuatha Dé Danann, before the battle they first played each other at hurling. The Fir Bolg won the match but lost the battle. This would have been some 1200 years or more before Christ. Part of the legend of Cúchulainn has it that he was not only the nation's greatest ever warrior but also the greatest ever hurler. According to the Irish national epic poem *Táin Bó Cúailnge* (*The Cattle Raid At Cooley*), in which Queen Medb of Connacht takes an army to steal the magnificent brown bull of Cooley from the Ulstermen, Cúchulainn was a bit of a prodigy to say the least. At the age of six, when still known by his real name of Setanta, he was studying military tactics and the mechanics of warfare, and the following year he took up arms. As far as I can recall, at the ages of six and seven I was mostly prodding curiously at my testicles and aiming to eat my own body weight in chocolate buttons.

At seventeen Cúchulainn set off for Ulster carrying a shield, a sword, a hurley and a sliotar. He spent much of the walk driving the sliotar ahead of him, then throwing the hurley after it in order to knock it out of the sky. When he arrived at his destination he charged straight into the middle of a game of hurling, nabbed the sliotar, stuck it between his knees and carried it over the goal line for a goal, rather in the manner of a teenager attempting to impress his girlfriend by running into the middle of a bunch of small kids playing football in the park, belting the ball between the jacket goalposts and celebrating as if he'd just lashed home the winner in the World Cup Final. Naturally the other players, all fifty of them, took exception to this unwanted intervention and each of them fired an arrow at Cúchulainn. All fifty thudded into his shield. Then they each struck a sliotar at him, all of which he gamely stopped with his chest. Finally, they launched a volley of fifty hurleys at him, each of which he slashed and smashed to smithereens with his own.

Soon afterwards he took on 150 of them at hurling single-handedly and, of course, won comfortably. In fact it was as a result of hurling that he took the name Cúchulainn: he killed the dog of the blacksmith Culainn by walloping a sliotar down its throat with his hurley.

The opening minutes of the game were hard and uncompromising. Players from both sides needed treatment for knocks until the deadlock was broken by Kilkenny's Henry Shefflin, arguably Ireland's greatest current hurler, who knocked an easy free hit over the bar from close range after a foul by a Tipperary player. The pace was frantic: if they could keep this up for the full seventy minutes it was going to be some game. Tipp began to find their rhythm and clocked up some early points to go into the lead. It was hectic stuff: more than one hurley was broken and there was at least one bloody nose requiring treatment in the first quarter alone. It wasn't all blood and thunder though: the hurling was of the highest quality and not one of the thirty players on the field was having anything less than a terrific game. It was already better than the previous year's final, when Kilkenny walloped Waterford, not just beating them but utterly breaking their spirit with a relentless and merciless display of hurling in what many described as the best team performance in the history of the game. Waterford were overawed from the start; Tipperary were playing as if their opponents were mortals like themselves and it was working. They were playing Kilkenny at their own game, harassing them, closing them down. In the first half alone the lead would change hands six times as first Tipperary then Kilkenny would nose in front only to be overhauled as the sliotar flew over the crossbar at each end.

Beyond mythology there are references to hurling in the earliest annals of Irish history. It appears in the Statutes of Kilkenny of 1366, which were designed to bring the Norman aristocracy into line as they risked becoming 'more Irish than the Irish themselves' while they integrated with the local population, adopting

their manners of dress and even their hairstyles. It appears that the
Normans also adopted local sports and pastimes: 'horlinge'
became a proscribed activity for its 'great evil and maims' as a
result of playing with 'great clubs and ball'. The Anglo-Norman
authorities wanted to encourage more gentlemanly pursuits, like
archery. It clearly didn't work, as further legislation in the ensuing centuries proved: the 1527 Statutes of Galway also tried to
ban hurling, and in the 1695 Sunday Observance Act you could
earn a heavy fine or a two-hour session in the stocks for 'hurling,
communing, football playing, cudgels, wrestling and other sports'.

Such was the full-blooded nature of the final that it practically
encompassed each of those pastimes, and when the half-time
whistle sounded and the crowd could finally unclench their collective buttocks Kilkenny were slightly ahead by thirteen points
to eleven. It had been a blistering half of the highest quality hurling. Out there in the far west of Ireland, the width of a nation
away from Croke Park, I exhaled for the first time in nearly
forty minutes.

If we thought the second half couldn't match the intensity of
the first, the opening minutes proved us quite wrong. Early in
the half Tipperary worked the ball down the right flank. It
arrived at Tipp forward Séamus Callinan barely a dozen yards
from goal, with only Kilkenny's stocky goalkeeper P. J. Ryan to
beat. In one movement Callinan caught the sliotar, released it
into the air and swung his hurley, catching it sweetly and sending a fierce shot arrowing to Ryan's left and heading for the net
just inside the post at about shoulder height. The Tipperary fans
prepared to rise as one; the net was about to billow. But somehow, with reactions that bordered on the superhuman, Ryan set
himself, sprang to his left, got his hurley across and deflected the
ball wide of the post. The commentator was silent for a moment,
the 'g' of 'goal' still formed in his throat, not quite sure for a

split-second why the sliotar wasn't spinning among the mesh of the net. It had been an astonishing reflex save – even more so considering that Ryan's hurley was in his right hand and thus had to pass across his body to deflect the ball wide.

The hurling goalkeeper has arguably the hardest and most thankless role in any sport. The sliotar comes flying at him from all angles, spinning, bouncing, arcing with deceiving flight, out of the sun or out of blinding rain, with the thunderous footsteps of onrushing forwards waving big sticks close behind. The goal-keeper has no extra protection, no padding, no gloves, just his body and the carved length of ash in his hands. Even if he gets his stick to the ball, there's often no telling where it might end up: flying up over the crossbar for a point (while saving two), dollying over his head and dropping into the net, deflecting wide of the posts, dropping to the ground either to be cleared by his defence or pounced upon by a forward. When steepling, looping balls fly towards him from seventy yards away, looming grey out of the grey sky, he has to concentrate on nothing but the crescent-moon shadow of the incoming sliotar, forgetting all about the dozen or so players of both sides converging on it and him. He's then expected to pluck that ball out of the air like an apple from a tree and send it immediately spinning back whence it came to launch another attack.

To illustrate how tough hurlers are, and the rough deal goal-keepers get, here's the story of a Limerick goalkeeper called Joe Quaid. In 1997 he was in goal in a league match against Laois, when Limerick conceded a penalty. The penalty was hit with force and bounced just in front of the plunging Quaid. Suddenly the ball was spinning in front of him so he knew he'd saved it, that it had hit some part of his body. It was scrambled to safety, which is when the pain started. The sliotar had smacked him squarely in the knackers. This was in the first half, and he played out the rest of the match in searing pain. Midway through the second half he signalled to the bench that he needed to come off. They refused. After the game the pain and swelling became so bad that he was taken to hospital, where it was discovered that the impact of the ball had – and all the men reading prepare to cross your legs – split one of his testicles completely in two. Six weeks later, he was back in goal for Limerick. It was a tradition of toughness that harked back to hurling's early days and put me in mind of a late-seventeenth-century account that detailed how the 'players seldom come off without broken hands or shins, in which they glory very much'.

Ryan's save might have broken lesser teams than Tipp: Kilkenny give away few opportunities for goals, so when what looked like a certain score was denied by a quite brilliant save many teams would be forgiven for thinking that the game was up, there was just no way through. To their credit, however, Tipperary not only rallied but hauled back Kilkenny's lead and nosed ahead with a trio of points, refusing to be intimidated and cowed in the same way the sport itself had done over the previous centuries.

Despite the Statutes of Kilkenny and Galway, hurling thrived, and indeed became popular in the eighteenth century with local landlords who would pit 'their' teams of tenants against rival landlords for wagers that often topped 300 guineas. One baron kept a team which boasted a player who could strike the ball over Loughroe Castle, run around the building and catch it on his hurley before it hit the ground. Matches were played between teams of all kinds of provenance: married men vs bachelors was a curiously popular contest, while the first inter-county matches were mentioned around this time.

The inter-county match unfolding in front of me in the grainy pictures of the portable television was ebbing and flowing magnificently until Tipperary managed to self-inflict a grievous wound on their hopes of victory. Benny Dunne, a young Tipperary substitute, had only been on the field a few minutes when suddenly and inexplicably, as he and Kilkenny's Tommy Welsh waited beneath a high ball, he turned to Welsh and smashed his hurley into the grille of his helmet. To Welsh's credit, although he was floored by the impact, he was immediately back on his feet with none of the histrionics that you often see on the soccer field, but the referee's hand went straight to his breast pocket to pull out the red card. It was an extraordinary, apparently unprovoked assault from the Tipperary man and served only to make his team's task harder. Kilkenny are difficult enough to play against with a full complement, but with a man down? Impossible, surely.

Apparently not. Tipperary nosed ahead again, opening up a three-point lead at one stage as the sliotar flew from one end to the other. Then, with Tipp ahead by 21 points to 19, came the moment that would define the game. With eight minutes remaining Kilkenny surged towards the Tipp goal. Richie Power tried to battle his way through into the box, was resisted by a Tipperary player and the referee gave a penalty. It was a contentious decision: the grappling had begun outside the box but the referee deemed the offence he objected to had taken place inside. The match had cried out for a goal; would it now take what appeared to be a soft penalty decision to provide it? Standing over the ball was Henry Shefflin: socks around his ankles, breathing hard, eyeing the goal where the Tipp goalkeeper and two defenders stood between him and Kilkenny taking the lead. Shefflin, the man they talked about in whispers as being as good as Ring.

There can be few sports where one man towers above all others like Christy Ring in hurling. Most agree that Pelé was the world's greatest footballer but people can make the case for others. In hurling there is no dissent: Ring was the greatest. His finest years were in the forties and fifties, years when Ireland struggled against rampant poverty and when the boats left packed with emigrants. Down in Cork though, the short, stocky, golden-haired Christy Ring helped people forget their troubles. His performances drew massive crowds and no discussion of hurling was complete without reminiscing about Ring's latest achievements.

He made the Cork senior panel for the first time at the age of nineteen in 1939 and within five years had won four All-Ireland titles in a row with the great Cork team of that era. Ring would go on to win four more All-Irelands with Cork; his tally of eight winners' medals has only ever been equalled by Johnny Doyle of Tipperary.

Ring's greatness wasn't defined by a medal tally, however. He had that indefinable something extra that only the truly great sportsmen have. Ring could add thousands to a crowd just by being there. Off the field he was quiet and modest without a hint of flamboyance. He was never happier than when he had a hurley in his hand and would spend hours practising. But as soon as he stepped on to the field for a match, something happened; there was a presence about him. Ring's peak years were dark days for Ireland in many ways. But on the hurling field, with his balding wisps of blond hair and wearing the bright red jersey of Cork, Christy Ring brought a brilliant colour to the worlds of those watching from the sidelines. Everyone dreamed of being Christy Ring; he was the living embodiment of sporting fantasy. To watch him, small, fast and strong, racing around the field, producing the performances of dreams and pulling off the impossible – in those moments on the hurling field life suddenly didn't seem so hard. He was the human manifestation of every boy's dreams. Even his contemporaries on the field recognised his greatness: in 1956 Ring played his last All-Ireland final against Wexford, chasing his ninth winners' medal. In the event Wexford won, but at the final whistle the Wexford players, who had just achieved the ultimate accolade after a long, hard season, didn't leap around celebrating and congratulating each other, they ran straight to Christy Ring, hoisted him on to their shoulders and chaired him above the flat-capped crowds dashing on to the pitch. There he sat, looking faintly embarrassed, literally head and shoulders above the rest.

The following day he went back to work as usual as a driver for the Shell oil company.

Ring died suddenly at the early age of fifty-eight of a massive heart attack while walking through Cork city. Some sixty thousand people turned out for his funeral and today a statue of Ring in his prime stands in his home town of Cloyne. No one has come anywhere close to matching the legacy of Christy Ring, but today Henry Shefflin is a name often spoken in the same hushed tones.

Croke Park and the entire watching nation felt time slow down. Shefflin stepped forward towards the sliotar that lay on the grass. He bent down and scooped it up with his hurley, took a split second to set himself and sent a vicious strike towards the goal, travelling at head height and aiming for a spot between the Tipp goalkeeper and one of the defenders on the line. Someone got a touch on it, but the shot was too strong and it glanced off ash and rocketed into the roof of the net.

The Kilkenny fans leapt from their seats, thrashing, arm-waving pockets of black and amber around the stadium. Kilkenny were ahead by a point and had the psychological advantage of a goal. Three points in an instant, wiping out at a stroke three individual hard-fought Tipperary scores. A man down and a point behind to penalty for an offence that looked debatable even in replays, Tipperary needed to gather themselves and respond quickly. They pressed up the field from the restart but lost possession. The ball was sent flying down the Kilkenny left, deep into the Tipperary half. Two defenders went for it but neither could bring it under control. It flicked off a Tipp hurley and went straight to Eoin Larkin. Larkin quickly played a hand pass inside to Martin Comerford who caught the ball and quickly guided a shot low past the Tipperary keeper that bounced, rolled and trundled into the empty net. Kilkenny had scored two goals in the space of sixty seconds: with barely six minutes remaining, the Cats had opened up a four point lead. For the first time Tipperary looked broken. As the ball hit the net, some of their players were already flat on their backs on the grass. Others sank to their haunches, their hands clasped on the top of their hurleys as if at prayer. It was a cruel sixty seconds, a minute that looked set to unpick the work of an entire season.

To their credit Tipperary tried to hit back immediately. Almost from the restart Noel McGrath received the ball at a tight angle close to the Kilkenny goal. With a hint of a dummy he disposed of the Kilkenny defender in front of him and struck a fierce shot that looked to be heading for the roof of the net. P. J. Ryan, having the game of his life, thrust his hurley up into the air and deflected it over the bar, saving a certain goal at the cost of a single point.

The final minutes ticked down. For the first time Tipperary's determination had noticeably begun to wither. The Great Famine and emigration did likewise to the game itself from the 1840s. In 1841 a Mr and Mrs Hall from England came across a hurling match on their travels in Ireland.

'A fine, manly exercise,' they wrote in their account of their journey, 'with sufficient danger to produce excitement . . . to be an expert hurler a man must possess athletic powers of no ordinary character; he must have a quick eye, a ready hand and a strong arm; he must be a good runner, skilful wrestler and withal patient as well as resolute.'

Hurling, they said, was 'a matter of astonishment to those who are but slightly acquainted with the play'.

(I'd tried it briefly myself, incidentally. Jude had bought me a hurley and a sliotar for my birthday and when a friend came to stay bringing her eight-year-old son we took them to the beach where I'd show the young 'un a thing or two. Now, I explained, you don't hold it like a cricket bat or a golf club, your hands are the other way around. So you hit it like this. I lobbed the sliotar into the air, slashed at it so hard that I almost turned a full circle, and heard the thunk of the ball hitting the wet sand at my feet. I tried again. And failed again. This was repeated a few more times: swish, thunk, swish, thunk, swish, thunk, until I realised that the moment you truly know that you don't 'possess athletic powers of no ordinary character' is when you reduce an eight-year-old boy to helpless laughter while trying to hit a ball with a stick.)

Famine and emigration hit the areas where hurling was strongest and in the three decades that followed the famine the game suffered greatly. It was the GAA's recognition that hurling was deeply ingrained in Irish culture that saved it. A set of rules was codified and structured competitions introduced. The game became associated with Irish nationalism – at Charles Stuart Parnell's funeral two thousand men marched with hurleys over their shoulders draped in black crepe, and during the War of Independence in 1921 that led to the partition of Ireland, men used hurleys in military drills in place of guns: hence the hurley earned the nickname 'Tipperary rifle'. The game flourished as the years passed, reaching its pinnacle over the last decade bestrode by this remarkable Kilkenny side, moulded by their coach Brian Cody, in charge since 1998. Cody has a kindly, pale face decorated with two bright red cheeks. He has the air and appearance of a schoolmaster, probably because that's exactly what he is. A tactician of incredible perspicacity and a master psychologist, Cody is among the greatest coaches working today in any sport anywhere in the world. His achievements match and surpass those of any coach in any arena. And now he prowled the sideline, peering out impassively from beneath his ubiquitous baseball cap as his team mercilessly ground Tipperary down in the dying minutes. Eoin Larkin knocked over two late points that opened the lead to five and as injury time commenced with this resilient but depleted Tipperary side needing two goals to snatch the game, the Cats' supporters in the 82,000-strong crowd began to celebrate.

The referee brought the game to an end and Cody's expression finally cracked into a triumphant, roaring grin. His coaching staff descended on him, his players on the field raced to each other in delight. Kilkenny had become the first team since the great Christy Ring-inspired Cork side of the early forties to win four consecutive All-Irelands. Fans raced on to the pitch past the prone bodies of the distraught Tipperary players who had produced an extraordinary performance to run Kilkenny closer than anyone thought possible. The commentators were already hailing this game as one of the greatest hurling matches ever, and Tipp had more than played their part. But, to the players prostrate on the grass, some of them weeping openly, they'd be leaving with nothing. All those hard, cold nights of training under gloomy floodlights all season, the matches, the emergence through the provincial championships, the battle to the final, the superhuman efforts they'd all put in, when they got on the coach back to the home of hurling there'd be no silverware. The Liam

McCarthy Cup would be staying in Kilkenny. It would be on the road to Kilkenny city that the night sky would be aglow with the celebratory bonfires that traditionally line the route of a victorious All-Ireland team once they cross their county border.

I looked out of the window. The late afternoon sun caught on the ruined cottage in the field on the other side of the road, the sightless eyes of its windows in shadow as the sunshine warmed yellows from the stones. These old houses are constant reminders of the hard times, the emigrations and famines. In contrast, the eighty thousand people at a packed Croke Park watching two of the finest hurling teams ever produced put on the most dazzling display of the ancient and essentially Irish sport of hurling demonstrated to me that for all its hard times, Ireland always, always comes back to win.

CHAPTER TWELVE

For the first time ever, I felt like an outsider in London. Not in the same way John Connelly would have when he wobbled queasily off the freezing, sopping deck of the steam packet from Cork more than a century and a half earlier, but while everything was familiar, from the pattern of the seat fabric on the District Line to the floodlit brickwork of the Tower of London as I emerged from Tower Hill tube station, there was no longer the easy familiarity of the city where I was born and where I grew up. It was more a strange kind of grounded disorientation, if anything.

The Tower Hill Travelodge was probably a little more salubrious than wherever John had spent his first night, but geographically the locations probably weren't that far apart. As I climbed into bed that night, John Connelly's entire emigrant life lay spread out over a couple of miles to the east of me. I lay in the dark trying to imagine what it would have been like for John on his first night, in whatever godforsaken fleapit of a place he'd managed to secure a bed or, more likely, a bundle of filthy rags on a dirty floor in a room full of snoring, farting, stinking strangers in a building that looked fit to collapse in a pile of dust and timber at any moment. The knotted fear in his stomach, the immediate quest for work the following morning in a city whose geography, customs and rhythms he didn't know and were so far removed from his background as to be practically extra-terrestrial. For this displaced teenager who knew nothing much beyond the family homestead and the fields around it, a boy who was growing up fast and would have to learn fast to avoid being trampled on by the merciless life of what can be the loneliest city in the world, that first night must have been terrifying.

It was the same kind of nervous, sleepless first night spent by millions of Irish people who'd left their native home, whether spent in the slums of London, the boarding houses of Grosse Isle in Quebec or in quarantine at Ellis Island. The longer I spent on John's trail the more I realised that this was not just a recondite family history; this was a wider story of Ireland. In the great scheme of things he was nameless and forgotten; he doesn't appear in the history books, his portrait hangs nowhere, he left nothing behind, but John Connelly is as important an Irish figure as any household name purely because of what he repre-sents. His is a story of millions.

Over the next couple of days I intended to walk in John's footsteps, tracing possibly the happiest journey he ever made and then the last journey he ever made, trying to gain at least a sense of the man whose arrival in London defined the future of gen-erations of my family.

The next morning, barely two minutes from the doors of the Travelodge, I turned in to Royal Mint Street. In 1843 this was Rosemary Lane, home to the poorest of the poor, the ultimate in squalor, and where at number 86 John Connelly and Catherine Burke were living on the day they got married at St Mary's Church in Whitechapel. It had a long history, Rosemary Lane: in the seventeenth and eighteenth centuries it had been

Rag Fair, the site of a regular clothes market. Richard Brandon, purportedly the man who carried out the execution of Charles I in 1649, allegedly sold the orange studded with cloves that he'd taken from the King's pocket here for ten shillings and later died in a house on the Lane. It wasn't the finest of shopping experiences: one 1753 account describes the 'dunghills of old shreds and patches' and suggests that 'farmers wanting to buy clothes for their scarecrows might benefit best from the goods on offer'. In 1843 the famous Irish temperance leader Father Mathew had held a rally just off Rosemary Lane where apparently some two thousand people, possibly John and Catherine among them, took the pledge.

Today Royal Mint Street, as it was renamed in 1850, is quite different. It's a quiet thoroughfare linking Tower Hill to Cable Street and there's nothing left that John would recognise. Assuming the building numbering system would have been roughly the same, number 86 would have been on the left hand side as I walked down the street, the length of which is now a car park disappearing beneath the gently encroaching railway bridge bringing trains out of Fenchurch Street station. I paused and looked at the tarmac laid behind railings. It was from here that John Connelly would have left for the church on his wedding day. The market would have presumably been busy, the street noisy with trading. If it had been a hot August day it would probably have smelt pretty unpleasant. If he'd had a set of best clothes he would have been wearing them. He may have had James Taylor with him, the man listed as a witness on the marriage certificate. He would have been nervous and excited. He may have walked out on to the street, looked up and commented that at least they'd got good weather for it. James may have asked him if he was ready, received an apprehensive but firm nod, and then set off along the street just as I did. On the other side there was a convenience store and a pub named the Artful Dodger, from outside which a man had eyed me suspiciously as I stared at an empty car park and wandered around taking photographs. Further along the street on the right was a restaurant, its frontage painted turquoise and yellow, named Rosemary Lane in the only visible nod to the street's history.

I turned left, into Leman Street. On the island in the middle of the road, beneath the railway bridge over which trains rumbled threateningly on their way to and from south Essex, a man sat hunched, grey hair and beard, an old donkey jacket pulled tightly around him, elbows pulled in, hands clasped, forearms resting on his thighs, a green haversack next to him, the gold-coloured can of strong lager at his feet shining incongruously among the grey of the asphalt and paving stones. He stared sightlessly at the ground a few feet in front of him, oblivious to the thunder of the traffic and the rumble of the trains, withdrawn into a world of his own which I hoped was better than the one it seemed he'd landed in.

Leman Street is typical of modern east London: a collection of office buildings of various vintages and restaurants and shops offering Indian, Lebanese and halal specialities. Across the road was the Brown Bear pub, which looked old enough to have been there in John's day. It struck me that John may even have called in there himself for a stiffener to settle his pre-wedding nerves, so I crossed the road, pushed open the door and did likewise. It was early lunchtime so the clientele was mainly office workers, jackets off, shirtsleeves rolled up, jangling the change in their trouser pockets as they talked in small groups that burst occasionally into laughter. Sky Sports News played out silently on a flat screen television high on one wall.

I ordered an Irish whiskey and sat down, wondering if John had done the same, maybe even sat on this spot, staring nervously at his glass, his friend James telling other drinkers that it was his wedding day, fielding the jokes, the barbs and the good wishes of strangers, the handshakes and the thumps on the back. This young man, still a boy in so many ways, his Cork accent strong, his features yet to be wizened with age, poverty and hardship, marrying the girl he loved and who reminded him of home, a home that now seemed as though it might as well be on the other side of the world.

I carried on up Leman Street and turned right, cutting off the corner as John would have done and emerging at Commercial Road. On the left was a large old pub, attached to the outside of which were old Irish direction signs pointing to Kinnegad, Annaghdown and Dublin but in reality doing nothing more than waving vaguely at a notion of Ireland held by the expats that would drink there. Ireland: it's out there somewhere, lads, maybe that way, maybe over there, but when it comes down to it, you're here. Weeds grew out of cracks in the plasterwork; the only signs that the place was still a going concern were the poster of upcoming football matches in the window and the lights on the taps shining in the gloom inside.

A few minutes later I turned on to Whitechapel High Street and arrived at the small park where the church of St Mary Whitechapel had once stood. It's now Altab Ali Park, named in honour of a young Bangladeshi murdered near by in 1978, and the church is long gone, destroyed during the Blitz. A wide, sapling-lined path leads through the park, which is flanked on one side by the busy Whitechapel High Street and overlooked on the other by a modern block of flats. A few gravestones from the old churchyard still stand in one corner; a large and elaborate tomb at the other end against which sat two council workers in fluorescent jackets, eating sandwiches out of tin foil. As I walked across the grass, trying to imagine what it must have been like that day in 1843, I looked down and noticed something. It was a line of white bricks embedded in the grass, stretching away at a curious angle to the layout of the park. As I followed this narrow brick road it dawned on me that it represented the layout of the old church, its outline picked out in brick so that at least some acknowledgement remained that it had once stood there for hundreds of years. I paced around it, walking the walls of the old church, then walked up what would have been the aisle and stood approximately where the altar would have been when my ancestors exchanged vows. The green of the grass was burnished with the first golden leaf fall of autumn as I stood there, on the spot where this elusive ancestor of mine had stood, nervously repeating his wedding vows in his sing-song Cork accent that echoed around the stone walls and the high ceiling. I couldn't imagine that the ceremony had been particularly well-attended: if both were recently arrived there'd certainly have been no family there to speak of. It wouldn't have been the most sumptuous occasion east London had ever seen either, but standing there on a blustery autumnal day on a patch of grass that once held a simple, brief wedding ceremony, one among thousands that would have been performed there over the centuries, I felt a surge of exhilarated happiness charge through me. For the first time I felt a connection with John Connelly. It wasn't, as I thought it would be, somewhere in Ireland but in a busy, urban part of east London a few short miles from where I'd grown up.

He was happy here on that day, hopefully a gloriously sunny one that cast coloured lights across the pews and floor as it shone through the stained-glass windows. Catherine would have looked as beautiful as he'd ever seen her and he would have felt that they may have been poor, their lives may have been as hard as any in London, they may have been a long way from home, but on that day none of it mattered. From what relatively little I knew of John and the life he led, it was on this spot that he was happiest, happier than he'd be at any other time in his life. I laughed out loud, which attracted a couple of curious looks, and at that moment a dove, brilliant white, swooped down low across the park, gliding almost over my shoulder, flew gracefully and languidly around the park, soared into the air again and headed off in the direction of the city. I watched it shrink until it became a speck and disappeared.

The following morning I made my way east along The Highway towards Wapping. In John's time, The Highway would have been St George's Street, where he'd lived for a while in the poor man's boarding house, and in a previous incarnation it was the notorious Ratcliff Highway, one of the most dangerous streets in London, the haunt of thieves, brigands and murderers. Today it's home to News International. Their buildings sit on the site of the old London dock where John laboured for his whole working life. Back then this part of London would have been dominated by warehouses four storeys high and carved with seafaring frontages. Tea, rice, wine, brandy, tobacco: goods would arrive from all over the world at the London docks, its vista a thick forest of masts and rigging, men like John dashing to and fro, the shouts of the stevedores, the clank of iron chains and cranes, the cries of traders: this was the world John would have known.

When I reached Shadwell I turned right into Wapping Lane, passing the vast and now deserted converted warehouse of Tobacco Dock, once the self-styled Covent Garden of the Docklands and now a shell of empty retail units. Eventually I turned left into Raine Street, a short road that seems to go nowhere, meandering round to the right and stopping dead at a block of flats. Just over a century earlier the journey along Raine

Street would certainly have led somewhere but it wasn't anywhere you'd want to go: Raine Street led to the St
George-in-the-East workhouse, the place where John ended his
days wracked with tuberculosis in the workhouse infirmary.

It's a quiet part of the East End. There's a large church there
among the modern flats and garages, and there's nothing to indi-
cate the thousands of poor, wretched lives that played out here
and, as in John's case, ended here. I spent a while walking
around, estimating exactly where the workhouse had stood
thanks to an old map of the area. Nothing appeared to remain of
the workhouse itself but as I was about to set off back up the
road towards Shadwell I noticed, at the rear of some shops, a
large, sturdy, dark brick wall that was older than most of the
other masonry in the area. It had pillars and a substantial gateway
that certainly didn't look as though it was built with the intention of bringing up the rear end of a bookies. I couldn't be
certain, but this was in all likelihood all that remained of the
workhouse, all that remained of the place where John Connelly
died. The high wall, all dark brick and crumbling mortar,
seemed to have a forbidding austerity even today. I walked up to
it, placed my hand against its rough surface, shuddered slightly
and set off on John Connelly's last journey.

A couple of days before I'd left for London I'd had a stroke of
good fortune. While rummaging on the internet trying to find
out exactly where the workhouse would have been I'd somehow
stumbled across the record of John Connelly's death from the
Raine Street records. Don't ask me how I did it, because I don't
know. What I'd found was a scan of the 'memorial book' from
the workhouse and written in the hand of C. V. Sayer, the workhouse steward. There, on the page for February 1890, John's
death was recorded. He was listed, as on his death certificate, as

John Connell, dying on 21 February 1890 aged sixty-five. He was, a note at the bottom of the page revealed, one of twenty-eight workhouse deaths that month. What attracted my attention most of all was the column headed, 'where buried', which told me that John had been laid to rest in the East London Cemetery. It was a pauper's burial: like most of the others who died that month John's body hadn't been claimed.

It was drizzling when I emerged from West Ham underground station and set off for the cemetery. Before long I arrived at the main entrance, marked with traffic cones in black and white, and called into the office building on the right just inside the gates. I knew I wouldn't find a specific grave for John but hoped at least to find the part of the cemetery where the workhouse paupers were buried.

A young woman smiled at me from behind the counter as I walked through the door.

'Hello,' I said. 'Erm, I wonder if you could tell me where I might find the Victorian paupers' graves?'

She sent her right arm around in an expansive gesture and said, 'They'll be all around the outside edge of the cemetery.'

Ah.

'Oh, OK, well, I don't suppose you'd have individual records for workhouse burials, would you?' I asked.

'Well, yes we do,' she said, 'if you've got the full name and the date of death, I should be able to dig out the records and give you an idea.'

I ripped open the flap of my bag and pulled out the blue document wallet in which I'd brought all the relevant records. I leafed through them and handed over John's death certificate. She took it from me and looked at it, chewed her lower lip for a moment, nodded and headed away out of sight. Within a few seconds she'd returned with a massive old leather-bound ledger book clutched to her chest which she set down on a table with a whump. She heaved it open, turned over a crackling wodge of pages, leafed through a few more, found the one she wanted and ran her finger down it.

'Yep, there we are,' she said, opened a drawer, pulled out a piece of paper and came back to me at the counter. It was a photocopied map of the cemetery.

'Now,' she began, 'he's in this section here' – she circled a number thirteen on the map – 'which if you go up the main road as far as you can here and turn right at the war memorial, section thirteen is on your left set a little bit back from the path. If you look at some of the graves they'll have numbers on them starting with thirteen; that's when you know you're in the right place.'

This was more than I'd hoped for. Of course there'd be no headstone or anything, but at least I'd be able to visit a specific, moderately sized area of the enormous cemetery and know that John was there somewhere. I thanked her profusely and set out into the drizzle again. I followed the directions and walked up the tree-lined avenue, green still on the branches but a light carpet of fallen golden leaves lining the way. I passed the chapel where two men in suits stood sombrely, early for a funeral. I reached the war memorial and turned right, and made my way up through the wet grass between the graves until I found one with a number that began with thirteen. I'd found him at last. I'd arrived where John Connelly's journey from Cork had finally ended, a far corner of a soggy cemetery in east London on a bleak, cold, grey, rainy day. Most of the graves here appeared to be from the mid-nineties with a few from the fifties, but I knew John was here somewhere under this bumpy, uneven, unkempt patch of grass as far from the cemetery entrance as you could really get. It was probably a damp, drizzly day like this when

John was buried, presumably one of several workhouse paupers to be buried in one go, no family, no real ceremony, just put into the ground as quickly as possible with minimal fuss. It wasn't much of an ending for a hard life. I thought about how John Connelly had done a remarkable thing: he'd survived. He'd been born into poverty, some of the worst poverty in European history. He'd left to help secure the future of his parents and siblings, left for the unknown and a life that turned out to be every bit as miserable and hard as back home, but at least it was a life with the prospect of employment. He'd made a niche for himself, however poor; he'd married, had children, kept working, kept struggling, kept surviving against the odds. He'd known utter misery: widowed at forty, seen several children born and several children die. He'd found himself at the very bottom of the labour ladder, doing the worst jobs in the worst conditions you could imagine, yet he'd done it, he'd survived at least until tuberculosis took hold and killed him. Standing there on a patch of grass between the edge of the graves and the iron fence of the cemetery boundary I realised just how proud of him I was, this forgotten man who left no trace beyond a name on a few municipal records. He'd proven hard to find and at times I felt like he didn't want to be found at all, but here I was, probably his first visitor in more than a hundred years, possibly his first visitor ever. I'd found him and I was proud of him.

I rummaged in my bag and pulled out the things I'd brought. At Dublin airport I'd suddenly thought that I wanted to take something from Ireland to at least leave at the cemetery even if I couldn't find the spot where he was buried. The choice was limited, and in the end I settled for a small teddy bear dressed in the red and white strip of the Cork county GAA teams, while on the way to the cemetery I'd called in at an off-licence and picked up a bottle of Guinness (*Foreign Extra*, it said on the label, *Imported*). I took them out of the bag, found a small hump of raised ground near the fence and laid down the bear and the bottle.

I stood quietly for a moment and then trudged back towards the gate, skirting around the chapel where a funeral cortege was just arriving. 'DAD' said the yellow floral arrangement propped against the coffin through the rain-spattered windows of the hearse. The drizzle began again and the hearse was lost amid a flap of unfurling black umbrellas.

CHAPTER THIRTEEN

If John's was a story of Ireland in the nineteenth century it's also one that's still being played out to this day. When I thought of John I thought also of the people I'd met when I was wailing and hollering my way around the pubs of Irish London with my guitar. Here were the nineties equivalents of John Connelly, men and women forced to leave everything they knew and take the boat over to the closest neighbour, to dig ditches and stack bricks, to lay roads and mix concrete, literally to build the England in which I'd grown up. The statistics are astonishing: it's estimated that of every person born in Ireland between 1931 and 1941, *four out of five* would go on to leave the country, with 80 per cent of those heading for Britain. By the late fifties there were around sixty thousand Irish people arriving in Britain every year but they weren't arriving out of a sense of adventure or wander-lust: they were arriving because Ireland couldn't keep them. Indeed, it could be argued that those people saved the country: as well as removing themselves from burdening the Irish state, it's estimated that in the thirty years that followed the outbreak of the Second World War, the Irish in Britain sent home around three billion pounds, and that's not including people taking money home in person, nor sending it over as cash.

According to the UK census there were 850,000 Irish-born people in Britain in 2001. Many of those will have been elderly, and the elderly Irish in Britain are disproportionately concentrated in the poorest parts of the country. The state of their health is worse than the national average and the Irish in Britain are more likely to live alone in poor quality housing than any other ethnic group. John Connelly's life, one of backbreaking work, hardship, poverty, bereavement, ill-health and an ultimately lonely death, is being repeated many, many times over across Britain today, even as you read this. The slums may have been cleared, the newspapers may no longer describe the Irish as feckless, drunken simians, but while these days the paintwork on the walls might be better the story stays the same.

From the cemetery I travelled across to Archway in north London, traditionally a major hub for the Irish in the capital. I emerged from the tube and walked down the Holloway Road. I passed the Old Mother Redcap, one of my old Irish haunts with its *Cead Míle Fáilte* sign over the door and further on, standing on the corner of a side street waiting for me as he'd said he would be, was the man I'd come to talk to.

Brian Boylan is an outreach worker and former Catholic priest originally from County Cavan who's lived and worked in London since 1980, but left Ireland in the fifties. Having been a priest at a mission in the Philippines for some years he left the church, moved to London and began working with the homeless. Today he works among the Irish community in the London Borough of Islington, a rare voice trying to draw attention to the plight of the lost generations of Irish people in Britain; the John Connellys of today. I'd seen Brian on a television documentary shown in Ireland and he'd moved me greatly with some of the things he had to say.

'The Irish here,' he'd said, 'our whole identity, how we look at ourselves, is through the Irish eyes in Ireland. There's a sadness that we're separated from those people. There was a famine in Ireland and it's something that's long been acknowledged. This is a different kind of famine though; it's a famine of the spirit.'

If I was going to understand John Connelly a little more, not to mention get a handle on the reality behind the sugary image of Ireland, Brian was a man who could hold the key.

He smiled from beneath a head of thick white hair, an open, friendly face above a light-blue polo shirt, jeans and opened-toed sandals over white sports socks. We shook hands and exchanged greetings and he took me back to the community centre where he's based. We stood in the reception area and through a pair of internal doors I could see a large room set out for lunch, crowded with noisy, chattering Chinese people. In front of each was a small, high-sided bowl of blue and white and a set of chopsticks.

'Twenty years ago, this whole building was purely an Irish centre,' Brian told me. 'Upstairs and downstairs, all Irish; there was a bar in there,' he indicated the room where the Chinese were waiting for their lunch, 'and on Friday and Saturday nights you just couldn't get in here; the place was packed. Irish music, Irish dancing, it was membership-only and we were always over-subscribed. Now, there's nothing. The only Irishman here is yours truly, in that room, every morning from nine till eleven for tea and sandwiches.'

He indicated a door off to the side and took me into a large room with a sink and a cooker in the corner, a few tables and the kind of gold-painted chairs with scarlet cushions that you find in most hotels or social clubs these days.

'That's the Chinese community in there, there are about five thousand of them in the area,' Brian continued as he pulled a loaf of brown bread out of a carrier bag and set about cutting it into thick slices as the kettle boiled. 'Yet there are ten thousand Irish-born people in the borough of Islington and you never see them doing anything like this any more.'

He scooped dollops of margarine out of a catering-sized plastic tub and slathered it on to the bread. 'We just haven't got that much energy in terms of social involvement these days. Help the Aged have two beautiful centres in Islington and the Chinese, the Pakistanis, the English and the Bangladeshis, they'll all go there. But the Irish don't go.'

He unscrewed the lid from a pot of strawberry jam, spread it over the buttered bread, put the slices on to a plate, walked over to the table where I was sitting and placed it between us. As he did so the low growl and slow rhythmic clunking of a train rumbling lazily past, barely six feet from the window, all but drowned him out as he told me about the plight of the John Connellys of today.

'Some of the Chinese come here on walking sticks, yet we won't leave our little flats or bedsits,' he continued, hoiking teabags from two steaming cups and adding milk. 'We haven't got the life within us. The Chinese have got their own Chinese channel on the television in there, their own Chinese cooking, their own chefs – they put on forty meals every lunchtime and deliver more to people in the community who can't make it in. They have English lessons, t'ai chi, you name it, they've got it. And we Irish? I make a few sandwiches in the morning for a few individuals who come in, a handful, and sometimes we'll play bridge. That's it.'

Brian Boylan is a remarkable man. With his kindly face, neatly brushed white hair and sandals he is the nice neighbour who you say hello to and have a quick chat with on the way back from the shops and rely on to keep an eye on your house when you go on holiday. He's warm, kind and friendly. But beneath his wide,

ready smile and behind his sparkling eyes there burns a hunger
and an emptiness; the same hunger and emptiness that afflicts
many if not most of the Irish people who came to England in
the decades after the Second World War. The forgotten Irish,
forgotten by their home country and largely anonymous in the
country they now call home. Just as John breathed his last in the
workhouse, alone and destined for a pauper's funeral in a rainy
east London cemetery a long way from home, elderly Irish are
dying alone, forgotten and unloved across Britain. Brian attends
as many of the local funerals as he can; too often he is the only
mourner. He regularly visits a small part of a local cemetery
where the Irish for whom no relatives can be found are buried,
sometimes with nothing more than a wooden cross and a name
written in indelible marker pen to commemorate a life of displaced toil and ultimate loneliness.

This room, this sparsely furnished room shaken every few
minutes by passing rolling stock, is all that's left of the once
thriving Irish community centre of the eighties. The people are
still out there; they're just growing old and becoming more and
more insular, each nursing a pain in their heart they all share yet,
according to Brian, won't acknowledge. The Irish in Britain
still have a yearning for home, the home they left half a century
or more ago. When they arrived in Britain most of them
thought they'd be going home after a little while, when they had
some money, when things picked up again. But they never did.
The Ireland of home is now a cheap flight away, less than an
hour, yet they feel they just can't go.

'We're avoiding reality,' he says. 'I have contact with two hundred Irish people in the locality and in all the years I've been
involved here just one person has gone back to Ireland to live.
One. I've asked everybody about it and I've got the forms from an
organisation who have an agreement with the Irish government

that twenty-five per cent of social housing in Ireland will be available to returning Irish immigrants. They'd be interviewed here, when they went over somebody would meet them, look after them, sort out their medical benefits, their bus pass, everything, it would all be looked after, but nobody wants to go. Nobody. One person in all these years.'

The reason, he told me, was possibly the same reason that John Connelly never went back, why he stayed in that godforsaken, filthy, poverty-stricken couple of square miles in the poorest part of the East End for all those years.

'The thing is, the Irish are different from other ethnic groups here,' he explained. 'If I was from India, for example, and went back from here to India I'd be perceived as a rich person, a successful person, even if I was claiming benefits. It's the same for the Africans, the South Americans, the West Indians, the Bangladeshis, the Somalis, everyone. But if I go back to Ireland, the people there who didn't have a backside in their pants when I left are now affluent. By and large they're better off than we are here. Traditionally the immigrant goes back having made his money, as a success. We go back as failures. We're ashamed to go back because you, in Ireland, would be looking down on us. That is a tragedy. It's only in our heads, yes, but it's a part of us that we can't overcome. There's a yearning to go back, but we just won't face up to it.

'I've got a group here that plays bridge. They're all homeowners with families and we talk about all sorts of things, but we never talk about this hunger that's in us, we never go back. Yet you, with your distant Irish roots, you can go back to Ireland and it's easy. You don't have that baggage that we have. If you'd come over to England in the nineteen-sixties rather than your great-great-great-grandfather coming over, I guarantee you wouldn't be living in Dublin now. Guarantee it. You'd be here feeling that pain and hunger and shame. In our minds here we're still walking up and down the boreens of Ireland, places that aren't there any more; we don't face up to the reality: that the Ireland we left behind and still have in our fantasies no longer exists.'

Even when I'd been playing on the Irish music circuit in London in the mid-nineties there had been a strong Irish community presence in the city. The *Irish Post* and the *Irish World* would have whopping listings sections of events and meetings happening across London and the country every night of the week, but, when I picked up an *Irish Post* in Dublin before I'd left to see what was on while I was in town, to maybe revisit an old haunt, there was practically nothing. I was amazed at the changes in, and indeed the near disappearance of, the London Irish community since those days, barely fifteen years earlier, when I'd been a part of it. Where had everyone gone?

'The reality is, and research shows this to be true, that we Irish die younger than any other ethnic community in Britain,' said Brian. 'We die younger than the people here and we die younger than our brothers and sisters over in Ireland. We have a higher incidence of cancer, coronary heart disease and depression than anyone else in Britain. Getting on that boat has knocked, on average, five to ten years off the lifespan of everybody who came over here. Now, we enjoy the same privileges as people here who could trace their family back to the Battle of Hastings: we have the same healthcare provisions, welfare benefits, everything, yet we're dying up to ten years earlier than everyone else. And the reason why is,' he clenched a fist and held it in front of his chest, 'the reason is the pain that we all of us carry inside. The shame and the pain we all have in here.'

He was quiet for a moment. The hubbub from the Chinese in the next room still filtered through the doors.

'Another thing I find fascinating is that on the last British

census, in terms of home ownership, which in this country is the
hallmark of success and aspiration, the Chinese were around eighty
per cent homeowners, the Indians were seventy-something per
cent. Africans were twenty-nine per cent or thereabouts. The
Irish? Twenty-five per cent. Right at the bottom of the pile, and
we *built* most of the bloody things. It was our area of expertise
and yet we're right at the bottom of the heap for owning them.
We're top of the pile in terms of bad health and early death and
all that but when it comes to the marks of success we're right at
the bottom.'

I wondered whether this is tied in with what Brian had said
about the Irish in Britain still walking the boreens in their minds,
still convincing themselves that the option to go home was still
there. That maybe buying a house in Britain would be admitting
to yourself that you'd never go back.

'An awful lot of people who came over thought it would be
temporary, that they'd go back,' he said. 'That dream is gone.
There's an old guy living nearby, he's seventy-eight and living in
sheltered housing. I said to him recently, you've got family back
in Ireland, you've got part ownership of the family farm, why
don't you go back? He said, "They'll all be looking down at me."
I said to him, if Ireland was as poor today as it was in the
fifties . . . and he didn't even let me finish the sentence, he said,
"I'd go back tomorrow morning." There's a shame out there and
I don't think we're as thick-skinned as we'd like to pretend we
are. It's because of that shame and the feeling that they'd be
regarded as failures that they don't go home.

'Ireland only survived because we left,' he continued as
another train trundled past with a heavy metallic clunking that
made the windows rattle. 'The country didn't have to support us
once we'd gone. In fact, in the Dáil there are records of a
Minister of Finance saying back in the forties or early fifties that

the only way Ireland could get back on its feet would be if more people would emigrate: the population as it was then just couldn't be supported. So, by not only sending back money but by actually leaving in the first place we helped the country when it needed help most.'

The mindset is different in America. The Irish-American community is strong and influential, influential enough for Presidents to go and visit obscure patches of rural Ireland to commune with their roots. There's a unified pride in the Irish-American community, yet there's no equivalent for the Irish in Britain: there are no Irish-British or Irish-English. The shame Brian was articulating isn't in the Irish-American psyche and it's a lot to do with the difference between the perceptions of Irish emigration to America and Irish emigration to Britain.

'When you went to the States they'd have an American wake for you,' he recalled. 'We'd all gather and have a wake for your departure and raise some money for you to help you get started when you arrived across the Atlantic. On the flip side, going to England was seen by many as an act of betrayal: going to the old enemy, a godless country where you'd lose your faith. There was a totally different perception: you'd read stories in the papers back in the fifties where, say, I could have been up in court for stealing a bicycle. The judge would say, "Right, Mister Boylan, you've pleaded guilty to a serious offence and I'm going to give you a choice. You're either going to Mountjoy prison for six months or you're going to be on the first boat to England in the morning." So in the collective understanding of the Irish, going to England was only marginally less severe than being sent to prison.

'Now, don't get me wrong, this country has been good to us, no doubt about that. We're possibly in the best country in the world here in many ways: there's tolerance, the health service,

access to benefits and support that is almost unparalleled anywhere. I have poor Irish people here, people who've had
nothing, for whom I have to sign their name on cards for them
when they're sending things home, and they have lovely flats and
retain their sense of dignity. But these guys' feelings for Ireland
are deep and profound, so what are they doing with that pain?
How are they dealing with it? I'm fortunate: I'm relatively comfortable, I have a family here, I go back to Ireland four or five
times a year and my family and friends back home are great – but
I still carry this pain, this hunger with me. So what about the
people in a worse position than me? How are they dealing with
it? Some of them know that they'll never go back: how do you
cope with that realisation?

'There's a guy who comes in here, a dear, lovely man. I can
see the pain written on his face every time he walks in. He was
brought up in Ireland and his mother wasn't married. These
things happen; birth control was outlawed in Ireland back then.
When this man was a boy of seven his mother was offered marriage, a genuinely nice guy, a member of the *Garda Síochána*. She
loved him and he loved her, but in Ireland back then to enter
into marriage when there was already a child was frowned upon.
So she had him adopted. Total rejection for him at just seven
years old. So, he was let down by his mother and in exactly the
same way Mother Ireland has let the immigrants here down.
Mother Ireland threw me out, she couldn't support me and left
me with an inheritance of guilt and blame and pain, and it's in
all of us here, all of us. What makes it worse is that Ireland *did*
recover enough to take us back but now we're too ashamed to go
back. That's the tragedy. That's more sad and fundamental and
devastating than being in a ditch working twelve hours a day, the
sleeping in cold rooms with five other guys, the being turned out
of your lodgings every night because they didn't want you

hanging around there: that's all bullshit compared to what we go through now. On one level we've never had it so good, but down here in the soul, in the heart, we are utterly devastated.'

He paused as another train rumbled past. From the other room the noisy hubbub of Chinese conversation continued which only served to accentuate the silence and emptiness of the room in which we sat. As I looked around I realised that each chair, each empty, chipped, gold painted, scarlet covered chair in the room represented one of the forgotten Irish: for every one of those empty seats, I thought, there was somewhere out there a lonely Irish person, in poor health, living alone, feeling alone, and carrying this intense pain and shame that none of them could confront. People who should have been there at that moment, having lunch, talking, coming alive with company: on each of the empty seats in that room sat the ghost of what might have been, ghosts of the living, ghosts of the hopeless, forgotten Irish.

'Denying difficulty destroys you,' said Brian, 'and as a result the collective soul of the Irish community here is in a sad plight. I'm in good shape this morning, but I was talking to a student doing a master's on this kind of thing the other day and I realised I was coming across as really depressed; that in talking about it I was letting a sense of the community into me, making me a conduit for it. Me, I'm alive, I've never felt better, but when I let the feeling of my community in I'm immediately a depressed, confused and hopeless individual. It's there in me as it's there in everybody, but we don't complain about it or confront it, we stay quiet. We complain about other things, things that divert our attention from the sadness that's lying under those green fields back in Ireland and that's lying in our souls here. I see too many people here who are beaten. The old digging of the ditches didn't beat us; it's the sense of loss, abandonment and rejection that's done it. Ireland didn't *formally* reject us: there's no reason, physically, financially or whatever, no reason at all that thousands of us couldn't go back over there other than a deep-lying internal inability to make the move. And that's a tragedy. What can Ireland do? Well, give us the vote for a start. If we came from any other country we'd have the vote back home even as expats. But not in Ireland, which just adds to the sense of exclusion. But above all we've got to face up to the reality that the Ireland these guys think of when they think of home just doesn't exist any more.'

I thought back to my days playing in the pubs of London, playing to the very people Brian was talking about. Back then, with my starry-eyed concept of Ireland, I'd got it totally wrong. I thought these lads were all genuinely happy, deep down, properly happy. Sure they were hard up, some of them, but they were happy. They told great jokes and great stories, they'd sing along with passion and gusto and tell me tales from home and sometimes they'd even teach me some old songs. The pints would flow and the *craic* would be mighty and I took the whole thing at face value, heading back to the tube station afterwards thinking, this is Ireland, this is what it's about, this is my heritage, thinking I understood the image beyond the leprechauns and the blarney and the sugary nonsense of the Emerald Isle.

In reality I had no idea, none at all. I never suspected that for many of them all the laughter, the jokes and the stories, that it was all a front, a veneer to protect themselves from the terrible, guilty, shameful pain they were feeling, the disconnection, the partitioning of the soul that would never make that pain go away. Not ever.

That's not to say that everyone necessarily felt this way: I think back to some of the musicians I knew and friends I had back in London in the nineties and some of them were certainly happy, fulfilled, successful emigrants, be they building workers who played brilliant mandolin by night, venue bookers, pub landlords or part-time poets. Most had come over during the hardship of the eighties and maybe had more of a sense that they could go back home anytime, and certainly many of the emigrants from the forties and fifties will have settled happily in Britain, but everyone to some extent will have carried a sense of displacement, acknowledged or not, accepted or otherwise, and many of the elderly Irish in Britain are now almost consumed by it. There are the Brians of this world, happy, settled, comfortable with their identity, but there are also the Patricks, Bridgets, Michaels and Marys staring at the walls of lonely bedsits, literally pining away for a country so close and yet so very far away. For such a purportedly sociable nation, the paucity of the listings for Irish events in London in the *Post* where twenty years earlier there would have been pages of gigs, parties and community events demonstrated to me how much of the Irish community in Britain seemed to have lost its heart and had it replaced by this empty, lonely pain.

Brian walked out into the street with me to point me in the right direction back to the tube station. As we shook hands, he held on to mine.

'If most people went through half of what some of these guys went through they would have been bloody dead years ago,' he said. 'The Irishman here deserves a medal, he deserves to feel great about himself, he deserves to feel like a real man for being alive, for surviving. We must remember that these people have been through a lot; they've been through things that Wordsworth and the other poets could have articulated. Shakespeare could have written his greatest tragedies, equal to any of his greatest works, about the things that have happened to some of the people I see in this area alone, and I see them day in, day out.'

On the way back to the tube station I picked up a copy of the *Irish Post* and took it into the Mother Redcap. There was a handful of afternoon drinkers watching the racing on the television in the corner and I sat down at a table with a Guinness. Inside there was a feature spread across two pages about the new wave of twenty-somethings leaving Ireland in the wake of the collapsing economy. This is the most noticeable shift in the emigrant demographic: in the past the emigrant Irish were labourers, today the young Irish beginning to leave are graduates. They are more easily transplantable; they've grown up in an era of cheap and easy travel. One young graphic designer, just arrived in London, said, 'I'm living away but I don't feel like an emigrant; I don't feel like I'm not in a position to go back. I wouldn't say I was homesick, I just love Ireland and would be keeping an eye out for a good opportunity to go back there. In the meantime, I'm here.'

A few paragraphs further on a newly arrived architecture graduate said, 'I don't think anyone my age from Ireland that I've met feels like they're going to get stuck here – a lot would just say they're just here for a few years, for the experience.'

I drained my drink, folded up the paper and reached down for my bag. As I did so my hand brushed something cold and damp; it was the bottom of my jeans, still wet from the long grass that covered John Connelly's bones.

CHAPTER FOURTEEN

When I got back to Dublin I recommenced my possibly futile search for the place John had come from. For all the good fortune I'd had in bumping into Rob that day and finding he's now one of Ireland's leading genealogists I was aware that he was no magician. Short of bringing John Connelly back from the dead with the use of some seriously heavy juju and asking him outright, finding exactly where he came from was looking increasingly unlikely. So, while running into Rob had been an extraordinary chunk of good luck I was aware that if the information just wasn't out there, even Rob wouldn't be able to find anything. He certainly gave it a go, though. I gave him all the information that I had and a few days later, an email from him plopped into my inbox.

'OK, your Cork ancestor,' he said, 'I too had a look at some early Cork directories from the 1810s through to the 1820s and found no reference to a hatter called John Connelly or similar, but to be honest I wouldn't expect to. I'm afraid that if you were a client presenting me with the info you have I'd say all the money in the world won't find what you're looking for. Sorry for the bad news.'

It was no more than I'd suspected: the serendipity of running into an old friend in a different country didn't extend to miracles of genealogy.

'Leave it with me over the weekend,' he continued, 'and I'll do a bit of digging before I give you the final verdict. Don't hold your breath though.'

Whatever happened, even if Rob found nothing I knew that John would have left from Cork city for London. I'd always have that. I could at least stand at the quayside from where he'd departed: at least that would bring the story full circle. The following week Rob emailed me again to tell me he'd been doing some more rummaging. He'd searched a database of more than eight million Irish baptismal records and found twenty children in County Cork with similar names, born around the right time and, most excitingly, one child named John Connelly with a father also called John.

'Needless to say, I have absolutely no way of telling which if any of these is for the correct child – maybe none,' wrote Rob. 'It might be best to go with the only Connelly baptism, but to be honest you are not going to be able to establish with any degree of certainty if we have found the right fella. If you want my honest opinion, without any other corroborative details for John you are never going to be able to positively find where he came from.'

It was still something to go on, though. It was certainly more than I'd expected to unearth at that stage. There was at least a *chance* that this was the right person and in the absence of any other clues I'd have to at least pursue it. Rob pointed me towards the database he'd searched, reminding me that it didn't contain the complete records for Cork.

I ran my search and the results Rob had found appeared on the screen: there was only one John Connelly born to a father of the same name. It cost five euros to examine each individual record but having already shelled out an amount for the ancestry website that might well have saved an Icelandic bank, anything more was a drop in the Irish Sea at this stage anyway. I tapped out my card number, hit 'pay', waited for confirmation my fiver had been cyber-trousered, then clicked on the 'view record' button. A box appeared with the heading 'Church Baptism Record'. There he was. John Connelly. Date of baptism, 27 March 1827: later than the UK censuses had been led to believe but not preposterously wrong. There was his father, John Connelly, occupation left blank. His mother's name was given as Honora Connelly, née Cronin. And then the important part: where he was baptised. In capital letters, next to the words 'parish/district' was the name Youghal. I scrabbled for my road atlas of Ireland and scanned the Cork pages. There it was, on the coast in the east of the county not far from the border with Waterford at the mouth of the River Blackwater.

I tried not to get too excited, tried to rein in any sense that this was it, I'd found the town where the story started. This was just one record that matched in broad terms what I knew, a record among records that were incomplete and probably not kept completely perfectly in the first place. Sitting in front of the screen I wondered if there was any way, any way at all that I could perhaps arrive at a more definite conclusion. It was a long shot, but I thought of something. When I'd been at the National Archives, Helen had suggested that maybe John and Catherine could have travelled to London together; that they might have known each other. Also, given that Irish communities abroad tended to gravitate towards their own, there's even a chance that they met in London as part of a community drawn from the same part of the country.

I typed Catherine's name into the birth records search and again only one record stood out as a good match. In went the credit card details again and click went the 'view record' button. A couple of seconds thinking about it and the screen filled with the record. Catherine Burke, daughter of Patrick Burke and Mary Burke, formerly O'Neal, baptised 24 November 1829 in Killeagh. I searched on the map again. And there was Killeagh – a village no more than five or six miles west of Youghal on the main road to Cork city.

I allowed myself to get a teensy bit excited. I may even have used the combination of wooden floor and stockinged feet to do a little pirouette. One possible stumbling block was their ages: the baptism dates made them up to three years younger than the ages they'd given the census-takers. It also meant that they would have been around sixteen and fourteen when they married, which seemed unlikely until I learned that right up until 1929 the age of consent for marriages in Britain was fourteen for boys and just twelve for girls. Now, if you were under twenty-one you needed parental permission but this would have been practically impossible for John and Catherine. I wondered whether the church might have been a little more relaxed over the issue: they were married in an Anglican church, which seemed odd until I learned that the Protestant charity missions were particularly active and strong in the East End at this time and did a lot of work among the poor: most Irish couples in London at the time were married in Anglican churches. Maybe the church had agreed that in the circumstances immigrant couples could marry without official parental sanction.

So, while I'd not found any proof these were definitely the right people, neither had I found anything that suggested they weren't: everything still broadly added up. I scanned the other records that came up as possible matches, but none of them seemed anywhere near as strong as John from Youghal and Catherine from Killeagh.

The next thing I tried was Griffith's valuation, a survey of property carried out in Ireland in the mid-nineteenth century that is the closest we have to any kind of census for that period, and there I found a John Connolly [*sic*] living in the parish of Killeagh in a townland called Ballycurraginny at the right time. On the map it was located between Youghal and Killeagh, about a mile and a half north-east of the latter. You couldn't even call it a village: it was a smattering of buildings on the modern OS map. This could be it, I thought. I handed over what I'd found to Rob, and he said he'd see what he could come up with.

'I've tried to do some digging,' he said a few days later, 'and although the results are very inconclusive you might have grounds for making a case that this is the area that John origi-nated from.'

This sounded good. It sounded very good.

A couple of weeks later Rob took me to Dublin's General Record Office, sat me down and called up an original map of the townlands and a thick, old, leather-bound volume that con-tained the lease records for Ballycurraginny going back to the time when John would have been a boy there and beyond. The handwritten records showed that John senior, my great-great-great-great-grandfather, had had a Patrick Connelly, probably a brother, as a neighbour in the 1840s. Ten years later however, Patrick was living in the same building as John, with the house Patrick had occupied being listed as a ruin.

'I think we're dealing with some very poor people here,' said Rob. 'I can tell by the dimensions listed that these really were the most basic domiciles, hovels really, and look,' he placed his finger under the relevant record, 'Patrick's is listed as a ruin here: basi-cally he had to move in with John because his own house fell down.'

We compared the details given in the lease records with the

huge, beautifully drawn, thick paper ordnance survey map from the time. On it Rob was able to point out the exact building, a little black rectangle drawn on an ancient map, in which the people most likely to be my ancestors had lived.

This was more than I could possibly have hoped for, even at my most optimistic when starting out on this historical forage. I'd have been happy with a town or a village, and as Rob's finger stabbed at the map and he said, 'that's the one', even though he kept reminding me that we'd never be completely certain, I felt elation. There was every chance that these people, these poor, wretched people in their collapsing hovels trying to scratch an existence barely one level up from starvation, were the people from whom I was descended. These survivors against the odds, whole generations of them, who had never given in, had fought against deprivation and poverty and, in John's case, given up everything he'd ever known to make it easier for his family to survive and forge an existence in London. That little black rectangle on an old map, the building that, by the sound of things, was fortunate even to be standing: that was where the trail ended. On this wet Dublin morning in a neon-lit, city centre office, an old friend who'd cropped up after nearly two decades in exactly the right place and at the right time and with exactly the right skills and experience to lead me here, to this room, to this map and to this little black mark on the map, had provided me with the key to so much. It was the answer to a thousand questions, the root of a thousand stories, the place that started the journey I was completing.

It was a typical story of Ireland as well. There were millions like it, millions of John Connellys and Catherine Burkes who had fled poverty and hardship, deducing that anything, anything at all had to be better than this. I thought back to the old pubs of Kilburn, Hackney and Stockwell, the places where I'd belted out the songs the ex-pats wanted to hear. As I sang about the fields of Athenry, the cliffs of Dooneen and the hills of Donegal, the old men and the young pups, emigrants all, they could all think back to their own little rectangle on a map, their own Ballycurraginny, Athenry, Galway Bay, Dooneen, Donegal, Dublin in the rare oul' times. I'd taken all those songs literally, assumed they were specific to each individual place. It was only now, years later, standing over a giant, beautifully drawn map, gazing over Rob's shoulder to where his finger pressed the heavy-duty old paper, that I realised those songs were about everywhere and everyone. All the passion and heart I thought I was putting into them, for all that time, however many times I'd thrashed at my guitar and belted them out, I'd had it wrong all along. It was only standing there that day in the Dublin branch of the Irish General Records Office that I started to understand the yearning of exile, the pain and hunger that Brian had told me about and that he carried with him. I didn't have that hunger, hadn't carried that pain, not for me anyway, but now that I knew almost certainly where John Connelly had left from, I could, deep down somewhere inside me, feel a little of his.

I took one last look at the map and I knew at last where this particular story would end. If nothing else, I might, at last, finally ease the hunger John Connelly carried from the moment he left Ireland and the pain he took to his pauper's grave.

CHAPTER FIFTEEN

Before I could think about heading for east Cork there was somewhere else I needed to go, something I needed to see if I was to get a further grip on one of the aspects of my adoptive country that I struggled most to understand.

I am not a religious man. I probably should be, having gone to a school that was founded on religious lines, but it's just not something I've ever pursued. I don't get it. I can certainly understand people who do and would never dream of criticising anyone's faith – with the possible exception of Crystal Palace supporters – but it's just not for me. I find that kind of spiritual sustenance elsewhere. Despite my antipathy to religion however, the prospect of owning a two-foot-high, pale green, glow-in-the-dark figurine of the Virgin Mary was proving difficult to resist.

There is an entire parade of souvenir shops lining the main street of the village of Knock in County Mayo, but these are no ordinary souvenir shops. Their wares are holy. The gonks and figurines don't grin inanely or even just look a bit cute; they look pious, with downcast eyes. The postcards and fridge magnets don't boast saucy cartoons and bawdy slogans, they announce 'I lit a candle for you at Knock'.

It's a grotto of twinkling, conspicuous religiosity. There were figurines of a whole calendar of saints (although Mary seemed to be the only one available in a luminous edition). A candle holder featured a plaster representation of what was presumably meant to be Christ looking holy but which looked to me more like the bass player in a band from the lower reaches of the Woodstock bill. I could have picked up a solar-powered luminous grave marker bearing the legend 'In Loving Memory Grandma'. There was an entire wall of little ceramic holy water fonts ('please do not move fonts from display: breakages must be paid for'). You could also keep your holy water in the plastic screw-top bottles helpfully inscribed 'holy water' that lay in various sizes and prices in big baskets outside most of the shops in the same way that barbecue charcoal is displayed on garage forecourts.

There was a big tub full of sticks of Knock rock and a whole rack of pink ceramic piggy banks wearing sunglasses. I couldn't work out the biblical connection – was there a *Letter from St Paul to the Blind Porkers* that I'd missed at school? – but they had one with my name on.

In the window of one shop, in the midst of the Padre Pios, Virgin Marys and backlit portraits of Pope John Paul II in front of a moving waterfall was a plastic Liverpool FC clock. While I'm sure there are many people who could put a strong case for Fernando Torres being some kind of deity, his image here, blond locks flying next to a ticking chronometer, was a little incongruous among the sanctified.

Inside one shop a woman picked up a plastic figure of the Child of Prague and asked the assistant, 'Would this be right to give somebody who's just moved into a new house?'

'It would,' came the reply, with a firm nod. 'In fact, that's our biggest selling model of that particular type at €17.99. We do have some cheaper ones over here, but that's the most popular. I'd say they'd love that.'

Ring-a-ding-ding went the till. I had never seen anything like these Knocking shops, although they did remind me a little of something but it took me a while to remember exactly what. This punting of tackiness and tat born out of extraordinary reverence and devotion put me in mind of somewhere else I'd been. Ah, that was it, the Elvis souvenir shops opposite Graceland.

There is a reason for these shops existing and existing here, in a little village in the heart of Mayo. Knock has been a place of pilgrimage for more than 130 years, ever since the Virgin Mary, St Joseph and St John the Evangelist appeared to a group of villagers one rainy night in August 1879. It's been such a place of worship in fact that Ireland's first and only basilica now stands close to where the holy trio manifested themselves and, a few miles up the road, there's an international airport built to serve the needs of the world's pilgrims in bringing them to the west of Ireland for the opportunity to buy thigh-high glow-in-the-dark figurines of the Holy Mother. Yet Knock itself is a small village of barely eight hundred people; essentially one long street and little else.

I walked up the street into the biting wind being strafed by bullets of freezing rain, heading for the old church and forsaking for now the modern – and frankly hideous – basilica that holds up to twelve thousand people, to see what had caused all this fuss in the first place. The old Knock church looks faintly incongruous in front of the modern concrete plaza beyond with its basilica and the signs directing you to confession, holy water fountains, the tourist office and an Irish craft shop. There's an air of slight bewilderment about the old grey church, like that of a kindly pensioner who's wandered into a bordello by mistake. At the south end against the gable wall there's a modern addition, like a massive holy conservatory that dwarfs the church itself. Inside is a small chapel where three brilliant-white life-size plaster statues

of two men and a woman stand. To their left, in the centre of the
wall is an equally brilliant-white small altar on top of which sits a
lamb and a cross. Plaster angels fly around them. In bas relief, I
mean, not literally (but wouldn't that be something?). This display, the mega-conservatory, the souvenir shops, the basilica, the
glow-in-the-dark Marys and the international airport are all here
because of what happened on this spot one rainy night in August
1879.

Ireland was not in great shape back then. The effects of the
Great Famine were still being felt, there were occasional partial
failures of the potato crop and the island was gripped by the
Land Wars. Knock was typical of most villages in the rural
Ireland of the day: it was poor, with people trying to scratch an
existence on tiny plots of land, and many dwellings stood empty,
the legacy of famine and emigration. 21 August 1879 started out
as a day like any other, with people cutting turf and attending to
the meagre produce of their smallholdings. It rained for most of
it. At around 7 p.m. Margaret Beirne went to lock the church
doors and was aware of a bright glow at the far end, behind the
south gable. She thought nothing of it and didn't investigate.
About half an hour later the priest's housekeeper Mary
McLoughlin hurried past the church in the drizzle and noticed
figures there that she hadn't seen before. Again, she thought
nothing of it other than that the Archdeacon hadn't mentioned
that he'd bought a bunch of statues from Dublin, and continued
splashing on her way. Another half hour went by without incident until Mary returned with Margaret Beirne's daughter, also
Mary, and pointed out the new statues. The younger Mary
stopped dead.

'They're not statues, they're moving,' she said. 'It's the Blessed
Virgin!'

The three figures on the left of the scene were St Joseph,

who appeared inclining towards Mary in reverence, Mary herself in a white cloak and crown, holding her hands up at shoulder height, palms facing each other like a fisherman describing the trout that had narrowly eluded him, and St John the Evangelist, holding what appeared to be a Bible and with his hand raised as if teaching. The women knew it was St John the Evangelist, they said later, because he looked exactly like a statue of St John the Evangelist they'd seen in a church in another part of Mayo.

The whole scene was bathed in a bright glow, a glow seen from half a mile away by a farmer who wondered what kind of eejit would have a bonfire that close to the church. The vision lasted for a good couple of hours and was seen by about twenty people who came to kneel and pray in the rain and mud, while noting that, although the rain was blowing in towards the south end of the church, none fell on the figures or the wall. When the villagers tried to move closer, the figures moved back. An elderly woman tried to kiss the feet of the Virgin, but her lips met nothing but the crumbly mortar of the gable wall.

One of the women ran to tell the priest, but, bizarrely, he decided not to come out and have a look. He'd been out most of the day and was drying his soggy vestments by the fire. The prospect of heading out into the elements again was not one he cared to entertain, even if the Holy Mother and a couple of major saints had chosen to manifest themselves by the wall of his church a couple of hundred yards away.

Now, when I was a child, I was taken one night to see the circus on Blackheath. As we sat waiting for the ringmaster to come bounding out, cracking his whip ready to start the show, a glow appeared on the canvas walls of the tent. It was orange and it flickered. The word went around: a generator had caught fire outside. The place emptied as people scrambled to go and see the burning mass of cogs and wheels, shadows moved against the wall of the tent in the light thrown on to it by the fire. My dad asked me if I wanted to go out and have a look. I said, nah, I'm all right here thanks, and I've regretted that decision ever since. If I've spent the intervening three decades kicking myself for not bothering to go out of a big tent to see a generator go up in flames, imagine how the Knock priest must have felt later when he realised that he'd missed out on seeing the woman to whom he had dedicated his entire life and career on a rare occasion when she'd dropped by this mortal coil for a visit with a couple of premier league saints, literally just around the corner. That must have had him waking with a start in the dead of night for the rest of his days.

Either way, as Marian manifestations went this was a corker. The holy figures hung around for two hours (and must have had a minor panic when the first couple of people hurried past without taking any notice) and were seen by people of all ages and both genders (fifteen of whom were interviewed by a church inquiry afterwards and found to be, in the opinion of church officials, telling the truth). When you think of other alleged visitations, from images on pieces of burnt toast to a Limerick tree stump, you can see why this one had the world all of a tizz.

It wasn't long before people began arriving from all over the region, the country and then from abroad as word spread about the miracle at Knock, with invalids apparently walking again and the blind having their sight restored. The cement of the south wall was believed to have imbued miraculous healing properties leading to so much of it being chipped away by the faithful there was for a while the very real danger of the wall falling down. Within three years of the vision Knock had been visited by bishops from as far afield as Toronto and Tasmania.

The Pope visited for the centenary in 1979 and raised the

status of the newly built church to basilica, one of the few basil-
icas outside Rome and certainly the only one in Ireland. In the
early eighties the local priest, James Horan, began a campaign to
build an airport. Many thought building an international airport
in Mayo to serve a shrine was a crazy idea that was doomed to
fail, but Father Horan was a determined man and, in 1985, the
airport was opened. Some people have suggested that NATO
may have come up with some of the cash, seeing it as a potentially handy stopover for military flights, but either way you
could argue that what is now known as Ireland International
Airport (West), providing a gateway to the west of Ireland that
has stimulated local economies and provided valuable employment, is the real miracle of Knock.

I peered through the glass at the figures in front of the gable
wall. There was a service of some kind going on inside, sparsely
attended but being addressed with arm-waving vigour by a priest
in scarlet vestments from a lectern to the right of the apparition
statues. Behind me were the holy water fountains, a long row of
engraved concrete blocks with taps dispensing the blessed liquid
to the queues of pilgrims arriving at the peak of the pilgrimage
season in the summer, all holding their plastic 'holy water'-
embossed bottles purchased from the shops down the way. Today,
there were no takers. There was only a handful of people around.
Three young women got out of a car nearby, struggling in black
high heels, black leggings, black leather jackets; the dripping
gold of their enormous earrings, necklaces, handbags and
bracelets the only brightness on a dull day until night would fall
and a hundred shop window Marys could begin a-glowing.

'What time's Our Lady appearing?' said one.

'Three o'clock again,' replied another.

You see, I hadn't come to Knock on the off-chance of buying
a two-foot-high glow-in-the-dark figurine (although if I'd

known about them in advance, there's a good chance I might have). I'd travelled to the wilds of Mayo on this freezing, inhospitable, wintry day because the Virgin Mary herself was due to show up again. And you don't see that very often.

Ireland was going through a rough time. The economy was a shambles and the nation's Catholics and the public at large had recently been rocked by an inquiry into systematic child abuse in the Dublin archdiocese that betrayed an horrific tale of cover-ups, bullying and collusion among the priestly ranks right up to the Vatican itself, and even allegations that the Gardaí had covered up sexual abuse of children by priests over a period going back over thirty years. There were calls for bishops to resign at the very least, there were mumblings of regret and admissions that 'mistakes were made' when literally thousands of children's lives had been ruined, their childhoods stolen from them, their innocence kidnapped and disposed of by men they were supposed to call 'Father', men whom they were supposed to respect and look up to, men who were supposed to provide spiritual guidance, to tell them the right thing to do and the right way to live their lives.

It was an utterly shocking report that, as well as the horrific revelations it contained, underlined the power the Catholic Church in Ireland once had. It had the capacity to ruin lives and devastate entire families if anyone spoke out. Things are different now: while Ireland is not and will never be a secular nation, the Church's power has diminished greatly in recent years. What influence it has is now down to the faith of its flock rather than the actions of the institution itself. That flock is certainly imbued with faith too – Ireland has one of the highest church attendance figures in the world. During the boom years those figures declined but around the time I headed down to Knock statistics were released showing that attendance at Mass was on the increase again and had been since the start of the recession. Sixty-five per cent of the population were attending Mass at least once a month (in Britain the equivalent church attendance figure is around 15 per cent). All of which made the Joe Coleman phenomenon even more intriguing.

A fifty-five-year-old Dubliner from Ballyfermot, Coleman had shot to fame with his claims that he had the ear of the Virgin Mary herself, that she was going to make appearances at her 'beloved Knock' and that she was very angry with the church. Coleman had worked laying asphalt until 1979, when he fell off a roof. Told he would never walk again, he defied that prediction but has never worked since, living on incapacity benefits and donations from people he counsels (he strenuously denied allegations that he charged €60 for an hour's session but did admit to accepting the odd donation, something that when he revealed it on a national radio phone-in had the Irish Revenue raising a quizzical eyebrow).

In 1985 Coleman ended up in hospital again after falling down a flight of stairs and shattering his ankle. While undergoing an operation to repair the damage he claims that as the result of being given too much anaesthetic, he 'died' for fifteen minutes. It was during this time that the Virgin Mary first spoke to him, a dialogue they've kept up ever since. Coleman kept his holy pal to himself until announcing earlier in the year that he'd had a word with the Holy Mother and she was going to make an appearance at Knock in early October. Some five thousand people arrived in the village and many claimed to have seen a strange shimmering around the sun at the appointed time which they took to be the apparition of the lady herself.

She wasn't finished yet, revealed Coleman. During the apparition, she'd told him that she would return a few weeks later at the same place. 'She is very angry,' said our man. 'She told me she will rock the foundation of the church if the people do not listen, from Rome back down to where we are, down to Knock. And the gates of heaven will be closed.'

He suggested that fifty thousand people would attend this second purported manifestation and that Mary would appear to those who arrived 'with an open heart', at which the Knock authorities began to knuckle their brows at the prospect from a logistical point of view, let alone spiritual.

In the event around ten thousand people turned up for the second coming. Joe wasn't happy though. Mary had asked that a priest accompany him at the appointed time and he worried that the basilica wouldn't be unlocked for his arrival. There was no priest, but the manager of the shrine pointed out that on the contrary, the basilica would be open just as it normally is.

Joe had informed the world that Mary would appear in the basilica at three o'clock. An hour before the appointed time he arrived in front of the altar with another healer he'd picked up along the way, a younger man called Keith who, in hooded duffle coat and with shaved head and gold jewellery, could have passed for a holy rapper. Keith had only been a healer for a few short months – so was perhaps Joe's work experience clairvoyant – but either way they paraded into the basilica side by side, flanked by two women carrying crucifixes, and knelt at the altar to begin praying. The place was packed almost to capacity, largely a mixture of older women and members of the Irish travelling community. There was quite a hubbub, mobile phones kept ringing and camera flashes lit up the basilica. The atmosphere grew more intense as the hour approached. At three o'clock, Joe looked up from his prayers at the ceiling and smiled. He mouthed words that nobody could hear. He appeared to be talking to someone. A tear ran down his cheek. Suddenly from the door a cry went up: 'She's outside! She's outside!' and everyone stampeded for the exit. Babies were left in their pushchairs as everyone fought for the opportunity to catch a glimpse. Some people claimed to have heard a loud noise like a thunderclap coming from the clear sky. The crowds outside stared at the sun with many claiming that they saw it dancing and shimmering and changing colours.

Inside, Joe finally murmured, 'Thank you, Mother' and later revealed that his celestial correspondent had asked him to 'thank all my children for responding' and that she asked 'for peace. I ask for prayers every day for my son's apostles. I pray that they will listen and I pray and ask for unification of the faith across the globe.'

The crowds dispersed. Apparently a small boy's blindness had been completely cured but nobody knew who he was or where he'd come from. My heart sank a little to think that the first thing he might have seen was a two-foot-high, pale green, glow-in-the-dark figurine of the Virgin Mary.

Joe also said that Mary would be back again a few weeks hence, which is what had brought me to Knock. As far as I could see around the village the attendance looked like it would be well down on last time and there didn't seem to be any great sense of excitement. Despite Joe's mass invitations, on the two previous occasions the Holy Mother had, it seemed, become a little shy in front of the crowds.

I went for a bite to eat in a café across the road from the old church. A television camera crew sat in the corner looking bored. Pairs of elderly women drank tea with their handbags on their laps. Young families in sportswear and gold earrings sat around sullenly picking at bowls of chips. Through the steamed up windows I saw the occasional bright flash of colour as an umbrella scurried towards the sanctuary of the basilica; a trickle of devotees and the curious that eventually became a stream. I pulled on my coat, headed out of the door and made for the squatting white basilica. I splashed through the pools of water and took a short cut through the Stations of the Cross, where two young traveller girls were praying and touching the images in the pouring rain. I dashed past a handful of hooded press photographers, their lenses pointing at the ground as they waited for Joe's arrival, and took a seat near the front inside the vast basilica. Raked banks of chairs climbed away from the central altar, the lights were dim and there was a curious prevailing smell of wet dog. The place was nearly empty, there were just pockets of people scattered around the building, but it was still early. Most surprising though, given that we were in a church, were the half dozen or so burly men and women in yellow high-visibility jackets with 'security' written across the back. One had an earpiece. The Knock authorities were taking no chances after the stampede that characterised Joe's last visit.

As the time ticked by a few more seats were filled but there were just a few hundred at most in the place. A woman in a red anorak scuttled past, hissing at us, 'Spread the word, we're going to say the rosary,' a message she imparted to all the scattered folk in a circuit of the building. Sure enough, away to our right a murmured chanting went up.

About twenty minutes before the appointed hour there was a commotion at the doorway. Flashbulbs were going off and we stood and craned our necks in the direction of the hullabaloo like a football crowd following play down to a corner flag. It was Joe arriving. He walked into the basilica surrounded by photographers, journalists and the just plain curious. His neatly cut grey hair made him stand out in the crowd, above a black cagoule and blue jeans. A few paces inside he suddenly dropped to his knees, clasped his hands together and prayed silently to himself. Then he was up again and walking purposefully with a slight limp. In his hand he held a military style forage cap which he would occasionally lift to face level as if half-heartedly attempting to shield himself from the cameras. Keith walked behind him in a beige duffle coat, the thick gold chain around his neck glinting in the camera flashes.

Joe walked right past me, close enough for me to see the tiny crucifix he was wearing outside his rain jacket swinging back and forth as he passed. He strode not as expected to the altar but to a place in the front row of one of the benches a few yards along from me. The photographers sprinted for position and a swarm of people suddenly gathered. Just before he disappeared beneath the scrum, I saw he'd dropped to his knees again, placed his hands together and begun to pray. People were proffering pieces of paper at him, either requests for healing and prayers or autographs, I couldn't tell. Whatever they were, he ignored them for now. The security guards, stationed close to the central altar, had been sold a dummy by Joe taking his place with us in the bleachers. While he'd been expected to head for the altar, as before, now the only way security could tell his location was by the position of the fluffy grey sound boom a television crew held over his head in the mêlée. A couple of security guards made futile efforts at stopping the rush of people making for the former asphalter but they were brushed aside as if they weren't there as people hurtled towards the grey-haired praying figure with urgent expressions that I couldn't differentiate between religious fervour and the thrill of proximity to celebrity. Eventually the security guards placed a line of chairs as a barrier against more of the faithful and everything calmed down a little. Thankfully there were no more than about six hundred people in the place or things may well have got tricky.

All through the undignified scrimmaging the rosary continued to be chanted. It made an eerie sound, echoing around the cavernous basilica, and the chanting became notably more urgent as three o'clock approached. A recital of the Lord's Prayer sounded more like the barked instructions of a purser on a sinking ship as the top of the hour ticked ever closer. The middle-aged woman next to me stood on her chair for a better view. She wobbled slightly and placed her hand on my shoulder to steady herself. In her hand was a camera; around her hand was wound a rosary.

Even I began to feel a strangely nervous welling of anticipation, the kind of feeling you get when sitting waiting to be called for your driving test or waiting outside the headmaster's office after some misdemeanour. I hadn't even thought about the possibilities of an actual manifestation of the Virgin Mary. I was here purely out of curiosity, but, it crossed my mind briefly, what if something really did happen? Three o'clock approached, and as the chanting grew more and more urgent and the wind and rain howled outside it started to feel like we were waiting for the end of the world itself.

Three o'clock arrived. I stood and looked over to where Joe was kneeling among the crowd, his grey head just visible. A woman in a knitted pink hat was standing next to him, leading the incantations and prayers. The people nearest had their eyes closed and their brows furrowed. Joe was looking at the ceiling and smiling, just as he had last time. There were more prayers and incantations. Cameras flashed. A few mobile phones started ringing. Apart from that, as far as I could see nothing happened, nothing happened at all.

Above the hubbub came the strains of people singing the 'Star of the Sea' and then 'Ave Maria' and it was around then that I realised how despite being in one of the holiest places in Ireland, if not the world, despite the chanting of the rosary and the singing of hymns and the recitation of prayers, this was probably the least religious occasion I had ever attended. There was nothing spiritual about this, nothing uplifting. I'd sat through school assemblies in a freezing cold chapel mumbling through 'The King of Love My Shepherd Is' and it had boasted more meaning and point to it than this. Behind me a man chatted away on a mobile phone. People stood on chairs taking pictures of a middle-aged man in jeans praying. This wasn't about God, or Mary, or Jesus – as I write this I realise that nobody mentioned God at any point through the entire day, not once – this was about one man, one self-appointed messenger who'd become the centre of attention with firm promises that he couldn't seem to follow through. The rush of people towards him as he sat down disturbed me; I thought about it for the rest of the day and beyond. What were people looking for? Was this about religion or celebrity? Or was it about something else; about hope in the face of a near-bankrupt nation and a Church that had blatantly carried out, tolerated and covered up some of the worst crimes imaginable over several decades? Were people seeking something, anything, to affirm that in spite of the economic throttling the country was enduring and the hideous scandal engulfing their religious institution, there was still somebody watching over them?

Suddenly there was movement. Joe and Keith were on the move. They strode off suddenly around the far side of the basilica towards the exit, barely visible in the scrum of photographers, television crews and the more determined devotees. They went through the doors and were gone. The rest of us looked around with a kind of general unspoken, 'Is that it then?', gathered up our coats and made our way towards the exit. As we squeezed through the crowd I heard a man say to his friend, 'She was there, she was definitely there, but she was invisible.' 'Arra, she's only visible to him, to Joe,' his friend replied. People wanted to believe in something. They wanted to believe that something incredible, something wonderful could happen in these terrible times. Wanted to believe that their faith and the efforts they'd made to come to Knock on a miserable, freezing, murky day had been repaid after all, and the word of the Virgin Mary was real and true, even if it had come through a middle-aged man from Ballyfermot.

I called in at one of the souvenir shops. I thought long and hard about the glow-in-the-dark Mary but settled instead for a Knock Shrine snow globe: a blue plastic dome containing white flakes and fluid that swirled around the figures of Mary, Joseph and John the Evangelist whenever you shook it. Mary appeared to have a handlebar moustache.

'Were you at the church?' the woman behind the counter asked as I handed over my €3.50.

'Yes,' I replied.

'Did you see anything?' she asked.

'No,' I said with a rueful shake of the head.

She visibly relaxed as she gave me my change.

Outside the shop stood two elderly men beneath a golf umbrella. They were holding a large sign that they brandished at everyone leaving the basilica. 'Bible prophecy,' it read. 'The signs of the times, the time of the end. Jesus the only name by which anyone can be saved. Friends, it is the Devil masquerading as the Blessed Virgin Mary at all apparition sites. Apocalypse soon.'

I took a photograph of the sign and the man holding it smiled widely, nodded and said, 'Thank you very much.'

A short while later I was standing outside a corner shop by the roundabout that sits at the entrance to the village. Through the window I saw Joe Coleman talking to the shopkeeper. Both men were pointing in a way that suggested Joe was asking for and receiving directions. It looked like he bought a bar of chocolate. He came out of the shop, walked past me, got into the back of a waiting car and roared off. He may have the ear of the Blessed Virgin, but he needed more earthly assistance to get out of Knock.

I took the snow globe out of my pocket and gave it a shake, the white flakes and figures shining in the darkness. Mary really did appear to have a moustache.

CHAPTER SIXTEEN

When you mention Charlestown to someone in Ireland it garners one of two reactions. One, 'I think I've driven through it,' and two, 'Oh, the place John Healy wrote about?'

The origins of Charlestown are like those of no other town in Ireland: it was born out of a tremendous bloody-mindedness and determination to make a point but its story has turned out to be a typically Irish one, one that seems to be repeating cyclically to this day. But first, the frankly brilliant story of how Charlestown came to be.

It was the mid-1840s and the nation was in the grip of the Great Famine. Mayo as a county suffered more than most with 90 per cent of its population solely dependent on a potato crop that was annually failing. In the north-eastern corner of the county the local landlord was a Lord Dillon, an absentee landlord and not a bad one as it happens (certainly not when compared to some), but the boggy land here had only a few hardy tenants. Just over the border with Sligo, which also marked the boundary of the neighbouring estate owned by the Knox family, was the village of Bellaghy, a well-appointed place that was a centre for local market trading and which had a sanctioned set of weighing scales for produce. It was here that

Dillon's tenants had to take their barley and grain, picking their way through a bog to Bellaghy where they would join the queue for the weighing scales. The thing was, the rule in Bellaghy was that Knox tenants always had first dibs at the scales: no Dillon man could have his produce weighed until the Knox traders were finished, ensuring that the Knox traders always obtained the best prices for their produce by being first to market.

The Dillon people would protest to their land agent, Charles Strickland, but, frustrating and unfair though it was, there was nothing he could do. Things got worse when, at an official function, Lord Knox said something that grievously offended Strickland and left him with a burning determination to get even and show that pompous Sligo arse that he was messing with the wrong bloke.

Charles Strickland went home that night, brooded a while, and came up with a plan. A plan that must have sounded mad even to him, even after a couple of brandies at the height of his spluttering indignance at whatever Knox had said. He would have got up the next morning and realised that yes, it still sounded mad, but that didn't mean he couldn't pull it off. It would, he thought as he sliced the top off his boiled egg, teach him one heck of a lesson. I'm going to do it, he thought, I'm going to build my own town. On bogland. In this unremarkable corner of north-east Mayo. At the height of the Famine.

Strickland was a man of sheer bloody-minded determination. Building a whole town anywhere was a tall enough order, not least at that point in history, but he sat down and started planning straight away. The layout would be simple, bringing three roads together at a central square: one road to Sligo, one to Ballina and the other to Dublin. A mile from Bellaghy there was good firm ground which, if this madcap scheme was ever going to work, would have been ideal. But no. Strickland was going to stick it to Knox and Bellaghy and he was going to rub their noses in it big style. He was going to build his town literally next door, right up against the border, so close that the last houses in the street would be almost within touching distance of the first houses in Bellaghy. The town would rise from the boggiest, least suitable land in the district, land that could only be crossed by a series of stepping stones, to eclipse its snooty neighbours and show that nobody, but nobody, messes with Charles Strickland.

In order to carry out the building and encourage people to come to this most unlikely of new towns, Strickland came up with a genius idea. He announced that the builder of the first house to have a roof and a fire lit in its hearth, one whose smoke he could observe coming from the chimney, would win one hundred acres of land, rent free, in perpetuity. Not only that, each house in the town would have its own little piece of land to go with it. At a time of hardship when many landlords across the country were throwing starving tenants off their land or charging exorbitant rents, this was an extraordinary opportunity.

No accounts survive of what must have seemed like a small-scale recreation of the great land race of America, but the story goes that when it came down to the wire in that summer of 1846 two houses were in the frame. One had its roof slates but was still not quite ready to go ahead with their placement, while the other had its eaves up ready for a roof but was still waiting for the slates to arrive from Ballina, some thirty miles away. It was effectively neck and neck and, appropriately for a story that began with tremendous nose-thumbing ingenuity, the winner triumphed through subterfuge. The owner of the house with the slates piled next to the building knew that if he could delay the arrival of his rival's slates even by a day it would be enough for his men to scurry up to the roof, lash on the slates, spark up the fire and claim the hundred acres. If those slates arrived on schedule however, the cause was lost. He sent some of his men to Swinford to head off the men with the slate delivery, tell them the race was over so there was no rush and, basically, get a few pints in them. A rare old session was had, the slates stayed in Swinford and Charles Strickland had his winner.

To celebrate, he erected a set of weighing scales outside that first house: no longer would his tenants have to wait their turn across the border. Lord Knox went to court and won an order for Strickland to take the scales down. Which he did, then put them up again two feet away. Knox sued again and Strickland took down the scales. And put them up again two feet away. When it happened a third time, Knox asked that Strickland just be fined automatically every time he moved the scales. Strickland pointed out that no fine could be administered until it had been established in court that he had broken the law. At which point Knox gave in and Strickland moved the scales one last time, to the very centre of the town square where they remained right up until the seventies.

Strickland named the new town Dillonstown after his boss and before long the Dillonstown market was a rampaging success, drawing people from across the district. A few yards away Bellaghy's fortunes went into a swift decline. Its residents noted the large number of pubs in Dillonstown, and that the landlords were fairly easygoing when it came to administering closing time, and more and more of them spent more and more time across the county border until the Bellaghy constable began prosecuting the landlords. However, when they came before the local magistrate he quickly established that the pubs all had separate private entrances and anyone who passed through those entrances was regarded as a guest, not a customer, and therefore the licensing laws didn't apply. Case dismissed. Thinking ahead, when he'd planned the town Charles Strickland had insisted that each pub have this facility in case of just such an eventuality. After all, the local magistrate hearing the cases was a certain Charles Strickland, so he had a good idea of how these things worked.

He'd won. In arguably the most magnificent rejoinder ever to being insulted by a galumphing, pompous arse, Strickland had stuck it to Knox and stuck it to Bellaghy. As the kids might say, he owned Knox, like, totally owned him. On Strickland's death Dillonstown was renamed *Baile Cathal*, Charlestown, and the town would go on to inherit the resilience and determination of the man whose name it carried.

I'd come to know Charlestown reasonably well, as it's where Jude is from. Her mother's family have lived in the area for hundreds of years, beyond the existence of the town itself, so she's utterly steeped in the place. 'It's odd,' she once told me, 'there's you with no idea of where you come from, but me, I can practically walk out of my parents' house and show you the primordial swamp we first crawled out of.'

I like Charlestown a lot. In Finan's it has one of those magnificent Irish country pubs that's a shop as well: you walk in from the street, pass through the shop, open a door at the back and find yourself in a small, cosy bar jammed with ephemera and memorabilia. On one wall is a framed local newspaper cutting, yellowing now, of two fresh-faced young lads, over from England visiting family in the town, boasting about how one day they're going to be part of the biggest band in the world. Ah, they'll be Peggy Gallagher's boys, Noel and Liam, over from Manchester, grand lads altogether. Going through the shop and into the pub at the back at first feels like you're entering some kind of speakeasy, that you should know a password or a special knock, but the conviviality of the place soon rids you of that feeling and, after a couple of pints, when you leave through the shop again, it's amazing how you can be suddenly gripped by the urge to buy a broom or a soup ladle. It's exactly the kind of establishment and ambience that thousands of Irish pubs abroad have sought to recreate, only this is the real thing.

The town is still laid out just as Charles Strickland had planned it; spread spaciously around the market square at the centre of which are some stone cows to commemorate the trading that used to go on here. Many of the old buildings still stand. There's the odd concession to the Celtic Tiger: a 'business centre' offers office space to rent thanks to a big red sign on the front of the building punting 'Charlstown' [*sic*] as the ideal location, but Charlestown remains at heart a quiet country town.

If you walk up towards the old railway line – the station closed in 1975 but the platform is still there – you come to the border with Bellaghy. It really is very close: literally a train's width separates the two villages in two different counties. A small stone sign says 'Bellaghy', facing Charlestown in what seems to be a pyrrhic gesture at the neighbour that rose from the bog and bested them. Charlestown station may be closed, but the big sign on the platform is still maintained and its large capitalised CHARLESTOWN facing Bellaghy shouts down its neighbour.

Charlestown may have triumphed at its birth but it had its years of struggle. These were documented in a series of articles in the *Irish Times* by a son of the town, John Healy, published in 1967 as a groundbreaking book called *Death of an Irish Town*. In it, Healy opens by talking about how he'd come home from Dublin and hear a litany of shops that had closed and the names of the latest people to emigrate to England or America. He rails against the stagnation and decline of the west of Ireland. He finds the register of his 1944 primary school class and works out that of the twenty-four boys listed just three are still living in the town twenty years later. Fifteen have left the country altogether. Emigration had become a fact of life; most people left as soon as they could. The heart was ripped out of the town, as it was from many small towns like Charlestown across the country.

Despite Healy's pessimism, and to a large extent because of his subsequent agitation of the powers that be for the cause of the neglected west, Charlestown survived. He died in 1990, and while he would still recognise the town today as the town of his youth, he'd approve of the changes: the new library, the swimming pool, the new housing: Charlestown flourished. Young people may have left, but they often only went as far as Dublin and would return at weekends: if you wandered through the pubs on consecutive Saturday nights you'd see the same faces, not knowing that they spent the rest of the week in the capital. A new bypass opened recently to ease the traffic pressure on the little town and now bears John Healy's name. An annual literary weekend takes place there in his honour.

When the recession hit, Charlestown held its breath a little. Would it happen again? While there are a couple of empty shopfronts looking out at the main square the place seems to be doing OK. The cafés and pubs are busy and there's a cheery countenance to the place, especially on a wet weekend at the end of November, when Charlestown is gripped by cup fever.

The local Gaelic football team, Charlestown Sarsfields, had become the champions of Mayo. It was a title that put them into the semi-finals of the Connacht championship, which, if they won that too, would mean an All-Ireland semi-final and a crack at playing in Croke Park to become the club champions of the whole of Ireland. In their Connacht semi-final they'd come up against Castlerea from Roscommon. In injury-time Charlestown were a point behind in a game they'd been expected to win. In the dying seconds Castlerea burst forward into attack. As the ball broke loose, the Charlestown goalkeeper John Casey charged out of his goal and in the ensuing mêlée was knocked unconscious. The ball broke to a Castlerea forward barely twenty-five yards out: all he had to do was knock the ball between the posts and the match was Castlerea's. He lobbed the ball goalward and watched as it curled in the air, seemingly for an age, and pinged back off the post into the arms of a Charlestown player who sent it straight up the field to start a slick, fast move that ended with an equalising point with the last kick of normal time. Charlestown triumphed in extra-time.

In the Connacht final, the biggest game the club had seen in some years, they would face Corofin from Galway, on paper a slightly stronger team than Charlestown, but the Sarsfields would be playing on their own ground. On the day before the game the town was bedecked in green and white. Shops and pubs were festooned with bunting, signs wishing the team luck were on display in nearly every window and someone had painted green and white stripes on the road all the way up to the football ground. The national papers published extensive previews and interviews with some of the Charlestown players. Jude and I travelled down the day before the match and the talk in the town was of little else and had been of little else since the Castlerea game. We walked around the town and Jude bumped into people from school she'd not seen for years, back for the game. One girl had even flown over from London. Shops sold scarves, hats and flags. Television trucks had started to arrive, ready for the live transmission of the game. It was the biggest thing to hit Charlestown in a long time. The day before the match was a cold, wet one and we took refuge for a while by the fire in Gerry Murray's pub in the fading light of late afternoon. The talk among the handful of people at the bar was all about the match, of how Corofin were strong but there's something about this Charlestown team this season, that they could pull it off.

The phone rang in the pub, and the young man behind the bar answered it. 'You're kidding,' I heard him say. 'Ah well, OK, grand so, thanks.'

He placed the receiver back in the cradle and sighed. He turned to the bar and gave the bad news.

'The game's off,' he said. 'Called off.'

Ireland had been suffering a week of torrential rain that had caused serious flooding in many parts of the country. The bus we'd come down on had in places been up to its wheel arches in water. It was so bad that I was sure I'd seen Noah walk past the window with a mouthful of nails and a worried expression. Galway had been badly affected and it looked as though many of the roads up to Mayo might be impassable. The pitch was also utterly drenched so the decision had been taken early to call the whole thing off. The match would take place the following week. The pub was silent for a good while as the disappointment set in.

'Ah sure, it'll give the injured lads a bit of extra time to recover,' said one man.

'Beat them tomorrow, beat them next week, it's no different,' said another.

The following Sunday the match was shown on national television. It was one of those sunny days where the sun stays out
but can't seem to heave itself fully into the sky and it casts long
shadows across the cold ground. The little stadium was packed
with about four thousand people, five times the population of
Charlestown itself, and the place was buzzing by the time the
green-shirted gladiators lined up on the field.

They were hammered. Annihilated. Given an absolute hiding.
Corofin scored a goal inside the first two minutes and Charlestown
never recovered, never pulled together the fluency and doggedness
that had got them as far as they'd come. The game was over as a
contest almost by half-time. Admittedly the Sarsfields were missing a couple of key players, but even so, it was a walloping.

John Healy had played in goal for Charlestown and in one of
the most engaging passages of his book had described how, as a
boy, he and his contemporaries had worshipped the local hero,
Danno Regan. A Charlestown half-back, Regan had played for
the Mayo county side and brought home an All-Ireland winner's
medal in 1936. Healy described trips to see Charlestown play
away matches, about being jammed in the back of a flatbed
truck with other supporters going to the match singing 'Up the
Sarsfields' all the way, about not taking his eyes off Danno for the
whole match, about how at half-time as the team would come
together in the middle of the pitch for their instructions the kids
would sprint on to the field and squeeze between the players'
legs to offer Danno an orange for his half-time refreshment and
how, if he took your orange, you'd feel like the king of the
world.

Half a century after John Healy played in goal for Charlestown,
John Casey was wearing the number one shirt, getting knocked
out in the semi-final and having no chance with the Corofin
goals.

In his early twenties John Casey was the Danno of his day, the Charlestown hero. He wasn't a goalkeeper then though, he was a rangy, pacey, skilful forward for the Mayo county side, bursting with the confidence of being young and blessed with remarkable talent. He played in four All-Ireland finals before he was twenty-four, including a famous replayed encounter with Meath in 1996. Mayo were ahead by a point in the dying seconds when a hopeful punt by a Meath player bounced in front of the goal and looped heartbreakingly just over the crossbar to take the game to a replay. Mayo lost the replay and lost the final the following year to Kerry, to continue the Mayo curse of not winning an All-Ireland title since 1951.

At the age of twenty-four John Casey developed a nagging ankle injury, surgery on which prevented him from playing top class football ever again. It prevented him from playing outfield for his club too, so instead he took over in goal, still displaying the confidence, assurance and commitment he'd shown when performing in front of eighty thousand people and a worldwide television audience at Croke Park.

He works in the family business, a large hardware shop that looks out on to the market square in Charlestown. He built a house behind the shop, close to the river, which is where I went to see him a week after the Corofin game. He's friendly and relaxed, tall and fit. We sit in a large, high-ceilinged sitting room with a roaring fire, and soon it's clear that the GAA is something he could talk about for Ireland.

'In Ireland, if you don't know the GAA it probably rules you out of being friends with about eighty per cent of the public,' he said, sitting low on a sofa, his troublesome leg stretched out on a cushion. 'Just from being in business, in our shop, nine out of ten people will come in and talk to you about the GAA: the big topic of conversation is always what happened in the match last Sunday and if you're not up to speed on that you'll find you're a bit left out. Our family's steeped in it, it just runs through our veins, and with the town playing in the final just last weekend, things were hyped up even more. In the shop all week it was just GAA, people talked about nothing else.'

I commiserated with him on the result of the match. He shrugged.

'We met a team at the peak of their powers,' he said. 'I met a few lads who play for Galway who'd seen the game on television and they said Corofin have never played that well before in their whole lives. They decided to save their best ever game for us, which was unfortunate as we probably had our worst. It was a combination of those two factors that saw us get a right drubbing.'

It must have been hard to swallow though, I said, with all the build-up and the postponement?

'I didn't lose any sleep, not this time,' he replied. 'But I hate losing. I've lost a lot of big games over the years, won some more, but you wouldn't be doing it if you didn't love it. That's why you keep going back. I'm thirty-five now, with a young child, and still everything in the house is arranged around training and matches. Rita, my wife, she's a member of the *Garda Síochána* so she asks me what days she can work overtime, can I work next Sunday – overtime is where they make their living and every Sunday is taken up with the GAA for me so I'm practically telling her she can't work any Sundays. Your whole life revolves around the GAA and it affects family too.'

Despite playing at the highest level in his time, turning out in front of full houses at Croker, having millions watching on television, despite all the sacrifices he makes and his wife makes for him, John Casey has never been paid a penny for playing football. Every time he's played in front of those massive crowds, within days he's been back earning his corn behind the shop counter.

'The fact it's amateur is the thing that would completely baffle anybody in the UK or elsewhere.' He laughs. 'Nothing crosses our hands, we're not reimbursed. Nobody plays for monetary gain which in many ways is probably why the GAA is so strong. A few years ago, when I was playing for Mayo, we had some fellas over from John Moores University in Liverpool, they'd worked with the Everton soccer team in the English Premiership. They took us to Athlone for the weekend and rigged us up to machines and monitors and we're thinking, all we're used to is, "There's two posts, sprint to them and back as quick as you can," we weren't used to this at all. They recorded our fitness levels and body fat and everything and told us that we were equal to any Premiership player they'd ever come across. They'd compared me to Francis Jeffers, who was at Everton at the time and played for England, and the levels were all pretty much the same. They found it phenomenal that we were amateur sportsmen.'

I did wonder whether he ever cast an envious eye across the Irish Sea at the millions being earned by footballers and the fact that players in other sports could make their living, a comfortable living, doing the kind of thing he did out of working hours, with babysitting issues and long hours on the training pitch, after a full day at work.

'When I was eighteen and brought into the Mayo county squad for the first time, they were talking about making it professional so I fully expected at that age that I'd be getting some sort of monetary compensation for what I was doing eventually. Did it bother me? No it didn't. At the time I was thinking, Jesus, this is great *craic*, and if someone's going to give me a few quid for it, so much the better. But to me I wouldn't consider it as being paid, more as compensation. Premiership players are paid, GAA players are looking for compensation for the sacrifices they make. Can't go here, can't go there, getting babysitters . . . we're made to take days off work when we have to play matches in midweek. We've four Gardaí in our team, and the hassle they have getting time off work is unbelievable. Those fellas deserve something, you know?

'At club level you don't even get your travel expenses. You do at county level, minute expenses. I think back then it was 18p a mile we used to get, but if you were bringing a teammate with you it was 23p. So what we used to do was invent fake people and arrange who had "brought" whom – if there were three lads in one car we'd say that one had come with me so I could get my extra 5p a mile. One particular lad used to put in his expenses saying he'd been carrying this fella who'd been dropped from the county panel the year before, and he was still using his name to claim his 5p a mile!'

Even at club level the level of commitment shown by the GAA lads is incredible. A few weeks earlier John had come tearing out of his goal and been knocked out cold. Another key Charlestown player, David 'Ginger' Tiernan, had been injured seconds later in setting up the equalising score, breaking a bone in his foot. It's a tough game and can be a tough life, especially when the supporters start giving you grief.

'Yeah, I got knocked out in that game and also my back was going into spasm,' he recalled. 'I thought I was dying, I came round and I could barely get my breath. I ended up having lots of physio, hours of work on this back injury as well as going into work and looking after my daughter, and people don't see that, they just see you when you're out there on the field. We had a customer come into the shop after that game who told me that

I'd have no excuses the next time and that my "lies would catch up with me". I was fuming. He actually said I'd pretended I'd been knocked out, that I wasn't injured at all. I said to him, do you realise I've had twenty-eight physio sessions since that game? I've had a physio in my house for four hours working on my back one night and I've driven to Castlebar and back twenty-seven times on top of that for physio? Telling me I was lying on the ground pretending to be knocked out, and me out cold, coming round and my back is in spasm. Premiership players are being paid a fortune when they have to listen to that kind of stuff, we're not.'

I ask him about the injury that ended his county career.

'In 1999 this problem started,' he said, rubbing the back of his leg. 'I used to call myself Christy Brown because every injury I had seemed to concern my left foot: ankle ligaments, heel, Morton's neuroma, it was all there. Since I've got older of course it's all over the place, but back then it was always my left foot.'

In the 1999 season John developed a pain in the ball of his left foot that turned out to be Morton's neuroma, a knot of nerve tissue between the third and fourth toes that causes extreme pain. Subconsciously he began running differently to keep the pressure off the ball of his foot, which led to a heel problem.

'I didn't want to go complaining about it, because it used to come and go,' he said. 'But eventually it was decided that I needed surgery. I played all that year right up to the All-Ireland semi-final in August: I played with two cortisone injections before every game. I got a special boot made to try and ease the pressure on my heel, so I had that and the two jabs getting me through the games. The boys were getting sick of me – I'd walk into the dressing room limping and two minutes later I'd be like a spring lamb. I'll never forget Liam McHale saying, you're an effing eejit. But I'm twenty-four, I'm saying, it's going to be fine, when the season is over I'm getting it sorted out surgically and I'll be back next season. Little did I know, I'd never play for Mayo again.

'The first two operations weren't a success, then a second surgeon came along and took my Achilles tendon off my heel to get at the bone. Before the op I was able to run the hundred metres in just over ten seconds. I was fast: your Achilles tendon helps you with that speed so when the damage was done in the operating theatre I lost that sharpness. And that's what did for my county career. At twenty-four John Casey was on the scrapheap, never to play again.'

Even now, more than a decade on, the frustration and regret in his voice is palpable.

'God, if you'd told me then that day, that at twenty-four that was to be my last game in the Mayo jersey, I'd have said you were crazy,' he said, staring up at the ceiling. 'Although I was young I'd played for seven years for the county, and as far as I was concerned that was just the start of it. I thought I was in for a long and probably distinguished career with Mayo. Actually I still have nightmares about it now, where I'm playing for Mayo again but I haven't done any training, I'm like I am now, a thirty-five-year-old who can't run, and I'm been thrown in at the deep end in an All-Ireland final and I'm going to be a laughing stock. I'm thinking, Jesus, why are they doing this to me?'

It would have been a massive blow to anyone, having something they loved taken away, especially when they were clearly so gifted at it. Although John Casey lived out the dreams of thousands of Irish schoolboys by being a star player in a team that graced All-Ireland finals, it was a cruel blow to an

immensely talented young man who had yet to realise his full
potential.

'It does play on my mind a little bit, what might have been,
but I'll take playing over not playing any day, no question,' he
said. 'I've had nearly as long a career in goals now than I had out
on the field, so nobody under twenty remembers me as an outfield player these days. There are kids who'll point to me in the
street and say look, there's the Charlestown goalkeeper. It makes
me feel like saying, did you know I got Man of the Match
against Kerry in the 1996 All-Ireland semi-final, do you know I
played in four All-Ireland finals? I wonder, when my obituary
comes to be written, will I be remembered as the Mayo forward
or the Charlestown goalie?'

There was one thing I wanted to know, the small boy in me
and the adult who's watched All-Ireland finals with their
pageantry, their eighty-thousand crowds, the anticipation, the
streets of Dublin packed with people in team colours. My
dream was always to score the winner for Charlton Athletic in
the FA Cup Final: the drawback was that I was hopeless.
Similarly, every Irish boy dreams of playing in the All-Ireland
final and John Casey had done it, more than once. It was a
question that he must have been asked a thousand times, but I
still had to ask it. What's it like playing in the All-Ireland
final?

'It's a weird feeling,' he said. 'The weirdest part of it for me
was that in 1996 I'd got Man Of The Match in the semi-final so
I was getting extra-special attention from the media. I was only
twenty-one and I didn't know me head from me elbow. I had
RTÉ, Eurosport, everyone in my house every other day, I had
every radio station in the country on to me, every sports journalist and to me it was like, God, what am I doing here? What's
going on?

'The final itself bypassed me, to be honest with you. I had a poor game and it got to me. I don't know why I had a bad game, things just didn't click. It's your ultimate goal, every boy wants to play in an All-Ireland final, it's everything you want in life. Nobody gave us a prayer that year, we were in Division Three in the league and we were scraping wins against teams in that division, yet four months later we were in an All-Ireland Final. It's unheard of for a Division Three team to get to the final so there was so much hype and it was crazy, totally crazy. I don't really remember much about it: I remember the coach and the police escort to the match through the crowds, and coming round the corner of the stadium and seeing about fifty people from Charlestown, five or six of my friends home from America for the game, all outside this pub and I was looking out of the window and giving them a wave and thinking, those bastards are having great craic and here's me sitting here shitting it, that's not fair, they're here enjoying themselves and I've got to go and run around in front of eighty thousand people, with everyone watching my every move.

'It was an experience, certainly, but it's one I feel I didn't grasp. I wish I could have done it as a twenty-five- or twenty-six-year-old, when I could think, right, it's only a game of football, I'm going out there to enjoy it, I don't care about the crowd, the surroundings or what the occasion is. It upsets me a little: that I didn't get to play in an All-Ireland as an older player, to get the biggest day in the game as an experienced player. That hurts me a little bit.'

It must have been odd, I said, that having been the centre of national attention, being constantly in the spotlight, the autograph hunters, the interviews, the hype and the hoopla, to come back to Charlestown and go back to work, back to the mundane and the everyday.

'We went on our little benders, of course, two- or three-day ones, then things soon got back to normal,' he recalled. 'I found it hard to take. I'm not a good loser at the best of times, but at the time I was the pin-up boy and great white hope of the county and I hadn't shown up, we'd lost the game. Did I blame myself? Not completely. Did I think we could have done better? Of course I do and it's always going to be on my mind. A ball bounced over the bar in '96 and cost us an All-Ireland. A football-starved county like Mayo who love their sport, love their GAA and love being at Croke Park, a ball bouncing over the bar cost us the whole thing: that makes me sick to the core even to this day. I've never watched the games and I couldn't, I never will, they'd make me sick.

'A professional sportsman goes back to the training ground, we go back to work. That's reality for you. It's what makes the GAA so special, you know: you play the game and you get on with your life. We talked about that in the dressing room after the Corofin game, about how nobody had died. We didn't do ourselves justice, but nobody died.'

The fact that the whole town turned out for the match, the green and white bunting everywhere, the 'Good Luck Sarsfields' signs on the roadsides, it all demonstrated to me just how important the GAA is to a town, to a community, even to Ireland and a sense of Irishness. The GAA reaches into a community like no other sporting association in the world.

John has spent most of his life in Charlestown. He went away to boarding school and was at college up in Donegal, but mostly he's been in the town and now runs the family business. At thirty-five, he remembers the eighties, the stream of young people leaving the town for Britain or America, and I wondered whether he'd noticed it happening again.

'Floods of people left the town in the eighties,' he confirmed.

'It was said back then that Charlestown could field a better team in New York than they could here in Charlestown. There was a mass exodus of the next generation – my generation – too. I'd say there were seven fellas from my class at school who'd all headed to New York. It wasn't as bad as in the eighties, but it was bad enough, like. And now it's happening again: we've a few fellas unemployed in the team now, six that I can think of off the top of my head, and there was a feeling that this season was an opportunity we needed to grasp before everyone went their separate ways. One lad is definitely going to Australia in January, and there are two more who've been over to England for job interviews in recent weeks. So there's going to be another exodus, yes, but what can you do if there's nothing to stay here for?'

The cycle continues. From one Sarsfields goalkeeper to another fifty years apart, the story reinvents itself. As Healy himself had looked up to Danno Regan, the young kids of Charlestown today point out John Casey in the street and talk in hushed tones of the Sarsfields goalkeeper. Their dads might fill them in on the lightning fast, lethal forward who took Mayo to successive All-Ireland finals and they might take those stories with them if and when they leave for Britain and America themselves. As John Casey himself puts his elbows on the shop counter and talks about the latest news and the latest matches, he'll be wondering whether his old bones will still be there when training starts again on a cold, dark night in January, and how many faces might be missing from the team that made it all the way to the Connacht semi-final, and whether those faces are in New York or London, imagining themselves going through stretches and sprints in the sleet and wind back home at Father O'Hara Park.

Charlestown is a town like many others in the west of Ireland.

Mention it to someone and they might have passed through it or they might remember the book that was written about it once. As I walked back into the centre of the town the green paint in the rain-shiny road up to the GAA ground was beginning to fade.

CHAPTER SEVENTEEN

We stopped by an old wall and pulled out the map. We'd been walking now in the wind and the rain for a good half hour and thought we'd be there by now. A gust waggled the branches of the skeletal tree above us sending big bulging drops of water plummeting to the ground. One went 'whap', right on to the spot on the map I was looking at; another smacked me on the back of the neck and became a trickle of ice-cold water creeping down inside my collar. A little further on at the end of this narrow, single-lane road we'd find a junction. If we turned right there we'd be at Ballycurraginny. The wind blew up fierce again and the rain got heavier, flinging heavy drops into our faces. We hunched down into our coats and started walking again. It never happened like this on *Who Do You Think You Are?*

A day earlier we'd arrived in Youghal, the historic harbour town where, if my research was right, John Connelly had been baptised. It's a sleepier, more genteel town than its two Chinese takeaways called the Pak Fook and the Ho Inn might suggest. It sits at the mouth of the River Blackwater, about thirty miles east along the coast from Cork city and, having once been a thriving medieval port, is now a popular summer destination for Irish holidaymakers who head in their droves for the long sandy beach that stretches away south of the town.

We'd booked into a guesthouse at the south end of the main street, a huge Georgian building where we were given a room right at the top, in the roof. After doing all the new-room-in-a-hotel-or-guesthouse things like opening and the closing the wardrobe doors, looking out of the window, saying 'ooh, nice big bathroom' and finding out that the television channel numbers listed in the little folder by the bed bore absolutely no relation to the television itself, we set out for a walk around the town.

The long beach means that Youghal stretches along the coast for a fair distance, but the heart of the town is still contained within the boundaries of the old medieval walls. It's hunched up against a steep hillside and concentrated on a narrow main street divided by the large, sandstone Georgian clock tower that straddles it and is Youghal's most recognisable feature. It's easy to tell that this was once a prosperous town by the architecture; some fine Georgian houses line the streets while the main street itself is agreeably free of modern development. We made a circuit of the town centre and passed the forbiddingly closed gates of Myrtle Grove, famous as once being the residence of Sir Walter Raleigh. Raleigh is an example of someone who in Britain is regarded as a bit of a good egg, a national hero, a favourite of Elizabeth I and a fine sea captain, even if he was eventually executed for treason, but in Ireland he's viewed in a radically different way. In 1579 he'd been sent here to quell a rebellion, something he set about doing with murderous enthusiasm. A force of Italian and Spanish mercenaries had arrived late at Smerwick in County Kerry in order to support an uprising that had already been all but defeated. Hence most of the English forces in Ireland were able to surround the new arrivals and deal with them pretty much as they stepped ashore. Raleigh separated the Italian and Spanish officers, as they'd be worth significant ransoms, and then set about sorting out the rest, the mercenaries and all the inhabitants of the town. First he had all the pregnant townswomen hanged and then set about the remainder, some six hundred men, women and children, in a relentless slaughter that went on for two days and from which skeletons are still occasionally unearthed to this day. As a deterrent to anyone thinking of staging an uprising in or invasion of Ireland it was effective, as an act of barbarity even for those less enlightened times, it still rings down the centuries. As a reward for putting down the rebellion, Raleigh was given forty thousand acres of land in Ireland, a grant that included Youghal. Although it was unlikely, given his reputation, that Raleigh spent much time in Youghal, two of the most famous stories associated with him are purported to have happened there.

Myrtle Grove is a fine big Tudor house, still occupied by private residents and only really visible from high up in the churchyard next door. According to legend it was here that Raleigh planted the first potatoes in Ireland, hoping to develop the crop as a good source of sustainable food that, as it grew underground, would be protected from burning by rebels and raiders.

The story goes that Raleigh invited a number of dignitaries and landowners to dinner to sample this revolutionary new vegetable. Unfortunately, the former privateer's kitchen staff hadn't been informed that the actual crop was in the ground and so they carefully harvested the green leaves that grew above it, boiled them and served them to the big cheeses in the dining room. Unfortunately, potato leaves have a similar toxic reaction to deadly nightshade, and before long Raleigh and his guests were doubled up with stomach cramps and vomiting copiously. It wasn't the best impression under any circumstances, but with Raleigh's reputation he was immediately suspected of trying to poison his guests in order that he might seize their lands.

Also possibly apocryphal is the story that most of us learnt at school: that as Raleigh sat in the house one night enjoying a pipe of his newly discovered tobacco, a servant nearby, not realising what was happening, threw a bucket of water over his boss in the belief that he was on fire. Both stories are creaky and full of more holes than a Swiss cheese packaging plant, but basically anything that makes Raleigh look a bit of a knob is generally going to go down well over here.

Funnily enough, Youghal is also associated with the man whose name still provokes more opprobrium than any other in Ireland.

In 1997 the new British Foreign Secretary, Robin Cook, inspected the room where he'd be receiving foreign heads of state and high-ranking dignitaries. Hanging on one of the walls was a Victorian portrait of a high ranking official from the British Raj or somesuch. Thinking that such imperialist nonsense was no longer appropriate in this new era, Cook had it taken down and replaced with a large portrait of Oliver Cromwell. As an anti-monarchist and generally sound republican, Cook thought, he was an ideal subject to hang in the big space on the wall.

One of the first heads of state to visit was the then Irish Taoiseach, Bertie Ahern. Cook showed him into the room where Ahern immediately turned on his heels, walked out, and announced that he wouldn't be returning until 'that murdering bastard' had been removed from the wall. As a diplomatic faux pas it was up there with the best, as in Ireland Cromwell, even nearly four hundred years on, remains probably the most reviled figure in a nation that has a fair few people in its little black book.

Cromwell had arrived in Ireland in 1649, ostensibly to restore order after Catholic forces began to mass ready for an invasion of England to restore Charles II to the throne, but also to punish the Irish for atrocities committed against Protestant settlers nearly a decade earlier. During his time in Ireland Cromwell would be responsible for the deaths of an estimated two hundred thousand Irish people, most notoriously in the siege of Drogheda and sack of Wexford. It's a dark stain on Irish history and an aspect of the New Commonwealth I certainly didn't learn about at school.

The last place in Ireland where Cromwell set foot was Youghal. He probably wasn't sorry to see the back of the place either, as for all the sieges and battles of the previous months it was a good, sturdy Cork downpour that almost did for the Lord Protector once and for all. He'd presided over the funeral of Lieutenant General Michael Jones in the town – an officer who, it was discovered later, had been plotting against Cromwell at the time of his demise – got caught in a rainstorm and contracted pneumonia. He was bedbound for several weeks and reported as close to death on a number of occasions, but eventually recovered and was able to leave Ireland for ever and take a boat back to England from the quayside at Youghal.

I was woken early the next morning by the wind booming around the eaves. It was still dark outside but the telltale spatter of the rain on the window was all the evidence I needed that a particularly filthy day was dawning. In fact it had dawned already but the storm was attempting to hoodwink the town into thinking it was still the middle of the night. A bird scrabbled around on the wet roof tiles above, the persistent throaty squawk of a crow continuing for several minutes until I put the lamp on, swung my legs out of bed and went to switch on the little kettle on the other side of the room.

As I shook a couple of teabags to loosen the leaves I listened to the gusts of wind and the rain on the roof tiles and rued the fact that it wasn't an ideal day to take your great-great-great-grandfather home for the first time in more than a hundred and fifty years. My plan for the day was to visit the church in Youghal where John had been baptised, take the bus up the road to Killeagh where Catherine had been baptised and then walk in John's footsteps to the site of the little mud cabin he'd left some time in 1842 and to which he never returned. I had no idea what I might find. According to the modern OS map in my bag there were still buildings on the site where Rob had pointed out the little black rectangle to me on the map back in Dublin a few weeks earlier. I was pretty sure the same building wouldn't be there, given their apparent propensity to fall down even back then, but maybe there'd be a ruin I could stand in, a doorway I could walk through. There might even be a modern house there now, a path to walk up and a door to knock on, like my friend had found in Kerry, the warm welcome and being ushered in as family.

At breakfast the lovely lady who ran the place asked if we were down visiting family.

'Sort of,' I said, 'I've got ancestors from over at Killeagh so we're going to have a look round.'

I'd pronounced it 'Kill-ear', which I assumed was right even though I'd only ever seen the word written down. She looked puzzled for a moment.

'Ahh,' she said suddenly, 'Killer!'

At first I thought she was expressing approval with an impressive grasp of the modern urban vernacular for a middle-aged woman running a guesthouse in east Cork, and was about to reply with something along the lines of, 'Yeah, wicked innit?' when I realised that she was actually correcting my pronunciation. The village of my roots was pronounced 'killer'. We were the Connellys of Killer. I was a Killer Connelly.

After breakfast we headed up to the church. The wind was howling and the rain gliding through the sky in billowing pennants as Jude and I sloshed up the hill to the place where John was baptised. We turned off the street and stepped through the gates, and as we did so the wind gave what sounded like a deafening roar of pain, a sudden deep booming moan as it flew around the church, that was so loud that we both stopped, looked at each other, asked each other what the feck that was and laughed.

We continued up the steps and went through the doors into a large porch. We unzipped coats and unwound scarves for a moment and then Jude put her hand on one of the internal doors.

'Ready?' she said.

I nodded, and she pushed the door open and went inside.

It's a wonderful church. The gable end, where the wall behind the altar is painted pink from floor to ceiling, is decorated with pictures of saints and a beautiful white wooden gallery runs around three sides of the interior. It reminded me of a number of seamen's churches I'd been in before around the coast of Britain. Outside the wind continued to roar; the internal doors behind us opened and banged shut. We were the only people in the place and the only lighting beyond the murky daylight leaking in through the windows came from a couple of spotlights picking out the altar. Empty confessional boxes lined the walls and in the far left corner was a large nativity scene. Next to the nativity was the font, in all likelihood the very font in which John had been christened. The doors banged again, opening wide and crashing shut. The font was by the altar and I didn't want to trespass on the holiest part of the church so instead sat down in the front pew, possibly in the very place my great-great-great-great-grandfather had done at the christening of his son, and looked at the simple octagonal stone pedestal with a cross carved into its front. Here was where the infant John, just days old, was marked with holy water and sent out into the world. The doors banged again, the sound echoing around the empty building, and the wind made the eaves click as it rushed around and tugged at the roof outside. We sat for a few moments and the doors banged more insistently until we stood up and walked back out into the storm.

The bus-stop was crowded when we arrived. The bus to Killeagh was also the main route into Cork city and there was a fair-sized gaggle of folk heading for the post-Christmas sales huddled beneath the shelter. We shuffled in at the back, finding room underneath and probably nudged a couple of shivering pensioners out into the rain at the other end, but, you know, hey ho.

The grey sea churned up white foamy tips as the bus left Youghal along the coast. Before long we'd moved inland and the scenery gave way to fields, dark green in the dim light of the stormy day. It was barely ten minutes before the bus turned left over a small bridge and dropped us in the heart of Killeagh village. An enormous church looked down along the main street from a raised position, possibly the church in which Catherine would have been baptised. Killeagh didn't look its most homely that day, even to a distantly returning prodigal like me.

I'd planned to walk out to Ballycurraginny. Well, it was the only option of course, but also I'd figured that it was a journey John himself had made many times to and from the village and indeed, the return walk back to the village would echo exactly the first part of the journey he made one day in 1842, the journey that ended in London.

The road out of the village was uphill. We headed past the church and within a few yards were in countryside. The mud-brown rainwater ran down the hill in rivulets that sloshed over our boots and the rain spattered against our hoods. Every now and then a car would appear and we'd have to squeeze into the hedgerow. The rain seemed to fall harder the further we walked. After around twenty minutes we turned right, walked downhill and then uphill, passed a couple of houses and stopped to check the map where the big dollop of rainwater smacked right on to where we were going.

We pressed on uphill and the wind blew hard into our faces until we reached the junction and turned right on to the road which I hoped held all the answers. We'd reached Ballycurraginny.

There were more buildings than I'd expected. A clutch of farm buildings at the crossroads and some houses on the right, set back from the single track road. I tried to estimate on the map where the old homestead would have been as the rain fell harder and the wind whipped up again, moaning eerily and constantly in the telegraph wires overhead. We walked along the road a little way. It was muddy and narrow with a high hedge on one side and fields of pasture falling away down the hill on the other. We walked aimlessly up and down for a while, the melancholy of the telegraph harp strings and the buffeting wind a spooky and unwelcoming soundtrack. There was absolutely nobody around. The rain fell harder still. I walked into a field, yellow with cropped stalks, harvested recently enough. Pools of water had formed in the caterpillar tracks at the field entrance and I walked gingerly around them to look out across the field to the landscape beyond, thinking this was the view John would have remembered, the view he grew up with: was this what he recalled as he lay dying in the workhouse infirmary all those years later? It would have been no rural idyll for him for sure, but had he dreamed of returning, carrying for his whole life the pain and hunger that Brian Boylan had expressed so heartbreakingly and eloquently, of seeing this again?

Jude stood close to me and asked how I felt. I couldn't really answer, couldn't really speak. I felt . . . empty. Literally empty, an emptiness of the soul combined with a sudden fierce physical hunger. It may have been the weather and the constant moan of the wind in the wires, but I sensed something hopelessly mournful about where I was, a feeling that this wasn't a happy place. There was misery in the air, in the rain, in the ground, in the wind that pulled at my coat and sang of sadness in the wires.

'I shouldn't have come,' I said to Jude eventually. 'He left here for a reason, and I shouldn't have come back.'

The wind got stronger, the rain battered into our faces and the telegraph wires moaned some more. I had to get away, I just felt like I had to get away.

'Can we go?' I said to Jude, and she needed no encouragement. I had no desire to hang around, indeed, quite the opposite. I'd planned to knock on a couple of doors and ask if anyone knew of the Connellys but I'd lost all inclination to do that. It would have been an impertinence at the best of times, but suddenly I felt I was somehow letting John Connelly down. He hadn't wanted to be found here, he didn't want me asking questions, didn't want us to come back.

Jude put her arm through mine, led me to the road and we started walking back. I stopped after a few paces and turned around to look again.

'You shouldn't look back,' said Jude. 'I don't think he did

the day he left, and I don't think he wanted us to come here today.'

We got to the junction and turned left, heading down the hill and away from Ballycurraginny. A particularly strong gust of wind blew up behind us and forced us into a run for a couple of paces, like a hand in the small of the back speeding us on our way.

I felt bereft inside, almost as if I now knew what Brian and the forgotten Irish in England could feel, what John himself had felt as he walked this exact road for the last time, every step taking him further from everything he knew. I'd kept at the back of my mind a saccharine hope that he and Catherine had run away together, that this was a romantic story, but walking that road as he had I knew there was nothing romantic about it. This was poverty and desperation. Possibly even a sacrifice, voluntary or otherwise, to save the rest of the family as the potato crops failed and the prospect of employment shrank to nothing. John didn't want me here, he'd left this behind, he didn't want anyone living the kind of life he had or seeing what he'd had to leave.

I wasn't supposed to come back.

The further away we got from Ballycurraginny, the more the wind dropped and the rain eased.

'I don't think it's simply that he didn't want you finding this place, you know,' said Jude as we pulled our hoods down. 'I think it was just he didn't want to go with you. It was as if we were making him go back. It's to do with survival, I think. Sometimes people just shut down because it's easier to walk away from a situation where there's no nostalgia: it's easier to look forward than back; your family's always done that, that's why you didn't know anything about the past. It's as if they've carried this departure with them for generations without even realising it.

'Look at the whole day, that roaring howl of wind as we walked up to the church in Youghal: I always say some winds have voices and that one definitely did. The constant banging of the door in the church, this morning when we got up and the crow was on the roof, the crow: the very representation of a battered old man. Some people just don't want to be found. He left this place for a reason and he doesn't want that part of the story retold. You have a right to know who your family is and where they're from but you don't own them. Their story is not your story, and I think that's what this has been about. This man could have seen all sorts here and thought no, never ever again.'

This was the antithesis of the image of Ireland I'd grown up with. There was no comfy nostalgia here, no ruins, no pouting colleen, no boat in a field, no old house still standing, freshly whitewashed and recently re-thatched and with turf smoke easing from the chimney. This was the reality of the Irish past, the hardship, the filthy weather, the echoes of a grim determination to survive. There was no sense of looking back and longing here – John had left and never returned and, I felt, resented me going there. It was as if he was saying, I left this behind, it was no kind of life, it was a place of misery: I never went back so what are you doing there? Why on earth are you raking all this up after all these years?

That sense of emptiness and hunger stayed with me for the rest of the day. I felt like a husk of a human being. I could barely speak, barely think; I was just overwhelmed by a bitter and deeply unpleasant melancholy with a cavernous emptiness at its heart. In a way, in going there I'd been as guilty of falling into the picture-book nature of Ireland as I had back in London all those years ago. While I'd tried to keep an open mind before coming to Cork, I'd still subconsciously conjured up a rural idyll, a happy place where the sun shone and the crops were abundant, and while the family may have been poor they were happy, like the grinning, ruddy-cheeked peasants you'd see carrying armfuls of corn in Soviet propaganda posters. I'd even hoped I might feel like I belonged there, that some homing beacon deep in my genes had been sending out signals for as long as I could remember and had now been sated at last. But the minute I arrived I knew I didn't belong there, far from it. There was no epiphany. Instead I'd found a place lashed by rain and wind where a hungry, frightened family would have huddled together for whatever warmth they could produce in a mud hut, fearful and shameful that there was no work, that the pathetic potato patch outside was producing nothing but hunks of black, oozing, diseased matter that nobody could eat. They were being ground down, nudged slowly but irrevocably towards oblivion and there didn't seem to be anything they could do to stop it, which is when John either took it upon himself to leave or it was decided for him that leaving was the only option, removing a mouth to feed to help them all survive. Jude was right: I really had no business being there, it wasn't my story, it wasn't my place to rake up all those terrible memories, the heartbreak of exile still ingrained into the sodden earth, still moaning up there in the wires.

We walked up and down the main street in Killeagh one more time before the bus back to Youghal arrived. In Killeagh John might have heard stories of local men who'd left and noticed familiar faces missing from around the place. He might have heard about the men who'd taken the boat to London and were working in the docks – they'd see you right if you went over, John, they'd look out for you, we always look after our own here, John, even when the land itself can't. Sure, it might only be for a while, John, till things pick up again. Ballycurraginny will always be there, John, you can always come back, you know. You can always come back, John.

You can always come back.

CHAPTER EIGHTEEN

'I got a voucher for my eyebrows for Christmas. I went to get them done yesterday. There was nothing wrong with my eyebrows before but now I've to go back every five weeks.'

It was the morning of New Year's Eve and Jude and I were sharing a pot of tea in a café in Youghal before taking the bus to Cork city. I'd lost the emptiness and hunger of the previous day's stresses, not least thanks to the heartiest of Irish breakfasts at the guesthouse that ensured however hard the wind might blow that morning it wouldn't be knocking me over any time soon. I still felt a little down – you spend all that time tracking down a long lost and long dead relative and when you find him he effectively tells you to bugger off – but earwigging at the banter in the tea shop was doing wonders for restoring my spirits.

The woman with eyebrows and the sing-song Cork accent was buying a fruit scone. 'Is Mary open today?' she asked. 'She is,' came the reply from behind the counter, 'sure, what else would she be at?'

The Cork accent is possibly my favourite in Ireland. It bounces, it sings and it zings up and down the scale with its own brand of rhythmic syncopation. It can make funny lines twice as funny and has an honest, trustworthy tone to it that other accents can lack: a Cork person could look you in the eye and tell you that Bonnie Langford invented punk and you'd be thinking, 'Well now, there's a thing.'

(Cork people have, incidentally, gained a reputation of thinking they're above the rest of Ireland, that if you're from Cork you're privileged, special even. There's the old joke that tells of the Corkman with an inferiority complex: he thought he was as good as everyone else. Or the Corkonian who hears that Cork has been referred to as the 'Venice of Ireland' and responds, 'And why isn't Venice known as the "Cork of Italy"?' Jude once told me of how her uncle was driving out of Cork city one day and stopped to ask someone if he was on the right road for Dublin. 'Sure, what's wrong with Cork?' came the reply, entirely free of irony.)

I was sorry to leave Youghal. The previous evening I'd been cheered up by the atmosphere in its welcoming pubs as I listened in to a family gathering at one ('Oh, no Granny, this isn't my sister, she went home yesterday, remember? This is my girl-friend') and narrowly avoided joining in a sing-song – it was a close run thing for a while though – in another that was covered in memorabilia from the time Youghal harbour was used to rep-resent New Bedford, Massachusetts, for the 1954 John Huston film version of *Moby Dick* with Gregory Peck. Four fellas stood at the end of the bar, the only other patrons in the place, running through a selection of Elvis and Beatles songs and the appropri-ately seasonal 'Fairytale of New York' in a quartet of sonorous *basso profundo*. There was a friendliness to the place, this little town still adhering to its medieval layout, and a toughness ingrained in the stones of its buildings that sees it still thriving despite being long ago usurped by Cork as the major port of the south coast. When in the nineteenth century ships became too big for Youghal, Cork, which as Youghal folk will remind you used to be known merely as 'a small port near Youghal', utilised the wider inlets of the River Lee and became the main port for the south of Ireland. Yet Youghal is a place that won't be cowed; there's a strength to Youghal that reaches back through the centuries. It's not because most of its medieval defences are still intact, nor even the sign in the tea shop boasting that baguettes are available 'with a selection of filings'; there's just a sense that whatever happens Youghal will always reinvent itself, will always play to its strengths and find new ones. Which seemed to be the abiding theme of both strands of this story.

In Cork city we'd booked into the kind of hotel I'd ordinarily be turned away from with a sharp clip round the ear for my impertinence in even approaching the door, but this being recession Ireland we were welcomed with open arms at a bargain room rate. Even though we were sweating and panting profusely as a result of the hotel being sited at the top of a long and steep flight of steps at the top of a long and steep hill, the receptionist tried to coax us into booking their New Year's Eve dinner rather than assuming we were there to peel the vegetables for it.

From a room so large that it could have comfortably accommodated most of Hertfordshire and a bathroom capable of staging a full-scale game of rounders, we had a view right across the city to the hills beyond, which made a pleasant change from the usual view I get in hotels across the bins to the breaker's yard beyond.

After a quick game of rounders in the bathroom we abseiled down the hill into town, walking up Cork's majestic, sweeping St Patrick's Street. The post-Christmas sales were still on and the streets were busy; it was hard to imagine that barely a month earlier much of the city centre had been underwater after the floods that had swamped many parts of the country. The local paper and an enquiry at the tourist office had revealed that there weren't too many options for New Year's Eve – Ireland doesn't go wild in terms of public events at New Year – but we had a plan, at least for the last part. Anyway, by mid-afternoon we had found the Most Perfect Pub In Ireland so any other plans would have been shelved accordingly.

We'd nearly missed it altogether. It was situated near the town centre in a narrow lane and was so dark from the outside we almost walked past without noticing it was there. It was only the candles burning inside that gave the game away that it was a) a pub and b) open.

I pushed the door, we stepped inside and shot back in time around a hundred and fifty years. The place was long, narrow and dark. The wooden interior was of a brown so deep it clearly aspired to be black. The windows were small and leaded but as they looked out on to the narrow, high-walled dingy lane there wasn't all that much light to admit anyway. The tables were rickety and in the same dark wood of the panelling; on each was placed a lit candle in a whiskey bottle. In the soft light thrown by a few suspended lanterns it was clear the place was all but empty. We ordered a couple of pints and sat down at a table lit by the warm glow of a red candle emerging from an empty bottle of Bushmills. The wallpaper was dark and flocked, the pictures on the wall ancient prints of old Cork. The floor was stone. It was everything you could want from a pub, certainly from an Irish pub. This was perfection. I'm not going to tell you where it is either, but only because I can't remember how to get there and despite spending much of the afternoon and evening in it we never found out what it was called.

As I watched my pint of stout settle on the table in front me, the swirling brown clouds gently mutating almost imperceptibly into a sharply defined meniscus between black and cream, I realised that this was exactly what I'd wanted all those years ago.

I was in a perfect pub with a perfect pint and the perfect woman in the county of my forefathers. I knew exactly where I came from and above all I lived here, I lived in Ireland. The only difference was that I wasn't Irish and I'd never be Irish but that didn't concern me any more. I am not an Irishman and never will be, no matter how many books I read, places I visit, how good my Irish language might get, no matter how long I live here, how many times I throw things at the telly when Mayo crash out of the All-Ireland again, even if and when I have an Irish passport with my name on I'll always be an outsider here. But it doesn't matter. It's home.

'You're an Irish person in the sense that you've made a home here, that you chose to live here,' argued Jude. 'I suppose what you've done is a bit like the difference between a monarch and an elected head of state: it's a choice and sure, isn't that actually the best way to be? You've taken responsibility for where your life's going, just like your great-great-great-grandfather did, and you're not just relying on blood connections to define where and who you are and should be. And hey, none of us is all one thing; being one thing shouldn't define you completely. We're all just a big bloody mess of stuff.'

She thought for a moment, and added, 'I think I'll call that my theory of natural election.'

Reluctantly, as the afternoon became evening and the pub became crowded, we left the place to perform the final act of the year, to bring the story full circle. We headed along the river, crossed the footbridge and reached a paved section by the water in front of an early Victorian building fronted by a four-columned portico and topped by an idiosyncratically large statue of what appeared to be St George slaying a dragon. The building was once the headquarters of the Saint George Steam Packet Company and this was Penrose's Quay, the very spot from which

John Connelly had left Ireland some time in 1842. I walked
over to the door of the building: he'd probably walked through
those same doors to buy the ticket that secured his passage. Then
I walked back across the road to the river's edge. It was a clear,
cold night and the full moon sprinkled silver shards over the
water. The River Lee divides to the west of the city, making
much of Cork city an island, and reunites here to make its meandering way out past Cobh where the ships left for America and
on to the sea. I realised that the two strands of what I'd been
looking for came together in confluence here too: John's departure was the ultimate Irish reality, far distant from the sugary
image I'd lapped up in my younger days. Separation, emigration,
poverty and destitution; the ultimate sacrifice of giving up everything he knew, the heartbreak and heartache I'd felt for myself
just a day earlier and the same heartbreak and heartache being
felt by Brian and his elderly Irish in Britain.

There was a row of stainless steel pillars along the riverside
which were supposed to be 'listening posts' at which you could
hear recordings of emigrants' tales, but they weren't working. A
concrete plaque on the ground said they were 'to remember
the many thousands of emigrants who departed Cork and
Ireland from this quay'. In actual fact the silent posts probably
said more than the stories that were supposed to come out of
their speakers. The stilled voices of the nameless thousands who
left here for destinies unknown that remain lost over centuries,
and of those still to come – away to my left gleamed the floodlit white superstructure of the ferry moored there, recently
purchased to restart the Cork–Swansea route – their stories were
and will be just like those of my ancestor. Once again it was
brought home to me that the story of John Connelly is a story of
Ireland itself, stripped bare of the shillelaghs and leprechauns, the
postcard-perfect cottages and sugary songs.

It was a quiet, clear cold night and the moon gave the plaster-work of the old Steam Packet building a sharpened, blueish definition in the darkness. This peaceful scene was certainly a contrast to the day John left, when it would have been noisy and chaotic with hundreds of people milling about on the quayside, the funnels churning smoke, company officials struggling to keep order, the shouts of the passengers, the foghorns, the clanking chains, the farewells, the cargoes swinging overhead on cranes, the squabbles, the tears falling on to the stones. It must have been ridiculously busy: William Makepeace Thackeray visited Cork in 1842 and wrote of his arrival in the city that 'in the river and up to the bridge some hundreds of ships were lying and a fleet of steamboats opposite the handsome house of the Saint George's Steam Packet Company'.

Who knows, he might even have passed John on his way through, although if he did he probably wouldn't have been all that impressed: his coach attracted a lot of attention as 'a magnificent mob was formed round the vehicle and we had the opportunity of at once making acquaintance with some of the dirtiest rascally faces that all Ireland presents . . . Have they nothing else to do? Or is it that they will do nothing else but stare, swagger and be idle in the streets?'

I stood by the railing and looked down at the rush matting of moonlight on the rippled surface and then up at the sky. Orion twinkled back. I looked along the river, past the ferry and out into the night, the way the steamship would have taken John, probably huddled freezing up on a deck packed with people just like him. He hadn't wanted me around yesterday but here I felt calm and content: the quay represented the escape, the looking forward. He might not have wanted to go but the journey that began when he stepped off this very quay on to the gangplank and on to the ship was now over.

He'd done it; he'd survived. He'd made a life and a future. His old bones may lie cold and unmarked in a lonely spot far off in the East End of London, but here he was probably at his most alive, taking a ship to the unknown, gambling on a future that was not just his own. That one act, that one journey set in motion a chain of events that made sure I was born, that I was able to come here and bring everything home, to complete the circle.

I wasn't half proud of him.

The first firework was probably a bit early and whizzed and banged somewhere behind us. Then others began to pop and scream across the city with increasing frequency until the bangs and explosions reached an intensity that meant it must have been midnight. Suddenly the ferry to our left parped its foghorn and the sound bounced around the city among the staccato cracks of the fireworks. I reached into the pocket of my coat and pulled out the hip flask. I unscrewed the cap and offered it to Jude then took a swig of whiskey myself. Happy New Year, we said, and held each other for a long moment. I turned to the railing, held out the flask and upended it. A golden stream glugged forth and I heard it splashing into the river below.

'Here's to you, John,' I said. 'You did it. You really, really did it.'

ACKNOWLEDGEMENTS

When you write books that involve a certain amount of travel you're often in a pretty good position: you turn up somewhere for a few days, hang out, chat to a few people, have a few drinks, wander about a bit, do what you've got to do, disappear, write it all up like you're suddenly an expert and move on to somewhere else thereby handily avoiding any potentially tricky local consequences. This book is a little bit different in that I'm writing about where I live. I'm still here; I'm writing this long after the events described took place and I'm still only a hefty thwack of a sliotar from where the opening chapter concludes.

Luckily for me, Ireland is a copper-bottomed humdinger of a country: I consider myself very fortunate to live here and equally fortunate to have been able to write a book about the place. This has been possible thanks to a number of people whom I now owe several pints of Arthur Guinness's finest and probably the odd packet of Tayto cheese and onion to go with them.

The biggest thanks and most emphatic high fives go, as ever, to Lizzy Kremer, indisputably the best literary agent in the world and I'll wrestle anyone who disagrees with me naked and oiled in a barn in Somerset. The book would also not have been possible without the continued faith and support of big cheese and good egg – he's practically a walking dairy farm, in fact – Richard Beswick at Little, Brown for which I am always indebted. Thanks too to Zoe Gullen and Sophie McIvor at Little, Brown for helping to at least give the impression I can string a sentence together and for letting people know the book exists respectively. I also tip the hat to everyone in the Hachette Ireland office for showing such faith in the book from the earliest stages with special thanks to the one-of-a-kind Margaret Daly, publicist extraordinaire, and also to Ciara Considine who kindly, but probably unwisely from her point of view, offered to read the early manuscript from an Irish perspective. Special thanks are also due to Rory Mathews at Fáilte Ireland for all his help: in return would everyone please go on holiday to Ireland? Thanks.

There is a whole big bunch of folk I'd also like to thank for their support, whether practical, emotional, cyber, musical or alcoholic during the whole process and also for making me feel so welcome as a galumphing, clumsy stranger in a strange land. They are, in no particular order: Laura West, Shane Hegarty, Edel Coffey, Mum and Dad, Tristan and Olivia Manco, Michael and Sue Connelly, Michaela Stedman, the entire Leavy family, Maria Creaton, Karen Clayton, Steve Wicek, Nadine O'Hare, A. J. Lampe, Emily Dulohery, Tony Boland, Raven, Angie McLaughlin, Gary Fitzpatrick and the magnificent Sick and Indigent Song Club, Bob Johnston at the Gutter Bookshop in Temple Bar, James Harpur, Amanda Lyon, Ann Wheeler, Jill Zordan, Eddie Kelleher, Adrian Carty, Taragh Loughrey-Grant, Anna Rafferty, Arthur Mathews, Michelle Doyle, Steve and Danielle Morgan, Shay Byrne, Ryan Tubridy, Annie West, Bap Kennedy, Pete Howls, Ian Emmerson for his constant reminders of my heritage, David Heffernan, Chris Skudder, David Clancy, Peter Finn, Bernard Sumner, Rosita Boland, Abigail Rieley, Michael Stamp, the fine folk of the Ukulele Cosmos, Kez Piper,

Melissa May, Rob Woodward, Sarah Williams, Brian Boylan, Helen Kelly, John Casey and most notably the Irish Twitterati for keeping me suitably distracted – to paraphrase P.G. Wodehouse, without them this book would have been completed in half the time. A special mention also for Charlton Athletic, who thoughtfully went into spectacular freefall when I left Britain in a kind but futile attempt to make me miss them less.

Finally and most importantly all my love and thanks go to Jude, without whom . . . well, you know.

FURTHER READING

The preceding pages may not necessarily give that impression but I did actually do a great deal of reading in preparing this book. Ireland has been unfairly well-served with talented writers and has been equally well-served by people writing about the country. Hence I had to be necessarily selective in what I read, so what follows here is a rundown of some of the books I found useful and which I enjoyed most.

In terms of general histories of Ireland, Robert Kee's *Ireland: A History* gives a decent broad overview of a complex and difficult subject while his *The Green Flag* brings together his three-volume history of Irish nationalism in one book. I thoroughly enjoyed Shane Hegarty's authoritative and very readable *The Irish and Other Foreigners* (and probably scared him a little by repeatedly turning up at events where he was speaking about it) which relates Irish history in terms of the people who, like me, arrived in the country and the contributions they made, while Tim Pat Coogan's *Wherever The Green is Worn* tells the story of the Irish who left, a sad but vital narrative theme in the history of Ireland. Declan Kiberd's *Inventing Ireland: The Literature of the Modern Nation* is a brilliant and highly readable analysis of the perception of Ireland through its literature, while for an eye-opening account of Cromwell's Irish endeavours look no further than Micheál Ó Siochrú's *God's Executioner: Oliver Cromwell and the Conquest of Ireland*. For a slice of contemporary history, among the slew of books currently appearing about the Irish recession I found *Ship of Fools: How Stupidity and Corruption Sank the Celtic Tiger* by the respected Irish journalist Fintan O'Toole enlightening and, well, a little bit frightening.

For books dealing with everyday life in Ireland I enjoyed both David Kenny's *Erindipity: The Irish Miscellany* and Terry Eagleton's *The Truth About the Irish*. The latter is slightly dated now having been written in the early part of the boom years but is still a tremendous read, while *Erindipity* follows up having the best ever title for a book about Ireland by being perfect to dip into for quirky oddities about a country that brims with them.

Nearly every Irish bookshop has an entire section dedicated to the Easter Rising. The books I found most helpful were *The Easter Rising: A Guide to Dublin in 1916* by Conor Kostick and Lorcan Collins (and if you're ever in Dublin do take their guided walking tour) and *The Irish Times Book of the 1916 Rising* by Shane Hegarty and Fintan O'Toole. In addition, Mick O'Farrell's *A Walk Through Rebel Dublin 1916* is a tremendous self-guided walking tour while his *50 Things You Didn't Know About 1916* is a fascinating pocket-sized guide to some of the quirkier aspects of the rebellion.

For the ancestry sections I found John Grenham's book *Tracing Your Irish Ancestors* extremely helpful, while more generally the *Who Do You Think You Are? Encyclopedia of Genealogy* by Nick Barratt is invaluable for anyone tracing their family tree, especially from a standing start. If you think my friend Rob might be able to work the same magic on your Irish roots as he did on mine, his website is www.timelines.ie.

There is some fantastic writing out there about Irish sport but I'll mention just two books I particularly admire. To delve into the

anguish of supporting Mayo while at the same time understanding
the place of Gaelic sport in Irish society, try Keith Duggan's *The
House of Pain: Through the Rooms of Mayo Football* which, come to
think of it, is probably the best sports book I have ever read and
I've read a few. Christy O'Connor's *Last Man Standing: Hurling
Goalkeepers* is another brilliant read, both books going beyond the
sports themselves into a far wider context – as all the best sports
writing does.

For Connemara, look no further than the work of Tim
Robinson. His *Connemara: Listening to the Wind* and *Connemara:
The Last Pool of Darkness* are both extraordinary achievements in
topographical literature and are both beautifully written. Marie
Feeney's *The Cleggan Bay Disaster* is hard to find but is the fullest
account of the tragedy and its aftermath. John Healy's book
about Charlestown, *No-One Shouted Stop*, is equally difficult to
track down these days, but worth it if you can.

Ireland is well-served by travel books. As a huge fan of the travel
writer H.V. Morton it's probably no surprise that I'll hold up his
In Search of Ireland as a classic of this particular genre. Englishman
Morton travelled around Ireland at the end of the twenties, a raw
period just after the War of Independence and civil war, and
produces a sensitive, compelling and highly entertaining portrait of a country at a turning point in its history. More recently,
Lawrence Donegan's *No News at Throat Lake* recounts in terrific
self-deprecating style the author's renouncing of London life
for the wilds of Donegal, while *McCarthy's Bar* by Pete McCarthy
needs no extra endorsement from me as a wonderful piece of writing about Ireland. In *A Secret Map of Ireland*, the Irish poet and
writer Rosita Boland visits every county north and south of the
border to uncover some wonderful and moving stories in each that
are all beautifully told.

Finally, I'll finish tugging at your sleeve by casually mentioning

my website at www.charlieconnelly.com, while you can also follow
me on Twitter at www.twitter.com/charlieconnelly. If I don't see
you there I'll see you in The Sheds, Neary's or The Stag's Head.
Slán abhaile.